The Go-To Guide for

ENGINEERING CURRICULA, Grades 9–12

The Go-To Guide for

ENGINEERING CURRICULA, Grades 9–12

Choosing and Using the Best Instructional Materials for Your Students

EDITED BY

CARY I. SNEIDER

CORWIN
A SAGE Company

FOR INFORMATION:

Corwin

A SAGE Company

2455 Teller Road

Thousand Oaks, California 91320

(800) 233-9936

www.corwin.com

SAGE Publications Ltd.

1 Oliver's Yard

55 City Road

London EC1Y 1SP

United Kingdom

SAGE Publications India Pvt. Ltd.

B 1/I 1 Mohan Cooperative Industrial Area

Mathura Road, New Delhi 110 044

India

SAGE Publications Asia-Pacific Pte. Ltd.

3 Church Street

#10-04 Samsung Hub

Singapore 049483

Acquisitions Editor: Robin Najar

Associate Editor: Julie Nemer

Editorial Assistant: Ariel Price

Production Editor: Amy Schroller

Copy Editor: Kimberly Hill

Typesetter: C&M Digitals (P) Ltd.

Proofreader: Penelope Sippel

Indexer: Scott Smiley

Cover Designer: Gail Buschman

Marketing Manager: Amanda Boudria

Printed in the United States of America

A catalog record of this book is available from the Library of Congress.

ISBN 978-1-4833-0738-1

This book is printed on acid-free paper.

14 15 16 17 18 10 9 8 7 6 5 4 3 2 1

Contents

Foreword

Janet L. Kolodner
Georgia Institute of Technology

I have a dream. Nearly all our youngsters will graduate high school, and nearly all will be excellent readers, manipulate numbers and estimate easily, be able to argue a point using trustworthy evidence to back it up, make decisions informed by common knowledge, solve complex problems well, understand how scientists and engineers reason and be able to do some of that reasoning themselves, express themselves articulately, work well with others, recognize what they know and when they need to learn more, have passionate opinions backed by knowledge, and appreciate the roles they might take on (and love to engage in) as productive adults.

By middle school, students will begin to have some idea of the kinds of employment they might want to engage in as adults, and as a result of the experiences they are having in school and at home, they will evolve their interests over time and develop mature passions as they move through high school and beyond, imagining what they might be or be doing as adults, working toward aligning themselves with some of these possibilities, deciding they are interested in some and not interested in others, and eventually identifying how they will live their lives and achieve their goals. Some will be scientists or engineers; some will be writers or expressive artists; some will provide services; some will be technicians; but all will be gainfully employed doing something they want to be doing.

Plenty of research on how people learn suggests that engaging learners in achieving engineering challenges that they are personally interested in and capable of solving successfully (with help) can go a long way toward fulfilling my dream, which I hope you share. You can play an essential role in your students' lives by engaging them in design challenges that are relevant to their personal interests and helping them extract lessons from their work about how to define and solve problems and to imagine themselves as grownups who can solve important problems in the real world. A tall order, for sure, but not an impossible one. It won't happen tomorrow, and it won't happen at all if we don't seriously take on the challenge.

There are many reasons to be optimistic about the role design challenges can play in helping our youngsters grow and learn. First, it is not hard to make engineering design challenges fun, and it is not hard to help students see the value of math and science in their everyday lives if they are using disciplinary knowledge to address challenges they recognize as important. Achieving complex design challenges will not be easy fun for students, but if they are interested enough, they will put in the hard work. And if they see the value in what they are doing and learning and experience the success of learning and using science, more might enjoy science, more might see themselves as people who can engage well in thinking scientifically, more might understand the role science plays in our everyday world, more might become scientists, engineers, technicians, or policymakers who use science, and more might engage, during their adult lives, in thinking scientifically at times when that is appropriate.

Second, we know that developing deep understanding and masterful capabilities is hard and requires considerable time, but we also know that when somebody is really interested in what they are learning or in what they are attempting to do, and if the expectations are not so far beyond their capabilities that activities are overly frustrating, then people are willing to put in the time and effort. Learning something well, whether we are gaining understanding or learning how to do something, requires time and patience; it requires that we try our best to understand or achieve a challenge, that we pay attention to results and judge what is successful and not as successful, that we work on explaining when we don't understand something well or when we are not as successful as we want at solving a problem, that we develop new ideas and understandings, and that we have chances to try again (and fail again, and so on).

Achieving engineering design challenges provides opportunities for doing all these things—trying and not quite getting it right, observing what happens, explaining, developing new understandings, and trying again. When a science class is achieving engineering challenges together, the teacher and class can work as a unit to provide the help everyone in the class needs to engage successfully in all these processes. Not every student in the class will learn everything in depth or become masterfully adept at all skills and practices, but engaging together as a class in achieving engineering design challenges makes the classroom a place to help all students achieve as well as they can.

Third, engineering design challenges provide opportunities to use science, to engage in carrying out disciplinary practices, to engage in engineering design practices, and to engage in 21st century skills. When students get excited about achieving a challenge, they will want to develop the necessary skills well enough to be able to achieve the challenge; if they need each other's advice, they will want to learn how to give good advice and take advice well, and if they are working on a challenge that requires several kinds of expertise or perspective, they will want to learn to collaborate well. When a class engages in engineering design together, there are opportunities to reflect on and discuss how to carry out skills and practices well, and when students are eager to achieve the engineering design goal, they will also be eager to know how to do whatever is necessary to achieve that goal; they will take the time to reflect on what they are doing and work on refining the way they carry out processes if time is set aside for that and appropriate help is given.

Fourth, we know that learners become more engaged and interested and willing to work hard when they are able to take on agency—that is, when they are trusted to make choices. There are rarely optimal choices in achieving engineering goals; engineers are constantly involved in making trade-offs, and several engineers working on the same real-world problem might come up with very different designs. The context of achieving engineering design challenges is perfect for allowing learners agency. When different groups suggest different solutions, have a chance to present and justify their solutions for the class, and have a chance to argue with each other using evidence, learning opportunities are enhanced for everybody in the class, as each group gets to experience and think about not only their own ideas but also the ideas of others.

Finally, when learners are allowed to try on the shoes of scientists and engineers, they also can begin to imagine themselves in those shoes. Students who are helped to be successful student scientists and student engineers, as they are asked to do in achieving engineering design challenges, will also begin to develop understandings of the kinds of activities they enjoy and the kinds of work they might want to do later in life. If the set of challenges they attempt is large, encompassing a large variety of disciplines, life situations, and roles they might take on, they will have solid foundations to build on in imagining their futures.

Everything we know about how people learn and how to promote learning suggests that engaging our young people in achieving engineering challenges and solving engineering problems has potential to promote deep science learning and mastery of important disciplinary and life skills. The NGSS (NGSS Lead States, 2013), in encouraging curriculum approaches that foster learning STEM skills and practices along with science content, gives school systems and teachers permission to move in that direction.

* * *

This book documents 12 sets of curriculum materials for the high school years that integrate engineering design as a part of science. Although these materials were developed before publication of the NGSS, the authors of these chapters explain ways that they can be used today to support the NGSS at the high school level. And nearly all will be fine-tuned in the years to come as developers gain further experience with the NGSS.

Each of the chapters illustrates different ways that engineering design can help achieve my dream, starting with Chapter 1. "The INSPIRES Curriculum" is about a series of modules, designed to be integrated into science courses, or taught together in an engineering design course. Each module focuses on an engaging real-world problem. The chapter describes two of the modules: Engineering in Healthcare: A Hemodialysis Case Study and Engineering Energy Solutions: A Renewable Energy System Case Study.

Chapter 2, "Active Physics," is about a full-year high school physics course with a strong engineering component. A different engineering challenge for each chapter provides the context in which students will learn physics principles and transfer their knowledge to the completion of a project. Challenges include, for example, designing a vehicle safety device, a light and sound show, an appliance package for a family driven by a wind generator, a museum display, and a proposal to NASA for a sport that can be played on the moon.

Chapter 3, "Active Chemistry," is also a full-year high school science program in which scientific concepts in each chapter are introduced as needed to meet an engineering design challenge. In the Artist as Chemist chapter, for example, students learn various chemistry concepts, such as the physical properties of metals, behind art techniques, then apply those techniques by creating their own artifacts.

In Chapter 4, "Engineering the Future: Science, Technology, and the Design Process," students have an opportunity to see how science, technology, mathematics, and engineering (STEM) are part of their everyday world and why it is important for *every citizen* to be technologically and scientifically literate. The essential science concept of energy weaves through engineering projects related to insulating buildings, improving engines, and designing electric circuits.

Chapter 5, "Engineer Your World: Engineering Design and Problem Solving" from the University of Texas at Austin, is a full-year engineering curriculum that engages students in socially relevant design challenges intended to develop design skills and engineering habits of mind. Projects include designing a pinhole camera for artists with disabilities, designing safer buildings for an earthquake-prone region, and redesigning a human-powered flashlight.

Chapter 6, "Global Systems Science," concerns a set of curriculum materials for high school teachers and students that is centered on critical societal issues of global concern, such as ecosystem change, losing biodiversity, climate change, and energy use, all which require science for full understanding and thoughtful intelligent engineering for solutions. The curriculum is modularized to easily be used in existing high school biology, physics, chemistry, Earth science, or social studies courses to better support the NGSS.

Chapter 7, "Science and Global Issues: Electricity: Global Energy and Power, features one unit of a two-year high school sequence designed to provide a full year of biology and one semester each of physics and chemistry through units focused on the everyday application of science and engineering to everyday life. In the featured unit, students look at sustainability issues surrounding the generation and consumption of electricity, moving from global issues to local evidence-based decisions. During the unit students build, test, and redesign circuits focused on the storage of electrical energy. In a culminating activity, students meet a challenge to help restore power to an island that has suffered a catastrophic natural disaster.

Chapter 8, "Engineering by Design High School Courses," describes a sequence of courses that complete a K–12 curriculum sequence to educate *all students* about the world of engineering and technology and to inspire more students to pursue STEM fields. The six high school courses range from an introductory course for 9th graders, to an advanced capstone course for 11th and 12th-grade students. Each of the courses is briefly described along with the instructional model, assessment, professional development, and how the course can be integrated into the high school curriculum.

Chapter 9, "Science by Design: Construct a Boat, Catapult, Glove, and Greenhouse," is about a series of well-tested, hands-on product design challenges developed long before STEM was hot but which has now become a valuable resource for high school teachers wishing to implement the engineering side of the NGSS. The instructional modules, now combined in a single book, describe how to present these engaging design activities so that students learn the science behind the mechanisms as they develop inquiry and team-building skills.

Chapter 10, "Nature's Designs Applied to Technology," begins with an introduction to *biomimetics*, the practice of applying biological structures to engineering. Sample modules described in the chapter include Fur, Feathers, and Scales, in which engineers learn from animals about how to create the best insulating materials; and *biomechanics*, that includes lessons about bridge building from animal skeletons, and designing better flying machines by observing the ways that plant structures disperse seeds.

Chapter 11, "Voyages Through Time and the Evolution of Technology," is a course for students in the 9th or 10th grade that presents evolution on its grandest scale, from evolution of the cosmos as a whole, to the evolution of planets, life, hominids, and our technological world. The chapter features the last module of the course, which provides a broad overview of technology and how technological change affects society and the natural environment. In the culminating lesson, students choose a particular technology, study how it has changed through history, analyze current needs, and project how it may change in the future.

Chapter 12, "EPICS High Program," provides training and instructional materials to high school teachers who wish to use service-learning as a means to engage students in real engineering projects to meet needs in their communities. The chapter includes a number of examples, such as helping organize charitable donations, designing a butterfly garden for a museum, improving an exhibit at a zoo so the otters on display have a more natural living environment, and improving traffic flow in their own school building.

Although each project is unique, the chapter explains how they can be designed to help students develop the knowledge and skills in the NGSS.

* * *

It will not be easy to make traditional classrooms into engineering design classrooms. Some students who are used to reading and answering questions will balk at having to work hard; other students for whom learning comes easy will balk at having to work collaboratively with their classmates. If you are new to engineering education you will have to learn new ways of interacting with students and facilitating learning. It does not take long to draw students in if challenges are meaningful to them and if they are trusted with agency, but it will take a special effort to develop new ways of interacting with your students.

If this is your first time teaching engineering, you may not be as successful as you want immediately, but don't worry. As you learn to be a better facilitator of the engineering design process, your students will learn more deeply. If possible, work together with other teachers who are also learning to implement engineering or other project-based activities in their classrooms. And just as your students will be learning a new approach by attempting to solve a problem but not quite succeeding, getting help in understanding why their first approach didn't work, then redesigning, and trying again, it is very likely that you will go through a similar sequence of stages in your teaching. It will take time and willingness to work through possibly frustrating attempts to enact very different kinds of activities than you are used to, but it will be worthy and worthwhile work.

* * *

The many chapters in this collection provide advice and resources for using design challenges and problems to promote science learning. I hope that the chapters help readers develop imagination about integrating engineering design and problem-solving experiences into science classes, passion for moving forward to implement engineering design activities in their classrooms, and understanding of the conditions under which integrating such activities into our classrooms will lead to deep learning.

Choosing which of these instructional materials are right for you and your students is, of course, a huge part of the challenge. But it should be possible to identify likely candidates by reading the first three or four pages of each chapter, then reading the complete chapter for those that are most likely to meet your needs. As you do that, you might keep in mind several thoughts:

- Good education is not about "covering the material." Developing deep understanding and masterful capabilities is hard and requires considerable time. It is more important that students spend significant time on a few projects than that they do a lot of brief activities that cover a wide variety of topics.
- To sustain your students' interests over time, it is essential for projects to be sufficiently interesting and diverse to maintain your students' attention. Resources will provide some advice about how to do that, but you know your students better than curriculum developers; use your judgment to help problems come alive for your students, and if you see interest waning, figure out how to bring interest back. It's not hard to keep youngsters excited about things that impact their world and that help them experience worlds they've become familiar with from TV or the movies, but sometimes they need to be reminded why they are doing what they are doing.

- Judging the difficulty of a task will require your best judgment as a teacher. The requirements of a task should not be so difficult that it becomes frustrating so that students give up. Conversely, if what they are asked to do is too easy, students will not have opportunities to develop new skills or gain confidence in their abilities to tackle and solve really challenging problems. Some materials allow you to modify the level of the challenge to meet your students' needs.
- Opportunities for teamwork are evident in every one of these sets of materials. However, some are more explicit than others about how to manage teams and help students learn to work together effectively. What is important to remember is that working in teams should not just be seen as a way of managing the classroom but rather it is important for students to come to appreciate the benefits of collaboration and learn how to collaborate well. Help your students identify the understanding and capabilities they are gaining from teamwork and help them develop collaboration habits that they use and further develop across curriculum units and projects.
- Many of the materials described in this book expose students to the world of technology and a wide variety of career possibilities. Helping students recognize those possibilities provides a way of keeping them engaged and will aim students toward goals that are part of my dream (and I hope yours).
- In choosing materials to use in your classroom, remember that in addition to choosing particular curriculum units for the targeted content they address and the interests of your students, it is important that your students experience and appreciate the big ideas of science and technology. Curriculum materials used over a year or several years of school should build on each other in ways that allow learners to see the connections between topical areas and to exercise and develop their capabilities. Help your students see across curriculum units as well as digging deep into the content and skills targeted in each one.

I offer my best wishes and congratulations to all your efforts! I will be cheering for all of you and looking forward to meeting your many learned and mature-thinking students and experiencing the success of your endeavors in the decades to come.

—*Janet L. Kolodner, November 2, 2013*

Reference

NGSS Lead States (2013). *Next generation science standards: For states, by states, volume 1: The standards*, and *volume 2: Appendices*. Washington, DC: National Academies Press.

Janet L. Kolodner is Regents' Professor at Georgia Institute of Technology, where she served as coordinator of the cognitive science program for many years. Dr. Kolodner was founding director of Georgia Tech's EduTech Institute, whose mission is to use what we know about cognition to inform the design of educational technology and learning environments. Professor Kolodner is founding Editor in Chief of *The Journal of the Learning Sciences*, an interdisciplinary journal that focuses on learning and education. She is also a founder of the International Society for the Learning Sciences, and she served as its first Executive Officer. Her research has addressed issues in learning, memory, and problem solving, both in computers and in people. Dr. Kolodner's book, *Case-Based Reasoning*, synthesizes work across the field. Dr. Kolodner has focused most of her research on using the model of case-based reasoning to design science curricula for middle school, in which students learn science and scientific reasoning in the context of designing working arti-facts. More recently, she and her students are applying what they've learned about design-based learning to informal education—after-school programs, museum programs, and museum exhibits. The goal of these projects is to identify ways of helping children and youth consider who they are as thinkers and to come to value informed decision making and informed production and consumption of evidence.

Acknowledgments

First and foremost, I wish to thank the authors of these chapters, not only for taking the time to craft a compelling description of their curriculum but also for the foresight and persistence that it took to develop instructional materials in engineering, long before there were standards to support their efforts.

Recalling my early education that technology and engineering are allied with science but are also different in important ways, I want to acknowledge my early mentors, Robert Maybury, Harold Foecke, and Alan Friedman, as well as the leaders of the National Center for Technological Literacy at the Museum of Science in Boston, including especially Ioannis Miaoulis, Yvone Spicer, Peter Wong, and Christine Cunningham, as well as the many teachers and administrators in Massachusetts who were among the early adopters of what we now call Integrated STEM education.

I also appreciate the support of colleagues at Achieve, Inc., including the writers of the NGSS, Stephen Pruitt who led the effort, the brilliant and supportive staff, and the members of the NGSS Lead State Teams, for their steadfast dedication to crafting standards that fully embrace engineering as an equal partner to science. The current leadership of Achieve, Inc. is commended for granting permission to quote extensively from the NGSS.

Thanks also to the extraordinary personnel at the National Research Council, including the committee members and staff who developed *A Framework for K–12 Science Education: Practices, Crosscutting Concepts, and Core Ideas* and members of the Board on Science Education, especially Helen Quinn, Linda Katehi, and Heidi Schweingruber, who played crucial roles in the development of new science education standards.

Senior staff of the National Academies Press have also contributed to this work and to science education more broadly by making available free of charge the *Framework* and NGSS, along with many other important science education reports. The Press has given its permission to quote freely from the *Framework* and has asked us to publicize the availability of both the free downloads and hardcopy versions of the *Framework* and NGSS at its website:

http://www.nap.edu/catalog.php?record_id=13165.

Worthy of special thanks is the generosity of Jan Morrison, President and CEO of Teaching Institute for Excellence in STEM (TIES), whose major gift provided substantial support for this effort, and to the leadership of Corwin, who also provided financial support above and beyond the costs of publishing.

I also want to acknowledge Robin Najar and Julie Nemer, my Editors at Corwin, their assistant, Ariel Price, and the many other people at Corwin who made this set of volumes possible, as well as David Vernot, who volunteered to be an additional critical reader.

Although it is somewhat unusual for an editor to thank his readers, I also want to acknowledge your courage for being among the first to help bring the new world of STEM learning into being.

Publisher's Acknowledgments

Corwin wishes to acknowledge the following peer reviewers for their editorial insight and guidance.

Joan Baltezore, Science Instructor
West Fargo High School
West Fargo, ND

Arthur H. Camins, Director
Stevens Institute of Technology/CIESE
Charles V. Schaefer School of Engineering
Castle Point on Hudson
Hoboken, NJ 07030

Kelly Cannon, K–12 Science Program Coordinator
Washoe County School District
Reno, NV

Mandy Frantti, Physics/Astronomy/Mathematics Teacher
NASA Astrophysics Educator Ambassador
Munising Middle-High School
Munising, MI

Loukea Kovanis-Wilson, Chemistry Instructor
Clarkston Community Schools
Clarkston, MI

Sara Stewart, Educational Technology Specialist
Washoe County School District
Reno, NV

About the Editor

**Cary I. Sneider** is Associate Research Professor in the Center for Science Education at Portland State University in Portland, Oregon, where he teaches research methodology to teachers in a Master's degree program. In recent years, he served the National Research Council as design lead for technology and engineering to help develop *A Framework for K–12 Science Education: Practices, Crosscutting Concepts, and Core Ideas*, which has provided the blueprint for NGSS. He then played a similar role on the writing team to produce the NGSS, which was released in April, 2013. The recognition that teachers would need access to instructional materials to help them meet the new standards led Cary to develop the current series, *The Go-To Guide for Engineering Curricula*.

Cary was not always interested in engineering—or at least he didn't know that he was. For as long as he can remember, he was interested in astronomy. He read all he could find about it, and when he was in middle school his father bought him a small telescope. In high school Cary built his own telescopes, grinding mirrors and designing and building mountings. All this time he thought he was doing *science*. Today, he recognizes that, like many scientists, he especially enjoyed the *engineering* part of the work.

During his junior year at college, Sneider had an opportunity to teach at an Upward Bound program and found that he enjoyed teaching even more than research in astronomy. In subsequent years, he taught science in Maine, Costa Rica, Coalinga, California, and the Federated States of Micronesia. He returned to college, this time to obtain a teaching credential and eventually a PhD degree in science education from the University of California at Berkeley. He spent nearly 30 years in Berkeley, developing instructional materials and running teacher institutes at the Lawrence Hall of Science. He spent another decade as vice president at the Museum of Science in Boston, where he developed a high school curriculum called Engineering the Future, and finally moved to Portland, Oregon to be closer to children and grandchildren.

During his career, Cary directed more than 20 federal, state, and foundation grant projects, mostly involving curriculum development and teacher education. His research and development interests have focused on helping students and museum visitors unravel their misconceptions in science, on new ways to link science centers and schools to promote student inquiry, and on integrating engineering and technology education into the K–12 curriculum. In 1997, he received the Distinguished Informal Science Education award from the National Science Teachers Association and in 2003 was named National Associate of the National Academy of Sciences for his service on several National Research Council committees.

About the Contributors

Taryn Melkus Bayles is Professor of the Practice of Chemical Engineering at the University of Maryland, Baltimore County, where she incorporates her industrial experience to help students understand fundamental engineering principles. Her research interests include transport phenomena, engineering education, and outreach. She received her Chemical Engineering BS, MS and PhD degrees from New Mexico State University and the University of Pittsburgh.

Janet Bellantoni served for seven years as a high school physics teacher and administrator. She completed a bachelor's degree in mechanical engineering at the University of Rochester, a master's degree in science education at the University of Massachusetts Amherst, and graduate studies in deaf education at Gallaudet University. Since joining SEPUP in 2001, Janet has created over ten new units for the project and revised others. Her work includes leading the development of *Issues and Earth Science* and the physics units in *Issues and Physical Science*. She is currently developing the physics units for *Science and Global Issues*.

Philip Cardella is a freelance writer living in West Lafayette, Indiana. His writing interests include formal and informal education, sociology, religion, sports, and politics. He has degrees in writing and education.

Edna DeVore is the CEO and Director of Education and Public Outreach at the SETI Institute. She's an astronomy educator. Her work includes NASA's Kepler Mission, Astrobiology Institute, and Stratospheric Observatory for Infrared Astronomy, NASA and NSF Research Experience for Undergraduates, and Co-I for Voyages Through Time. She has served boards for the ASP, AAS and Foundation for Microbiology. She has published more than 30 papers on science and astronomy education and presented over 200 invited talks, teacher workshops, and short courses. She earned a BA degree at Raymond College, University of the Pacific, an MA in Instructional technology at San Jose State University, and a MS in Astronomy from the University of Arizona.

Arthur Eisenkraft, PhD, is the Distinguished Professor of Science Education, Professor of Physics and Director of the Center of Science and Math in Context (COSMIC) at the University of Massachusetts, Boston. He is past president of the National Science Teachers Association. He is chair and cocreator of the Toshiba/NSTA ExploraVision Awards, involving 15,000 students annually. His current research projects include investigating the efficacy of a second generation model of distance learning for professional development; a study of professional development choices that teachers make when facing a large scale curriculum change and assessing the technological literacy of K–12 students.

Cheryl Farmer is the founding project director of UTeach*Engineering*, which was launched in 2008 as the first engineering education-focused Math and Science Partnership of the National Science Foundation. In her role with UTeach*Engineering*, Ms. Farmer has led a diverse team in the development and launch of the Engineer Your World curriculum and supporting professional development programs, as well as the creation of degree programs for preservice and inservice teachers of engineering at The University of Texas at Austin. She is currently coleading a national effort to define standards for professional development for K–12 teachers of engineering.

Alan Gould directs the Global Systems Science high school curriculum project at Lawrence Hall of Science (LHS), UC Berkeley. He has over 36 years of experience developing and presenting hands-on science activities and 22 years of experience organizing and leading teacher education workshops. He is also Co-Investigator for Education and Public Outreach for the NASA Kepler mission, Co-Directs the Hands-On Universe project, Associate Director of the LHS Planetarium, and is coauthor of Great Explorations in Math and Science (GEMS) teacher guides. He is also on the Full Option Science System (FOSS) middle school course revision team. See http://www.uncleal.net/alan.

Pamela Harman is the Manager of Education and Public Outreach at the SETI Institute. Her work includes NASA's Kepler Mission, Astrobiology Institute, and Stratospheric Observatory for Infrared Astronomy, and the Voyages Through Time science curriculum. She has served on the steering committee for the San Mateo County biotechnology education partnership *Gene Connection* and as a National Lead Teacher, WGBH's *Evolution Project*. Pamela has authored and coauthored 20 papers and posters on science, astronomy, and astrobiology education and presented countless teacher workshops and short courses. She earned a BS in Civil Engineering from Iowa State University, and a California Biological Sciences Teaching Credential from San Francisco State University.

Mindy Hart currently serves as the academic recruiter for the Department of Technology Leadership and Innovation at Purdue University in West LaFayette, Indiana. Prior to this position, she was the EPICS High program coordinator and has spent time as a high school computer science teacher and K–12 Outreach Coordinator.

John Howarth is the Associate Director of SEPUP at the Lawrence Hall of Science. A 1995 recipient of the Presidential Award for Excellence in Mathematics and Science Teaching, John has been involved in science education for thirty-eight years. At various times he has been a high school science teacher, science curriculum supervisor, and Executive Director for Curriculum and Instruction. He has taught science in Wyoming, Michigan, Malaysia, Singapore, and Brunei. John received his bachelor's degree in biochemistry and postgraduate certificate in education from the University of Liverpool in England and master's degree in educational leadership from Western Michigan University.

Janet Kolodner's research addresses learning, memory, and problem solving in computers and people. She pioneered the computer method called case-based reasoning and uses its cognitive model to design formal and informal science curriculum. Learning by Design, her design-based inquiry-oriented approach to science learning, is a foundation of Project-Based Inquiry Science (PBIS), a 3-year middle-school science curriculum. In her informal science education endeavors, middle schoolers learn science through cooking and learn to explain while designing hovercraft. She is founding Editor in Chief of *Journal of the Learning Sciences* and a founder of the International Society for the Learning Sciences.

Amy Fowler Murphy currently serves as the Chemistry Education Specialist with the Alabama Math, Science, and Technology Initiative at the University of Montevallo. Prior to her role with this program, Dr. Murphy taught high school chemistry in urban and suburban settings for 10 years. Dr. Murphy is a National Board certified chemistry teacher and completed her Doctorate of Education in Curriculum and Instruction in 2012. The focus of her dissertation research was sustaining inquiry-based methods of teaching and learning in science classrooms. Dr. Murphy has been working with the Active Chemistry curriculum since 2004.

William (Bill) Oakes is Director of the EPICS Program and Professor of Engineering Education at Purdue University. He has been honored by the National Academy of Engineering, the American Society for Engineering Education and the National Society of Professional Engineers for his work with university and K–12 students related to engineering-based service-learning.

Lee Pulis, who earned his BA from Dartmouth, and MS from Cornell University, is coauthor of Science by Design, an NSF-funded curriculum developed by TERC, Cambridge, Massachusetts and published by NSTA. At TERC, Lee served as Principal Investigator and Project Director for several NSF and industry-funded high school STEM curricula. Lee is also coauthor of *Engineering the Future* by the Museum of Science, Boston. Recently he prepared the Teacher Guides for the Samsung/Scholastic Mobile App Academy. He teaches college transfer lab environmental science online and represents the Museum of Science and publisher, It's About Time, by presenting teacher professional development workshops and moderated online courses.

Susan Riechert is a UTK Distinguished Service Professor in Ecology and Evolutionary Biology at the University of Tennessee. She received her PhD in Zoology from the University of Wisconsin. Internationally recognized for her work in the field of behavioral ecology, she is a Fellow of both the Animal Behavior Society of America (ABS) and of the American Association for the Advancement of Science (AAAS). She is also the founder and Director of the Biology in a Box Project (http://biologyinabox.utk .edu), a collaborative effort with the National Institute of Mathematical and Biological Synthesis (NIMBioS), as well as Co-Director of the VolsTeach Program (http:// volsteach.utk.edu).

Julia Ross is Dean of the College of Engineering and IT and Professor of Chemical, Biochemical, and Environmental Engineering at UMBC. She leads a multidisciplinary research team in the development and implementation of the NSF-funded INSPIRES Curriculum (Increasing Student Participation, Interest and Recruitment in Engineering and Science). Dr. Ross is a Fellow of the American Institute for Medical and Biological Engineering and is the recipient of the ASEE Sharon Keillor Award for Women in Engineering and a NSF CAREER Award.

Jonathan Singer, PhD is Associate Professor and Director of Secondary Education in the Department of Education at University of Maryland, Baltimore County. He has established a research agenda that focuses on the professional development of STEM teachers' integration of technology to support student inquiry. He has been a Co-Principal Investigator on the INSPIRES project since 2008.

Greg Strimel is the K–12 coordinator in the Academic Innovation unit at West Virginia University. He also serves as a teacher effectiveness coach and curriculum developer for ITEEA's STEM Center for Teaching and Learning. In addition, Greg is a PhD student in Occupational and Technical Studies at Old Dominion University. In 2013, he was selected as a member of the Council on Technology and Engineering Teacher Education's 21st Century Leadership Academy. Greg formerly served as a technology and engineering teacher and career/technology education instructional team leader in Howard County, Maryland.

Jean Trusedell is a Nationally Board Certified Teacher with extensive experience working with K–12 educators and students. Her current project is working with the EPICS Program at Purdue University to create curriculum that can be used with students to integrate best classroom practices with engineering design. Previously, she was the Science and Technology Coach for MSD of Decatur Township in Indianapolis, Indiana. Ms. Trusedell is pursuing a PhD in Curriculum and Instruction with an interest in formative assessment and its relationship to student achievement.

Introduction

The NGSS (NGSS Lead States, 2013) have opened the door for engineering to join science as an equal partner in the classroom. What this will look like is still unfolding, but happily, we are not starting from scratch. Many talented educators have been developing instructional materials in engineering for a long time. That's what this book is all about.

The idea of integrating technology and engineering into science teaching is not new. More than 100 years ago, educators such as John Dewey advocated technology education for all students (Lewis, 2004). The call for integrating technology and engineering into science standards began with publication of *Science for All Americans* (AAAS, 1989) and has been featured prominently in standards documents ever since. A case in point is the NSES (NRC, 1996), which advocated that all students should learn about the relationship between technology and science, as well as develop the abilities of technological design.

Despite the many efforts to infuse science teaching with ideas and activities in technology and engineering, the call has been largely ignored. One of the reasons was simply momentum. Science education has traditionally included only the core disciplines of life science, physical science (including chemistry) and Earth and space sciences, so there has been little room for technology and engineering. A second reason is that, although state standards were commonly derived from the NSES and *Benchmarks for Science Literacy* (AAAS, 1993/2008), which also called for engineering and technology, each state crafted their own standards, and most ignored engineering and technology. As of 2012, only 12 states included engineering in their science standards (Carr, Bennett, & Strobel, 2012).

A third reason is confusion about the term *technology*, which most people only apply to computers, cell phones, or other modern gadgets (Meade & Dugger, 2004). There is even less understanding of the term *engineering*. If you've ever had difficulty with plumbing in a hotel room and reported the problem to the front desk it is likely that they called "engineering" to fix the problem. It's not surprising that most people think of engineers as people who fix things (Lachapelle, Phadnis, Hertel, & Cunningham, 2012).

Today the situation is entirely different. A blue ribbon panel of the NRC, which included Nobel Prize-winning scientists, engineers, university professors, and educational researchers have created a new blueprint for science—*A Framework for K–12 Science Education: Practices, Core Ideas and Crosscutting Concepts* (NRC, 2012). The *Framework* calls for engineering to be included at the same level as Newton's laws and the theory of evolution. Furthermore, the *Framework* served as the blueprint for the

NGSS, which are aimed at replacing the current patchwork of state science standards with a common core, as has already been done in mathematics and English language arts. To emphasize that these standards are not federal but rather an initiative of the National Governor's Association, the full title of the new standards is *Next Generation Science Standards: For States, by States.**

In the new world of science education that is being brought into being by these two documents, engineering is a true partner to science. There are several good reasons why this change may pay off at the classroom level in a big way.

The Value of Engineering to Reduce Declining Interest in Science

Most children love science, but it doesn't last. The majority of research studies have found that interest in science remains strong for most boys and girls throughout the elementary grades but begins to drop off in middle school (Osborne, Simon, Collins, 2003; Sneider, 2011). A few studies, however, have shown some decline as early as elementary school, and a consistent finding is that at all ages most girls exhibit less interest than boys and students of most minority ethnic groups tend to be less interested in science than Caucasian and Asian American students.

The introduction of engineering as a continuous thread in the science curriculum has the potential to change that trend and maintain students' interests in science as they transition to high school. There are several reasons why (from Cunnngham & Lachapelle, 2011):

- While many students who are competent in science view the subject as irrelevant for future careers or everyday life, some of these same students—especially girls and underrepresented minorities—respond positively to subjects such as environmental and medical engineering since these topics have obvious relevance to people's lives.
- Engineering involves students working together in teams, so design challenges appeal to students who enjoy collaborative activities.
- Engineering design challenges have more than one answer, and creativity is a plus. So the activities themselves tend to be fun and engaging.
- There are many more jobs available for engineers than there are for scientists. NASA, for example, hires 10 engineers for every scientist (NASA Workforce, 2013). So students see engineering as offering real future job prospects, especially when they see role models of different genders and racial backgrounds who enjoy their work.
- Failure of a design to work as expected does not mean being "wrong." Failure is a natural part of the design process, leading to improved designs, so students are encouraged to try out their ideas without worry.

In the past, few students were exposed to engineering as a school subject. In rare cases, when students were given engineering activities at school, it was likely to have been called "science," and engineering skills were not made explicit. Even in those cases where they *were* given engineering opportunities, it is likely to have been in the physical sciences, such as robotics or building bridges and towers that boys tend to favor rather than topics such as medical or environmental engineering that appeal equally to girls (Cunningham & Lachapelle, 2011).

So, now that we have science education standards that call for engineering to be deeply integrated into all science classes, how do we get from here to there? If you are reading this book it is likely that you are interested in an answer to that question. And not surprisingly, there is more than one answer.

How to Get Started

First, you will need instructional materials. Such materials do exist, and many of them can be found on the Web. A variety of websites with engineering activities are listed in Table 1. Each of the chapters in this book reference additional websites associated with a particular engineering curriculum.

Second, it will be helpful to have at least one colleague, and hopefully several who can work with you to comb through instructional materials, consider how your school's curriculum might change to implement the new standards, and perhaps establish a professional learning community to examine your first efforts as you try new approaches.

Third, you might be invited to spend a summer writing new curriculum materials that are fully aligned with the NGSS. Having spent a long career developing instructional materials in science and the related STEM fields, let me caution you to think carefully about how you might undertake such a project. Curriculum development is a labor-intensive process that often takes years, and the assistance of many other teachers, to develop an effective lesson that will engage your students' enthusiasm and that also has clear educational objectives and assessment tools. Nonetheless, I have found curriculum development to be a creative and rewarding experience, and you may too.

Fourth—and now we get to the reason this book has come into being—you will very likely find it to be a valuable and enriching experience to listen to the voices of the pioneers, the people who held the vision of "engineering as a partner to science" long before these documents were written and who have spent decades developing engineering curricula.

In the chapters that follow, you will see how engineering educators build on students' innate interests by presenting them with challenging problems, engaging them in designing creative solutions, and helping them understand how science and mathematics apply in their everyday lives. While many of the curricula do concern physical sciences, as a whole they span the entire spectrum of science disciplines.

How This Book Is Organized

Each chapter describes one set of instructional materials with vivid examples of what the curriculum looks like in the classroom, what learning goals it is intended to accomplish, how it can help you address the vision of the *Framework*, and the performance expectations in the NGSS.

Perhaps more importantly, the instructional materials described in these chapters do more than spark students' interests. They help students develop skills in defining and solving problems, in working on collaborative teams to brainstorm creative ideas, to build prototypes and use controlled experiments to compare different ideas, to design an optimal solution, and to learn about a wide variety of engineering professions.

All the materials in the collection have been under development for several years, tested by teachers and their students from a wide range of communities, and revised based on feedback. In many cases, they are also supported by research studies of effectiveness. A listing of all the curriculum materials included in this 3-volume sequence can be found in Table 2, which illustrates the full range of grade levels for which the curriculum can be used.

If you are looking for engineering curricula to try out, you will undoubtedly find something of interest on these pages. If you are part of a group of teachers interested in exploring engineering and science curricula, these chapters could provide stimulating topics for discussion. And if you are challenged with developing new instructional materials, these chapters will help you avoid the need to recreate the wheel.

As you read through these chapters, you may find that several strike you as top candidates for enriching your classroom or school science program. Although too many options is far better than too few, you may need some help in deciding among the top contenders. Happily, a new and very useful tool, with the acronym EQuIP has popped up on the www.nextgenscience.org website. Educators Evaluating the Quality of Instructional Products (EQuIP) Rubric for Lessons and Units: Science is designed to help you review and select materials based on how well the lessons and units align with the NGSS and provide instructional and assessment supports.

Before you can use the EQuIP rubric, you will need to have samples of the materials to examine. Contact information is provided in each chapter to allow you to do that. You will also need to be familiar with the *Framework* and the NGSS. The next section of this book provides an overview of engineering in these two important documents. If you are already familiar with these documents (which can be downloaded free of charge from the National Academies Press website www.nap.edu) and want to move on to the main business of this book, which is to learn about existing engineering curricula as described by the people who created them, you can get started with Chapter 1, The INSPIRES Curriculum.

The *Framework* and the NGSS have the potential to change the face of science education in the country but only if educators like you embrace the opportunity and begin to imagine what it may mean for the students in your care.

Table 1 A Selection of K–12 Engineering Education Websites

A Framework for K–12 Science Education—http://www.nap.edu/catalog.php?record_id=13165#

Building Big—http://www.pbs.org/wgbh/buildingbig/

Center for Innovation in Engineering and Science Education—www.ciese.org

Design Squad—http://pbskids.org/designsquad/

Discover Engineering—http://www.discovere.org/

Dragonfly TV—http://pbskids.org/dragonflytv/show/technologyinvention.html

Engineering Education Service Center—www.engineeringedu.com

Engineering Go For It (ASEE)—http://teachers.egfi-k12.org/

Engineering Our Future—https://sites.google.com/site/engineeringourfuture/

Engineering Pathways—http://www.engineeringpathway.com/

How to Smile: All the Best Science and Math Activities—www.howtosmile.org

Institute for (P-12) Engineering Research and Learning (INSPIRE)—http://www.inspire-purdue.org/

Intel Design and Discovery—http://educate.intel.com/en/DesignDiscovery/

International Technology and Engineering Education Association (ITEEA)—www.iteaconnect.org

Materials World Modules—http://www.materialsworldmodules.org/

Museum of Science, Boston (NCTL)—http://www.mos.org/nctl/

My NASA Data Lesson Plans—http://mynasadata.larc.nasa.gov/my-nasa-data-lesson-plans/

National Science Digital Library—http://nsdl.org/

Next Generation Science Standards—http://www.nap.edu/ngss

Oregon Pre-Engineering and Applied sciences—http://opas.ous.edu/resourcesEngCurricular.php

Project Infinity—http://www.infinity-project.org/

Project Lead the Way—pltw.org

Sally Ride Science Academy—https://sallyridescience.com/

Science Buddies—sciencebuddies.org

Spark Plug into Science: http://www.gse.upenn.edu/spark/sparkkits.php

Stuff That Works (CCNY)—http://citytechnology.ccny.cuny.edu/Design_Tech.html

Teach Engineering—http://www.teachengineering.org/

Try Engineering—http://www.tryengineering.org/

Women in Engineering—http://www.wepan.org/displaycommon.cfm?an=1&subarticlenbr=39

Zoom: http://pbskids.o rg/zoom/activities/sci/

Table 2 Instructional Materials in the *Go-To Guide for Engineering Curricula Series*

Book / Curricula	Elementary							Middle School			High School			
	P	K	1	2	3	4	5	6	7	8	9	10	11	12
E1 Seeds of Science/ Roots of Reading				X	X	X	X							
E2 Physical Science Comes Alive!	X	X	X	X	X	X	X							
E3 Engineering byDesign TEEMS, K–2		X	X	X										
E4 BSCS Science Tracks		X	X	X	X	X	X							
E5 A World in Motion		X	X	X	X	X	X	X	X	X				
E6 FOSS Full Option Science System		X	X	X	X	X	X	X	X	X				
E7 Engineering Is Elementary			X	X	X	X	X							
E8 Tangible Kindergarten	X	X												
E9 Engineering Adventures (OST)					X	X	X							
E10 Engineering byDesign ™ TEEMS, 3–5 & I³					X	X	X							
E11 Design It! (OST)								X	X	X				
E12 Junk Drawer Robotics						X	X	X	X	X				
E13 PictureSTEM		X	X	X										
E14 STEM in Action	X	X	X	X										
M1 Design Squad (OST)					X	X	X	X	X	X	X	X	X	X
M2 Models in Technology and Science							X	X	X	X	X			
M3 Everyday Engineering							X	X	X	X	X			
M4 SLIDER								X	X	X				
M5 Teaching Engineering Made Easy								X	X	X				

Book	Elementary							Middle School			High School			
Curricula	P	K	1	2	3	4	5	6	7	8	9	10	11	12
M6 Fender Bender Physics								■	■	■				
M7 Technology in Practice								■	■	■				
M8 IQWST								■	■	■				
M9 Project-Based Inquiry Science								■	■	■				
M10 Issue-Oriented Science								■	■	■				
M11 Techbridge (OST)								■	■	■	■	■	■	■
M12 Waterbotics (OST)								■	■	■	■	■	■	■
M13 Engineering Now								■	■	■	■	■	■	■
M14 Engineering byDesign™ 6–8								■	■	■				
H1 INSPIRES											■	■	■	■
H2 Active Physics											■	■	■	■
H3 Active Chemistry											■	■	■	■
H4 Engineering the Future											■	■	■	■
H5 Engineer Your World											■	■	■	■
H6 Global Systems Science											■	■	■	■
H7 Science and Global Issues											■	■	■	■
H8 Engineering byDesign™											■	■	■	■
H9 Science by Design											■	■	■	■
H10 Biology in a Box								■			■	■	■	■
H11 Voyage Through Time											■	■	■	■
H12 EPICS											■	■	■	■

Note

* *Next Generation Science Standards* (NGSS): *For States, By States* is a registered trademark of Achieve, Inc. Neither Achieve, Inc. nor the lead states and partners that developed the NGSS were involved in the production of, and do not endorse the *Go-To Guide to Engineering Curricula 9-12!* However, Achieve, Inc. has granted permission for the authors of this book to quote extensively from the NGSS.

References

American Association for the Advancement of Science (AAAS). (1989). *Science for all Americans*. Project 2061. New York: Oxford University Press.

American Association for the Advancement of Science (AAAS). (1993/2008). *Benchmarks for science literacy*. Project 2061. New York: Oxford University Press.

Carr, R. L., Bennet, L. D., & Strobel, J. (2012). Engineering in the K–12 STEM standards of the 50 U.S. states: An analysis of presence and extent. *Journal of Engineering Education 101*(3), 539–564.

Cunningham, C., & Lachapelle, C. (2011). Designing engineering experiences to engage all students. Boston: Museum of Science. Retrieved from: http://www.eie.org/sites/default/files/2012ip-Cunningham_Lachapelle_Eng4All.pdf

Lachapelle, C., Phadnis, P., Hertel, J., & Cunningham, C. (2012). What is engineering? A survey of elementary students. Boston: Museum of Science. Retrieved from: http://www.eie.org/sites/default/files/2012-03_WE_Paper_fo_P-12_Engineering_Conference.pdf

Lewis, T. (2004). A Turn to engineering: The continuing struggle of technology education for legitimization as a school subject. *Journal of Technology Education, 16*(1), 21–39.

Meade, S., & Dugger, W. (2004, September). The second installment of the ITEA/Gallup Poll and what it reveals as to how Americans think about technology. *Technology Teacher, 64*(1), 1–12.

NASA Workforce. (2013). Data on NASA workforce. Retrieved from http://nasapeople.nasa.gov/workforce/default.htm

NGSS Lead States. (2013). *Next generation science standards: For states, by states, Volume 1: The standards* and *Volume 2: Appendices*. Washington, DC: National Academies Press.

NRC. (1996). *National science education standards*. Washington, DC: National Academies Press.

NRC. (2012). *A framework for K–12 science education: Practices, crosscutting concepts, and core ideas*. Washington, DC: National Academies Press.

Osborne, J., Simon, S., & Collins, S. (2003). Attitudes towards science: A review of the literature and its implications. *International Journal of Science Education, 25*(9), 1049–1097.

Sneider, C. (2011, September). *Reversing the swing from science: Implications from a century of research*. Presented at ITEST Convening on Advancing Research on Youth Motivation in STEM, Boston College, Boston, Massachusetts. Retrieved from http://itestlrc.edc.org/youth-motivation-convening-materials, and from the Noyce Foundation at: www.noycefdn.org/news.php

Technology and Engineering in High School Standards

One of the most important contributions of the new standards documents has been to clear up the confusion among the terms *science*, *technology*, and *engineering*. According to the *Framework*:

> In the K–12 context, "science" is generally taken to mean the traditional natural sciences: physics, chemistry, biology, and (more recently) earth, space, and environmental sciences. . . . We use the term "engineering" in a very broad sense to mean any engagement in a systematic practice of design to achieve solutions to particular human problems. Likewise, we broadly use the term "technology" to include all types of human-made systems and processes— not in the limited sense often used in schools that equates technology with modern computational and communications devices. Technologies result when engineers apply their understanding of the natural world and of human behavior to design ways to satisfy human needs and wants. (NRC, 2012, pp. 11–12)

Definitions alone might not make a big difference, but combining these definitions with an entirely new approach to standards is very likely to be a game changer. Together, the *Framework* and the NGSS (NGSS Lead States, 2013a, 2013b) have the potential to change the way science is taught in this country.

To explain how technology and engineering are integrated in the new standards, it is helpful to understand the three "dimensions" introduced in the *Framework* and how they appear in the NGSS.

Dimension 1: Science and Engineering Practices

In the NSES (NRC, 1996), the set of abilities known collectively as "science inquiry"— what students should be *able to do*—were described separately from the list of what students should *know*. Although the NSES advocated combining inquiry and content, it did not specify how to do so. In contrast, the NGSS merges specific practices and core ideas. But before we describe what that looks like, we first describe what has become of inquiry in the NGSS. In its new form, the term *inquiry* has been replaced with eight "practices of science and engineering." Each of the practices is described in some detail and, what is most important for this book, each practice refers to both science inquiry and engineering design. Following is a description of the eight practices for the high school grades, with emphasis on engineering.

Practice 1: Ask questions and define problems. Just as science inquiry begins with a question, engineering design begins with the definition of a problem. With guidance from a knowledgeable teacher, students' interests in creating things can lead to the formulation of problems to be solved or goals to be met. With prompting, students in grades 9–12 can define a problem that involves the development of a process or system with interacting components and criteria and constraints that may include social, technical, and/or environmental considerations.

Practice 2: Develop and use models. Whether they are doing science or engineering, students frequently use models. As an engineering practice, students construct models to help them design and test solutions to problems. In grades 9–12, students should be able to develop and/or use a model (including mathematical and computational models) to generate data to support explanations, predict phenomena, analyze systems, and/or solve problems.

Practice 3: Plan and carry out investigations. There are many different kinds of investigations in science, ranging from controlled laboratory experiments to field biology investigations. In science, investigations are used to answer questions about the natural world. In engineering, students plan and carry out investigations to learn more about the problem they are trying to solve or to test possible solutions. In grades 9–12, students should be able to manipulate variables and collect data about a complex model of a proposed process or system to identify failure points or improve performance relative to criteria for success.

Practice 4: Analyze and interpret data. Science and engineering both involve analyzing and interpreting data. Students in grades 9–12 who are engaged in an engineering design project can apply concepts of statistics and probability to engineering problems, using digital tools when feasible. They should also be able to analyze data to identify design features or characteristics of the components of a proposed process or system to optimize it relative to criteria for success and to evaluate the impact of new data on a model of a proposed process or system.

Practice 5: Use mathematics and computational thinking. In addition to analyzing and interpreting data, mathematical and computational thinking includes representing relationships between variables with equations and using computers and other digital tools for automatically collecting, analyzing, and graphing data, and using simulations. High school students should be able to create and/or revise a computational model or simulation of a designed device, process, or system and determine if the results of a simulation "makes sense" with comparison to what is known about the real world. They should also be able to apply ratios, rates, percentages, unit conversions, and algebra to solve engineering problems.

Practice 6: Construct explanations and design solutions. In science, the end result is an explanation for a natural phenomenon. In engineering, the end result is a solution to a problem. High school students should be able to design, evaluate, and/or refine a solution to a complex real-world problem based on scientific knowledge, student-generated sources of evidence, prioritized criteria, and considerations of trade-offs.

Practice 7: Engage in argument from evidence. While in science, students use evidence to argue for or against an explanation for a phenomenon, in engineering students use evidence and reasoning to determine the best possible solution to a problem or to defend their choice of a given solution. In the high school grades, students should be able to make and define a claim based on scientific knowledge and student-generated evidence about the effectiveness of a design solution. They should also be able to evaluate competing design solutions to a real-world problem, based on scientific ideas and principles, empirical evidence, and/or logical arguments about relevant factors, which might include economic, societal, environmental, or ethical considerations.

Practice 8: Obtain, evaluate, and communicate information. Both science and engineering involve critical reading and the ability to communicate ideas in writing and speech. High school students should be able to evaluate the validity and reliability of information about a need or solution to a problem from technical texts or media reports. They should also be able to communicate their own process of solving an engineering challenge, presenting the information clearly in a variety of formats, including orally, in writing, graphically, and mathematically.

These eight practices of science and engineering are very important in the NGSS because they are woven into all the performance expectations, which comprise the heart of the standards.

Dimension 2: Crosscutting Concepts

The second dimension is a set of seven crosscutting concepts. These concepts were also present in earlier standards documents called "themes" in *Benchmarks for Science Literacy* and "unifying concepts and processes" in the NSES. The purpose of this dimension is to illustrate that although the different disciplines of science concern different phenomena, they represent a unified way of understanding the world. For example, although "energy" may be treated somewhat differently when studying chemical reactions, ecosystems, and the Earth as a body in space, the concept of *energy* is the same in each case. The seven crosscutting concepts described in the *Framework* and carried over into the NGSS are as follows:

1. *Patterns.* Observed patterns of forms and events guide organization and classification, and they prompt questions about relationships and the factors that influence them.

2. *Cause and effect: Mechanism and explanation.* Events have causes, sometimes simple, sometimes multifaceted. A major activity of science is investigating and explaining causal relationships and the mechanisms by which they are mediated. Such mechanisms can then be tested across given contexts and used to predict and explain events in new contexts.

3. *Scale, proportion, and quantity.* In considering phenomena, it is critical to recognize what is relevant at different measures of size, time, and energy and to recognize how changes in scale, proportion, or quantity affect a system's structure or performance.

4. *Systems and system models.* Defining the system under study—specifying its boundaries and making explicit a model of that system—provides tools for understanding and testing ideas that are applicable throughout science and engineering.

5. *Energy and matter: Flows, cycles, and conservation.* Tracking fluxes of energy and matter into, out of, and within systems helps one understand the systems' possibilities and limitations.

6. *Structure and function.* The way in which an object or living thing is shaped and its substructure determine many of its properties and functions.

7. *Stability and change.* For natural and built systems alike, conditions of stability and determinants of rates of change or evolution of a system are critical elements of study.

In addition to these seven crosscutting concepts, the writing team decided to add two other important ideas that were included in the *Framework* in a chapter on engineering, technology, and applications of science:

8. *The interdependence of science, engineering, and technology.* Without engineers to design the instruments that scientists use to investigate the world, modern science would be impossible. Conversely, new scientific discoveries enable engineers to invent and modify technologies. In a word, science and engineering drive each other forward.

9. *The influence of engineering, technology, and science on society and the environment.* Scientific discoveries and technological decisions profoundly affect human society and the natural environment.

Feedback from the public (and especially from science teachers) noted that ideas about the nature of science were missing from the *Framework* and the NGSS. Since concepts relating to the nature of science also cut across all the science disciplines, these ideas were also included along with the other crosscutting concepts listed above.

Dimension 3: A Small Set of Disciplinary Core Ideas

One of the criticisms of today's science curriculum is that it's "a mile wide and an inch deep" (Schmidt, McKnight, & Raizen, 1997, p. 2). The problem of too much to cover in too little time is not new for those of us who have been in science teaching for decades, but the advent of high stakes tests have brought the problem to the surface.

The *Framework* and NGSS are the first set of science standards to substantially reduce the amount that students are expected to learn. Furthermore, the content is more coherent than previous efforts. It is organized in just 12 core ideas that grow in sophistication and complexity across the grades. Eleven of the core ideas are in the traditional fields of life, physical, and Earth and space sciences. The 12th core idea is engineering design. In other words, students are expected to learn the essential process used by engineers to solve problems and achieve goals, just as they are expected to learn about the concepts of energy and heredity. The 12 core ideas that thread through the standards from kindergarten to grade 12 are listed in Table 0.1.

Table 0.1 Twelve Core Ideas in the Next Generation Science Standards

Physical Science	Life Science	Earth and Space Science	Engineering
• Matter and Its Interactions • Motion and stability: Forces and interactions • Energy • Waves and their applications in technologies for information transfer	• From molecules to organisms: Structures and processes • Ecosystems: Interactions, energy, and dynamics • Heredity: Inheritance and variation of traits • Biological evolution: Unity and diversity	• Earth's place in the universe • Earth's systems • Earth and human activity	• Engineering design

Each of the core ideas above are further broken down into components, and each of those are integrated into the NGSS in ways that are grade-level appropriate. By organizing the content in this way, teachers can see how their contributions build on the work in prior grades and lay the foundation for further learning.

A Progression of Core Ideas for Engineering

Table 0.1, above, lists "Engineering Design" as the 12th core idea for all students. Like the core ideas within the traditional science disciplines, these ideas grow in complexity and sophistication over time. Performance expectations for this core idea at all grade levels are shown in Table 0.2. Although this volume is concerned with the high school level, it is important for teachers and administrators to be familiar with the entire span of the learning progression.

Table 0.2 Learning Progression for Engineering Design

K–2	3–5	6–8	9–12
Ask questions, make observations, and gather information about a situation people want to change to define a simple problem that can be solved through the development of a	Define a simple design problem reflecting a need or a want that includes specified criteria for success and constraints on materials, time, or cost.	Define the criteria and constraints of a design problem with sufficient precision to ensure a successful solution, taking into account relevant scientific principles and potential impacts on	Analyze a major global challenge to specify qualitative and quantitative criteria and constraints for solutions that account for societal needs and wants.

(Continued)

Table 0.2 (Continued)

K–2	3–5	6–8	9–12
new or improved object or tool. Develop a simple sketch, drawing, or physical model to illustrate how the shape of an object helps it function as needed to solve a given problem. Analyze data from tests of two objects designed to solve the same problem to compare the strengths and weaknesses of how each performs.	Generate and compare multiple possible solutions to a problem based on how well each is likely to meet the criteria and constraints of the problem. Plan and carry out fair tests in which variables are controlled and failure points are considered to identify aspects of a model or prototype that can be improved.	people and the natural environment that may limit possible solutions. Evaluate competing design solutions using a systematic process to determine how well they meet the criteria and constraints of the problem. Analyze data from tests to determine similarities and differences among several design solutions to identify the best characteristics of each that can be combined into a new solution to better meet the criteria for success. Develop a model to generate data for iterative testing and modification of a proposed object, tool, or process such that an optimal design can be achieved.	Design a solution to a complex real-world problem by breaking it down into smaller, more manageable problems that can be solved through engineering. Evaluate a solution to a complex real-world problem based on prioritized criteria and trade-offs that account for a range of constraints, including cost, safety, reliability, and aesthetics, as well as possible social, cultural, and environmental impacts. Use a computer simulation to model the impact of proposed solutions to a complex real-world problem with numerous criteria and constraints on interactions within and between systems relevant to the problem.

Combining the Three Dimensions

The NGSS combines disciplinary core ideas, practices and crosscutting concepts in sentences called "performance expectations." These statements illustrate what students are expected to be able to do in order to demonstrate not only their understanding of the important ideas from the *Framework* but also how they should be able to *use* what they've learned. Each performance expectation begins with one of the practices and explains how students are expected to use that practice in demonstrating their understanding of the disciplinary core idea. Crosscutting concepts are sometimes explicitly integrated into these sentences, and sometimes the crosscutting concept is simply clear from the context.

Unlike the vague statements from prior standards, that generally began with the phrase "students will know that . . ." performance expectations specify what students should be able to *do* in order to demonstrate their understanding. Although performance expectations are not so specific as to designate a given teaching activity or assessment item, they are sufficiently specific to provide the same clear learning goals for curriculum, instruction, and assessment.

Recall that each practice could be used for science or engineering. Keeping in mind that science involves the investigation of natural phenomena in the traditional disciplines, while engineering involves designing solutions to problems, it is possible to figure out which refer to science and which to engineering. Table 0.3 lists several performance expectations from the NGSS. See if you can determine which ones are science and which are engineering. The first two statements are classified for you. Fill in the rest of the blanks to test your ability to distinguish science from engineering practices.

Table 0.3 Are these performance expectations science or engineering?

(The editor's preferred answers are at the end of the table.[1])

High school students who understand chemical reactions can:	This is an example of:
Develop a model to illustrate that the release or absorption of energy from a chemical reaction system depends on the changes in total bond energy.	Science
Refine the design of a chemical system by specifying a change in conditions that would produce increased amounts of products at equilibrium.	Engineering
High school students who understand Earth and Human Activity can:	**This is an example of:**
1. Construct an explanation based on evidence for how the availability of natural resources, occurrence of natural hazards, and changes in climate have influenced human activity.	
2. Evaluate competing design solutions for developing, managing, and utilizing energy and mineral resources based on cost-benefit ratios.	
High school students who understand ecosystems can:	**This is an example of:**
3. Design, evaluate, and refine a solution for reducing the impacts of human activities on the environment and biodiversity.	
4. Evaluate the evidence for the role of group behavior on individual and species' chances to survive and reproduce.	

(Continued)

Table 0.3 (Continued)

High school students who understand energy can:	
5. Design, build, and refine a device that works within given constraints to convert one form of energy into another form of energy.	
6. Develop and use a model of two objects interacting through electric or magnetic fields to illustrate the forces between objects and the changes in energy of the objects because of the interaction.	

[1] Answer Key: 1. Science, 2. Engineering, 3. Engineering, 4. Science, 5. Engineering, 6. Science

The layout of the NGSS is shown in the diagram below. Each set of performance expectations has a title at the top of the page. Below the title is a box containing the performance expectations. Below that are three foundation boxes, which list (from left to right) the specific science and engineering practices, disciplinary core ideas (DCIs), and crosscutting concepts that were combined to produce the performance expectations above. The bottom section lists connections to performance expectations (PE)s in other science disciplines at the same grade level, to PEs of the same core idea for younger and older students, and to related Common State Standards in mathematics and English language arts.

Structure of the NGSS

MS-PS3 Energy

Performance Expectations		
Science and Engineering Practices	Disciplinary Core Ideas	Crosscutting Concepts
Connections to: • Related core ideas at this grade level • Related core ideas across grade bands • Common Core State Standards in Mathematics • Common Core State Standards in English Language Arts		

Summary

The new standards are complex, so it's worth pausing for a moment to summarize the most important key ideas:

A Framework for K–12 Science Education (NRC, 2012)

- Was created by a blue ribbon panel of Nobel prize-winning scientists, engineers, university professors, and educational researchers.
- Provides the blueprint for the NGSS.
- Described three dimensions to be included in the new standards: (1) twelve disciplinary core ideas, (2) practices of science and engineering; and (3) crosscutting concepts.
- Calls for engineering to be included at the same level as Newton's laws and the theory of evolution.

Next Generation Science Standards: For States, By States (NGSS Lead States, 2013a, 2013b)

- Is organized by 12 core ideas in four disciplines: (1) physical science, (2) life science, (3) Earth and space science, and (4) engineering.
- Presents standards in the form of performance expectations, which combine disciplinary core ideas with practices and crosscutting concepts.
- Identifies which core ideas are to be taught at which grade, K–5, and by grade band in middle and high school.
- Provides clear and common targets for curriculum, instruction, and assessment.

Engineering is woven throughout the NGSS, which means that students must be able to demonstrate that they can *use* a given core idea in science to solve a practical engineering problem. Second, engineering design is also a core idea that all students are expected to learn at successively higher levels as they mature and move through the grades. In other words, engineering design is both a practice (what students should be able to do) and a disciplinary core idea (what students should know and understand).

Alternative Pathways for the High School Level

Although the NGSS specifies which core ideas should be taught at each level in Grades 1–5, there is no such designation in high school. The reason for this is that different states require different ways of organizing the science curriculum. Some states require that the disciplines be integrated so that life, physical, and Earth and space science are taught every year. Other states require that one discipline be taught in a single year. The NGSS accommodates these differences by specifying what students should learn by the end of 8th grade, with no required schedule for instruction.

Nonetheless, some topics lay groundwork for learning in other subjects; so some sequences are better than others. Consequently, the state teams that developed the NGSS have published recommendations for alternative pathways to guide the development of a curriculum sequence that is compatible with a state's requirements but that also enables students to learn in an optimal sequence. These recommendations are described in Appendix K of the NGSS (NGSS Lead States, 2013b).

While existing instructional materials will need to be modified to meet the new standards, and there are several examples of such modifications in the chapters in this book, thanks to the NGSS, the problem to be solved is far more specific—and therefore more easily solved—than at any time in the past.

References

NGSS Lead States. (2013a). *Next generation science standards: For states, by states, volume 1: The standards.* Washington, DC: National Academies Press.

NGSS Lead States. (2013b). *Next generation science standards: For states, by states, volume 2: Appendices.* Washington, DC: National Academies Press.

NRC (1996). *National science education standards.* Washington, DC: National Academies Press.

NRC (2012). *A framework for K–12 science education: Practices, crosscutting concepts, and core ideas.* Washington, DC: National Academies Press.

Schmidt, W. H., McKnight, C. C., & Raizen, S. A. (1997). *A splintered vision: an investigation of U.S. science and mathematics education.* Boston/Dordrecht/London: Kluwer Academic Press.

The INSPIRES Curriculum

Julia Ross, Taryn Melkus Bayles, and Jonathan Singer

University of Maryland, Baltimore County

Baltimore, MD

Students Working on Hemodialysis Module

Image courtesy of Ezana Dawit, Justin Santos, and Gabrielle Salib.

The INSPIRES Curriculum (INcreasing Student Participation Interest and Recruitment in Engineering and Science) is comprised of five standards-based modules for grades 9–12 that focus on integrating all areas of STEM. Our approach uses real-world engineering design challenges and inquiry-based learning strategies to engage students, increase technological and scientific literacy, and develop key practices essential for success in STEM disciplines. The curriculum is flexible and cost effective. Modules are independent of one another, so they can be implemented individually in an existing science or technology education course or together to comprise a full course.

The INSPIRES Curriculum is currently available by contacting the authors at inspires@umbc.edu.

Although the INSPIRES Curriculum was developed prior to the publication of *A Framework for K–12 Science Education: Practices, Crosscutting Concepts, and Core Ideas* (NRC, 2012), all modules align closely to this vision and the NGSS (NGSS Lead States, 2013) performance expectations related to engineering design. The curriculum modules target all eight Science and Engineering Practices and therefore provide a strong platform for discussion of the relationship between engineering and science. Each of the INSPIRES modules utilizes a different engineering design challenge and therefore targets different science disciplinary core ideas and crosscutting concepts.

Design Principles

Each module follows a common lesson plan structure and is based on the following curriculum design principles:

1. **Context.** Real-world, defined problem space that provides intellectual challenge for the learner

2. **Standards Based.** Publications that define the language and methods of the larger community, including the *National Science Education Standards* (NRC, 1996), *Standards for Technological Literacy* (ITEEA, 2000, 2005, 2007), and *Common Core State Standards* (NGA & CCSSO, 2010).

3. **STEM Practices.** As defined by *A Framework for K–12 Science Education*

4. **Collaboration:** Interaction between students, teachers, and community members to share information/designs, negotiate alternatives and build consensus

5. **Public Artifacts:** Public representations of ideas or practices that can be shared, critiqued, and revised to enhance learning

6. **Metacognitive:** Opportunities to explicitly (1) recognize the nature of STEM practices, (2) interpret key STEM concepts individually, and (3) revise designs and reports based on feedback

Principles 1, 2, and 3 are based on the theory of situation cognition—that knowing is inseparable from doing, and that knowledge develops in social, cultural and physical contexts (Linn & Hsi, 2000; Singer, Lotter, Feller, & Gates, 2011). Principles 4, 5, and 6 are based on the theory that making thinking visible by encouraging meaningful dialogue focused on science content will help students not only increase subject matter knowledge but also improve their reasoning abilities (Garet, Porter, Desimone, Birman, & Yoon, 2001; Lotter, Singer, & Godley, 2009; Rushton, Lotter, & Singer, 2011). Each of these principles plays out in the form of specific instructional strategies, as we will describe in two of the curriculum modules.

Where Does INSPIRES Fit in the High School Curriculum?

Each module is approximately six weeks in length (assuming a 45 minute class period) and is structured for students who have Algebra I competency. Modules have been tested for efficacy in various settings, including biology, physics, chemistry, allied health, and technology education classrooms. Table 1.1 suggests course placement for each module. In most cases, a single module is chosen for implementation based on the STEM content fit for the given course. Alternately, the modules can be grouped together to form a complete semester or full-year "Engineering Design" course.

Following are brief descriptions of two of the INSPIRES modules: "Engineering in Healthcare: A Hemodialysis Case Study" and "Engineering Energy Solutions: A Renewable Energy System Case Study." Design principles associated with the various activities are indicated in (**bold**).

Table 1.1 INSPIRES Curriculum Modules

INSPIRES Module	Science Concepts Currently Included	Recommended Course Placement
Engineering in Healthcare: A Hemodialysis Case Study	• Diffusion/Selective diffusion • Equilibrium • Membrane structure • Fluid flow/Flow rates	• Biology • Technology Education • Allied Health
Engineering in Healthcare: A Heart-Lung System Case Study	• Heat transfer • Fluid flow/Flow rate/Pumps • Anatomy and physiology of the heart and lungs	• Physics • Anatomy/Physiology • Technology Education
Engineering Energy Solutions: A Renewable Energy System Case Study	• Work/Power/Energy • Gears/Simple machines • Systems/System efficiency • Renewable resources	• Physics • Technology Education
Engineering and Flight: A Hot Air Balloon Case Study	• Forces/Force balances • Weight/Density • Buoyancy • Heat transfer • Material properties • Properties of an ideal gas	• Physics • General Physical Science • Technology Education
Engineering and the Environment	• Currently under revision to enhance fit in chemistry	• Chemistry • Environmental Science • Technology Education

Engineering in Healthcare: A Hemodialysis Case Study

An introductory video focuses on a teenage girl with kidney failure who undergoes hemodialysis on a regular basis. The video describes her treatment, introduces her doctor, and explains the function of a modern hemodialysis machine (**Context**). Student teams are given the challenge to design, build, test, and refine a system that mimics attributes and functions of a hemodialysis system, including the removal of a minimum of 2.5 mg of "waste" from simulated "blood." Design teams are challenged to maximize efficiency while minimizing system cost. The maximum system cost is set at $50 (**STEM Practices**). After watching the video and receiving the challenge, students use a "Think, Pair, Share" strategy to reach consensus (**Collaboration**) on key ideas as well as the criteria and constraints required to construct a design solution.

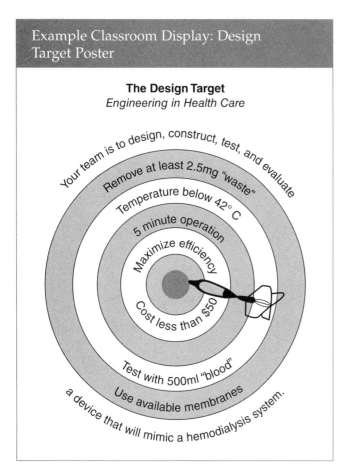

Example Classroom Display: Design Target Poster

The Design Target
Engineering in Health Care

Your team is to design, construct, test, and evaluate
Remove at least 2.5mg "waste"
Temperature below 42° C
5 minute operation
Maximize efficiency
Cost less than $50
Test with 500ml "blood"
Use available membranes
a device that will mimic a hemodialysis system.

Image courtesy of the University of Maryland.

As students attempt to solve the design challenge, they are introduced to the engineering design process as a rational and methodical cycle of steps (**STEM Practices**). The various steps are explicitly addressed during the lessons to ensure that students understand each process they use (**Metacognition**). A large classroom poster is used to facilitate these explicit connections (**Public Artifacts**). To understand the various design constraints and criteria as well as make informed design decisions, the students learn relevant scientific principles as well as mathematical equations to quantitatively assess and refine their design (**Standards Based**).

In this module, students learn concepts associated with (1) diffusion/selective diffusion, (2) equilibrium, (3) membrane structure and function, and (4) fluid flow. These science concepts are introduced in the curriculum through a variety of "just in time" phenomena-first activities (**Context**) and inquiry-based investigations (**STEM Practices**). First, student teams are presented with a mini design challenge in which they must design and test an apparatus to separate Rice Krispies® from a complex mixture of breakfast cereals. This hands-on exercise is used to introduce the concept of separating a component from a mixture in a way that is visual to the learner. It is also used to reintroduce the engineering design process (**Context/Standards**). Students must consider the physical properties of the various cereal components as they begin their designs and decide on properties that could be used as a basis for separation. Prior to receiving teacher approval to start device construction and testing, individual group members submit potential design solutions, then engage in small group discussion to build consensus (**Collaboration**) on a prototype design. Most student groups focus on size as the basis for separation, which is consistent with the overall hemodialysis design challenge. Group presentations of designs and design decisions link the exercise to the overarching hemodialysis design challenge.

Students then learn more about the function of the kidneys and how dialysis works. Fundamental concepts such as concentration, concentration gradient, molecular motion, and diffusion are introduced through a serious of hands-on exercises. Students visualize the concept of selective diffusion by observing the movement of a dye across a semipermeable membrane. Students then consider and explore various factors that influence the rate of diffusion and the total amount of mass transfer in a given time period. These factors include the effects of temperature, molecular weight, membrane pore size, and membrane surface area. Finally, students investigate ways to make fluid flow and learn how fluid flow is measured and described quantitatively. This allows design teams to consider how fluid flow may be used in the design of a hemodialysis system.

Following hands-on exploration, students use online models and animations to illustrate the "nonvisible" mechanism(s) driving many of the observed macroscopic events. Concepts of molecular motion and diffusion are stressed, linking the online visualization to the hands-on activities. Computer-based mathematical simulations are utilized prior to the final design and build phase allowing students to alter a variety of design parameters and quantify their impact on system efficiency (**STEM Practices**). Students then plan, build, test, and refine a "hemodialysis system" (**Integrates all principles**). Student teams present their final designs along with an analysis of design decisions in an open forum (**Collaboration/Public Artifacts**). Concepts and key ideas are reinforced and continuity between lessons is maintained through the use of a design notebook and by having students post artifacts representing their understanding (**Metacognition**) on a classroom artifact board (**Public Artifacts**).

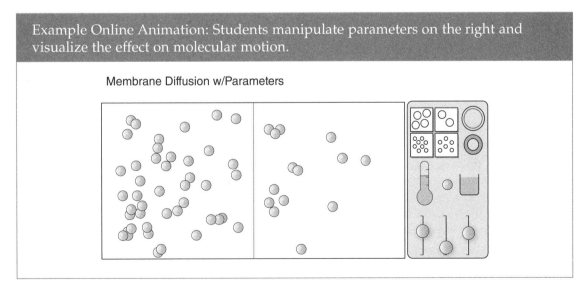

Example Online Animation: Students manipulate parameters on the right and visualize the effect on molecular motion.

Membrane Diffusion w/Parameters

Image courtesy of the University of Maryland.

Engineering Energy Solutions

A Renewable Energy System Design Challenge

An introductory video focuses on how society uses energy, the structure of modern energy systems, current and projected energy challenges, and the need for the development of renewable energy strategies. Students learn that many steps are involved in supplying energy to the consumer, including collection, conversion, storage, and transport (**Context**). Student teams are given the challenge to design, build, test, and refine an energy system that (1) collects energy from a renewable source (hydro, wind, or solar), (2) stores the energy, (3) transports the energy to a testing location, (4) converts the energy to a useful form, and then (5) powers a 0.4 watt light bulb for a minimum of 15 seconds. Design teams are challenged to maximize system performance while minimizing system cost. The maximum system cost is set at $100 (**STEM Practices**). After watching the video and receiving the challenge, students use a Think, Pair, Share strategy to reach consensus (**Collaboration**) on key ideas as well as the criteria and constraints required to construct a design solution.

As students attempt to solve the design challenge, they are introduced to the engineering design process as a rational and methodical cycle of steps (**STEM Practices**). The various steps are explicitly addressed during the lessons to ensure that students understand each process they use (**Metacognition**). A large classroom poster is used to facilitate these explicit connections (**Public Artifacts**). To understand the various design constraints and criteria as well as make informed design decisions, the students learn relevant scientific principles as well as mathematical equations to quantitatively assess and refine their design (**Standards Based**).

As in the Hemodialysis module, students are introduced to the engineering design process (**STEM Practices**). Through the activities unique to this module, they learn concepts associated with (1) work/power/energy, (2) gears/simple machines, (3) systems/system efficiency, and (4) renewable energy resources. These science concepts are introduced in the curriculum through a variety of just in time phenomena-first activities (**Context**) and inquiry-based investigations (**STEM Practices**). First, student teams are presented with a mini challenge in which they must design a system to use hydropower (2 qt. of water) to raise a weight as quickly as possible. This hands-on exercise introduces the concepts of work and power and reintroduces the engineering design process (**Context/Standards**). Students learn how to measure work in this system and calculate power, exploring the relationship between the two concepts. Prior to receiving teacher approval to start device construction and testing, individual group members submit potential design solutions, then engage in small group discussion to build consensus (**Collaboration**) on a prototype design. Group presentations of designs and design decisions link the exercise to the overarching energy system design challenge. Students next learn about gear systems and how they can be used to increase the work done by a system (mechanical advantage) and transfer motion or power from one moving part to another. Using hands-on activities, teams explore gear function and gear ratios. Design teams are then issued a follow-up mini challenge to incorporate gears into their systems to increase performance.

Students next learn about energy conversion through hands-on activities using a solar cell and windmill. In the first activity, groups use solar power to lift a weight, thereby learning how a solar cell works and how a motor converts electricity into kinetic energy. A second activity focuses on the conversion of kinetic energy from a windmill into electricity using a generator. Students learn how to calculate work, power, and efficiency. Students then learn about how energy is stored, how energy is transported and how each step in an energy system combines to yield the overall system efficiency. Mathematical calculations for efficiency are included.

After hands-on exploration, students use computer-based mathematical simulations to alter a variety of design parameters and quantify their impact on the system efficiency (**STEM Practices**). Students then plan, build, test, and refine a renewable energy system to meet design criteria (**Integrates all principles**). Student teams present their final designs along with an analysis of design decisions in an open forum **(Collaboration/Public Artifacts)**. Concepts and key ideas are reinforced and continuity between lessons is maintained through the use of a design notebook and the classroom artifact board (**Public Artifacts**).

Example of Hands-on Activity

Image courtesy of the University of Maryland.

Instructional Materials

Instructional materials for the INSPIRES Curriculum consist of a variety of components for each module as described below.

Design Challenge. Each module includes an overarching open-ended engineering design challenge that focuses on a real-world problem or need. The design challenges are written with quantitative design criteria and constraints and require students to make decisions about trade-offs as they move through the design process. The challenges have enough

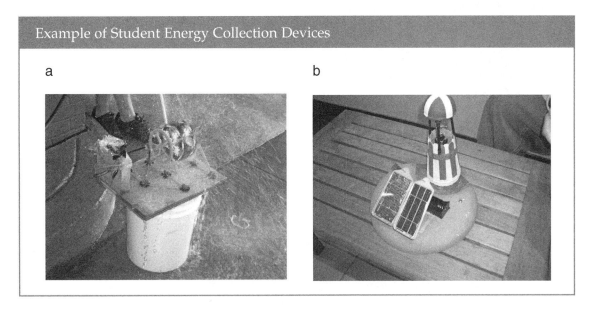

Example of Student Energy Collection Devices

a   b

Images courtesy of the University of Maryland.

specificity to allow solution within a week to two weeks of class time but are open-ended enough to allow for significant creativity in the design solution.

Lesson Plans. Complete lesson plans for each module include detailed instructions for presenting content and doing hands-on activities and suggest appropriate pedagogical strategies. Student handouts and worksheets are included to facilitate instruction.

Classroom Display. Electronic files suitable for printing at poster size for classroom display are available, including the "Engineering Design Loop" and a "Design Target" specific to each module.

Video Content. The curriculum uses professionally produced video segments to introduce students to the real-world application and societal need behind each engineering design challenge. Videos also introduce students to career pathways related to the module content.

Online Animations and Mathematical Simulation. All modules include an online mathematical simulation that allows students to vary parameters specific to the design challenge. In doing so, students explore quantitatively how these changes affect system performance. Selected modules also include online animations that allow students to visualize molecular level phenomena responsible for macroscopic behavior.

Assessments. The curriculum includes end-of-module multiple choice tests to assess student learning of engineering and science concepts. These tests can also be given before a module, if evidence of student growth is required. Scoring guides for assessing individual and team performance on engineering design tasks are also included in the curriculum materials.

Laboratory Equipment and Supplies. The INSPIRES Curriculum is designed as a low-cost solution to integrating engineering into the high school classroom. The curriculum does not require the purchase of expensive core equipment and relies heavily on common science lab supplies and materials often found in art rooms or woodshops. Almost all materials needed to complete the modules are available through retailers such as Walmart®, Target®, Radio Shack®, Home Depot® and Lowes®. Recycled and common materials are used as much as possible.

Tips for Maximizing Student Success

From the beginning, INSPIRES was developed as an integrated STEM curriculum that focuses not only on engineering design but also scientific and mathematical concepts and reasoning. The ultimate learning goal associated with the INSPIRES modules is to support students in making explicit connections among design decisions, underpinning STEM concepts and the contextualizing challenge. As a result, this integrated approach aligns very well with the NGSS. However, it also presents challenges for teachers not accustomed to teaching in this manner. To be successful, the classroom teacher needs to consistently keep the integration of Content, Context, and Practice (Design Principles 1–3) visible by employing instructional strategies consistent with Design Principles 4–6.

1. **Make explicit connections to the overarching design challenge during each lesson.** Student learning is maximized with the INSPIRES modules when students are pressed to provide rationales for their design decisions that are grounded in foundational STEM concepts and practices. These foundational concepts are learned throughout the modules using an inquiry-based format. Most science teachers are familiar with inquiry-based strategies such as a predict-observe-explain cycle that provides hands-on common experiences prior to introducing formal definitions. This type of strategy has been the accepted norm of high quality science education for decades. However, in the case of the INSPIRES Curriculum, taking an additional step to facilitate connections between the newly introduced idea and how that concept may be applied in the actual design challenge is key. Making such connections on a routine basis will help students keep focused on the overarching learning goals.

2. **Use simulation results to inform design decisions.** Each of the INSPIRES modules includes computer-based lessons that occur just prior to the final system design, build, and test activities. The computer-based lessons include a tutorial style program that reviews key concepts followed by a set of questions that must be answered correctly before continuing onto the next idea. An incorrect response prompts the student for further review. In addition, a mathematical simulation is included that allows the learner to systematically manipulate one design variable (e.g., flow rate in the Hemodialysis module) while holding the other design variables constant in order to quantitatively predict system performance. A data chart is generated showing the results of the simulation and can be used to make informed design decisions. The combination of computer lessons fulfills the same purpose as the meaning-making sequence required at the conclusion of each inquiry-based activity. The tutorial reviews the fundamental STEM concepts while the simulation applies that information directly to the design challenge. Teacher survey data have indicated that when teachers run short on time it is these two lessons that tend to be skipped. As a result, the design, build, and test phase often takes longer because students do not know what combination of design parameters are likely to lead to a successful design. Therefore, requiring students to justify design decisions based on results of the simulation will lead to less "trial and error" and shorten the time needed to enact the module.

3. **Emphasize planning and rationale for decision making.** When enacting lessons requiring students to plan, build, and test an apparatus, teachers tend to place too much emphasis on the "build" and insufficient emphasis on "plan" and "test." Many students approach design projects with an initial attitude of trial and error. When given a design task such as those described in the section above, students will enthusiastically start putting pieces and parts together to build something. This "rush to build" may also be inadvertently supported by the teacher in response to time pressures or the teacher's own enthusiasm for students' eagerness. As a result, many teachers focus on the actual building process and lose sight of the larger educational goals. This overemphasis on the building phase can also cause groups to become fixated on construction issues and lose sight of the larger purpose of the design challenge. For example, student groups may fixate on trying to repair a small leak in the hemodialysis system, even though the leak does not greatly affect system performance. As a result, students may spend a great deal of

time on activities that are not supporting new or deeper learning of STEM content. It is therefore imperative that the teacher be able to redirect groups and make a determination if the quality of construction is sufficient to collect the required design performance data.

In many ways, the building activity is less important than what should occur immediately before and after. Prior to building, students should be involved in a structured planning phase. In this phase, the teacher should require a plan illustrating and explaining how the design will be constructed as well as criteria that will be used to measure the level of design success. Requiring students to provide a rationale grounded in the understanding of STEM concepts and the results of the mathematical simulation is at the heart of the learning objectives. Similarly, at the conclusion of the building activity the teacher should organize a class discussion that explicitly makes connections to the importance of the systematic approach they used, connecting the approach to the accepted practices of the STEM field (e.g., Design Loop or Scientific Method). After testing, results should be related back to design decisions and STEM understanding.

Connection to the NGSS

In its current form, the INSPIRES Curriculum targets multiple aspects of the NGSS. Each module focuses on distinct scientific content. Therefore, coverage of NGSS performance expectations with respect to science concepts varies from module to module. Similarly, mapping to the NGSS Crosscutting Concepts varies from module to module. However, each INSPIRES module was developed to focus on engineering design and the approach to design is consistent across the curriculum. As a result, each INSPIRES Curriculum module targets all four HS-ETS1 Engineering Design performance expectations as shown in Table 1.2 and all eight NGSS Science and Engineering Practices as shown in Table 1.3.

Table 1.2 Mapping of INSPIRES to Performance Expectations in the NGSS

NGSS Performance Expectation	INSPIRES Curriculum Component
HS-ETS1-1: Analyze a major global challenge to specify qualitative and quantitative criteria and constraints for solutions that account for societal needs and wants.	Each INSPIRES module includes an overarching real-world engineering design challenge. While criteria and constraints are included in the challenge, students must prioritize criteria, consider trade-offs and include constraints that are specific to their classroom or situation.
HS-ETS1-2: Design a solution to a complex real-world problem by breaking it down into smaller, more manageable problems that can be solved through engineering.	In each module, student teams design and build an apparatus or system to meet performance criteria. Learning is scaffolded to focus on various technical aspects of the design independently prior to performing the overall design and build.

NGSS Performance Expectation	INSPIRES Curriculum Component
HS-ETS1-3: Evaluate a solution to a complex real-world problem based on prioritized criteria and trade-offs that account for a range of constraints, including cost, safety, reliability, and aesthetics, as well as possible societal, cultural, and environmental impacts.	After the student teams design and build an apparatus or system, they must test and evaluate performance based on design criteria, cost, and safety. Groups must document trade-offs and explain how constraints impact their design. If time permits, redesign is recommended. During final presentations, groups evaluate and discuss the design solutions of other teams in the class.
HS-ETS1-4: Use a computer simulation to model the impact of proposed solutions to a complex real-world problem with numerous criteria and constraints on interactions within and between systems relevant to the problem.	Each module includes an online mathematical simulation in which students vary several design parameters and investigate the effect the changes have on system performance and cost.

Table 1.3 Mapping of INSPIRES to Practices of Science and Engineering in the NGSS

Practice	Science	Engineering
1. Asking questions and defining problems		X
2. Developing and using models	X	X
3. Planning and carrying out investigations	X	X
4. Analyzing and interpreting data	X	X
5. Using mathematics and computational thinking	X	X
6. Constructing explanations and designing solutions		X
7. Engaging in argument from evidence		X
8. Obtaining, evaluating and communicating information	X	X

In addition to targeting specific engineering and science content knowledge, the INSPIRES Curriculum is designed to develop critical thinking skills foundational for student success in STEM fields. Each module focuses on the following skill sets:

- **The ability to effectively work in teams and communicate technical ideas** both orally and in writing.
- **The ability to solve an open-ended problem**. Students using the INSPIRES Curriculum address questions such as: Is the problem under- or overdefined? What do you need to know in order to solve the problem? Are you lacking necessary information? If so, can you get the information? Do you need to make assumptions or approximations to bridge the gap between what you need to know and what you do know? What constraints are there on the solution (i.e., what is the acceptable "solution space")?

- **The ability to synthesize** what is learned in science and mathematics classes **and to apply** the **knowledge** to a real-world open-ended problem. This skill asks students to transfer what they are learning in one environment and to use the information in another way.
- **The ability to describe the natural world using mathematics.** With the INSPIRES Curriculum, students learn how mathematics is *used* to aid in the solution of a complex open-ended problem. Students focus on questions such as the following: What calculation do we need to do? Why is that the appropriate calculation for this problem? What will happen to the solution if I change a certain parameter? How does this information help me solve the engineering design problem?
- **The ability to think creatively** with respect to the solution of an open-ended problem. Student teams are encouraged to develop a solution to the design challenge that is unique.

Conclusion

The INSPIRES Curriculum was developed by engineering and secondary education faculty at the University of Maryland, Baltimore County in collaboration with faculty from the University of Maryland School of Medicine. To date, the curriculum has been used by over 170 science and technology teachers impacting more than 4500 students in the mid-Atlantic region. Our research program has shown that the curriculum enables students to achieve significant learning gains in science and engineering.

References

Garet, M. S., Porter, A. C., Desimone, L., Birman, B. F., & Yoon, K. S. (2001). What makes professional development effective? Results from a national sample of teachers. *American Educational Research Journal, 38,* 915–945.

International Technology and Engineering Educators Association. (2000, 2005, 2007). *Standards for technological literacy: Content for the study of technology.* Reston, VA: Author.

Linn, M. C., & Hsi, S. (2000). *Computers, teachers, peers: Science learning partners.* Mahwah, NJ: Lawrence Erlbaum Associates.

Lotter, C. R., Singer, J. E., & Godley, J. (2009). The influence of repeated teaching and reflection on preservice teachers' views of inquiry and nature of science. *Journal of Science Teacher Education, 20,* 553–582. DOI: 10.1007/s10972-009-9144-9

National Governors Association Centers for Best Practices (NGA) & Council of Chief State School Officers (CCSSO). (2010). *Common core state standards: Mathematics* and *English language arts.* Washington, DC: Author.

NGSS Lead States. (2013). *Next generation science standards: For states, by states.* Washington, DC: National Academies Press.

NRC. (1996). *National science education standards.* Washington, DC: National Academies Press.

NRC. (2012). *A Framework for K–12 science education: Practices, crosscutting concepts, and core ideas.* Washington, DC: National Academies Press.

Rushton, G., Lotter, C., & Singer, J. (2011). Chemistry teachers' emerging expertise in inquiry teaching: The effect of an authentic professional development model on beliefs and practice. *Journal of Science Teacher Education, 22,* 23–52. DOI: 10.1007/s10972-010-9224-x

Singer, J., Lotter, C., Feller, R., & Gates, H. (2011). Exploring a model of situated professional development: Impact on classroom practice. *Journal of Science Teacher Education, 22,* 203–227. DOI: 10.1007/s10972-011-9229-0

2

Active Physics

Arthur Eisenkraft
University of Massachusetts, Boston

Illustration by Tom Bunk in Chapter 3 of *Active Physics*

Image courtesy of It's About Time Publishing.

*A*ctive Physics is a full-year comprehensive physics course that is suitable for all high
school students enrolled in a first-year physics course. It is accessible for physics students who have already succeeded in biology and chemistry as well as students (and
schools) that prefer a "physics first" approach. The question we now confront is how closely

our approach matches the philosophy and requirements of *A Framework for K–12 Science Education* (NRC, 2012) and the *Next Generation Science Standards* (NGSS Lead States, 2013).

One of the most important features of the *Framework* and NGSS that sets them apart from prior standards documents is the prominent role given to engineering. As a practice, engineering design in the NGSS is given the same level of importance as scientific inquiry, and core ideas about engineering are presented along with core ideas in the natural sciences as Newton's laws of motion and the theory of evolution.

Although *Active Physics* was developed long before the *Framework*, it is not surprising that it is compatible with the new standards since it has always been about engineering design challenges. Being the first (and perhaps only) project-based high school physics course, *Active Physics* has been engaging students in engineering since its field testing (as an NSF-supported project) in 1996 through its third edition in 2012.

The *Active Physics* Chapter Challenge

The *Active Physics* chapter challenge drives each chapter because it provides the context in which students will learn physics principles and transfer their knowledge to the completion of a project. The chapter challenges have been chosen (after polling thousands of students) because of their inherent interest to high school students, the requirement of physics and engineering content and practices to successfully complete the challenge, and the opportunity to display student creativity. Here are the chapter challenges that we've selected for the third edition:

Chapter 1. Driving the Roads. Challenge: Design and create a safe-driving manual.

Chapter 2. Physics in Action. Challenge: Create a 2–3 minute voice overdub for a sporting event that will help viewers understand the physics concepts involved in the sport.

Chapter 3. Safety. Challenge: Design and build an improved safety device for a vehicle.

Chapter 4. Thrills and Chills. Challenge: Design a roller coaster to meet the needs of a specific group of riders, such as daredevils, young children, or people with disabilities.

Chapter 5. Let Us Entertain You. Challenge: Design a light and sound show to entertain your friends.

Chapter 6. Electricity for Everyone. Challenge: Design an appliance package for a family that is powered by a wind-driven generator that has a constraint of 3 kilowatt-hours of energy per day and 2400 watts of power.

Chapter 7. Toys for Understanding. Challenge: Design a toy that uses either a generator or a motor.

Chapter 8. Atoms on Display. Challenge: Create a museum display to acquaint visitors with aspects of the atom and nucleus.

Chapter 9. Sports on the Moon. Challenge: Develop a proposal for NASA for a sport that can be played on the surface of the moon.

The chapter challenges all include engineering design. Too often, physics teachers limit any engineering infusion into the physics curriculum to the mechanics topics (e.g., forces, motion, and momentum) in brief design challenges (bridge building, bungee jumping, egg drops). These design challenges are used as illustrations of the physics as opposed to the *raison d'être* for learning the physics. As illustrated by the following description of Chapter 3 in *Active Physics*, engineering design is integral to learning physics.

Chapter 3: Safety

In Chapter 3, each student design team develops a safety system for protecting passengers in an automobile, airplane, bicycle, motorcycle, or train during a collision. This engineering design challenge—an improved safety system—is not going to be solved by trial and error by the students. One distinct feature of engineering that is often missing in the popular bridge building or egg drops is the identification and application of physics principles in the design. In *Active Physics*, students will devote an entire month to learning these physics concepts. And after each physics concept is learned, the knowledge is incorporated into their safety system.

The chapter consists of seven sections. In Section 1, students identify and evaluate safety features in automobiles and consider what safety features they could use for various vehicles and for their design of a safety system. This activity provides practice in defining a problem and identifying criteria, an important skill in engineering design.

In Section 2, students explain what happens to passengers during a collision using Newton's first law. They read about the concept of pressure and apply this concept while designing and testing a seat belt to safely secure a clay passenger in a cart undergoing a collision.

In Section 3, students conduct an investigation to observe how spreading the force of an impact over a greater distance reduces the amount of damage done to an egg during a collision. The class decides what kind of collision the egg carrying cart will undergo. It could be a collision with another cart or with a stationary object. The class also decides how fast the cart will be moving. As in real life, the design teams will not know the details of the future collision in the chapter challenge until after their design is completed. They describe and explain their observations using the work-energy theorem.

During Section 4 students explore the effects of rear-end collisions on passengers, focusing on whiplash. They use Newton's laws to describe how whiplash occurs. They also describe, analyze, and explain situations involving collisions using Newton's first and second laws.

After observing various collisions, in Section 5, the students are introduced to the concept of momentum. Through measurements taken during various collisions, they determine the mass of a cart. They then calculate and consider the momentum of various objects.

In Section 6, the students investigate the law of conservation of momentum by measuring the masses and velocities of objects before and after collisions. They then analyze various collisions by applying the law of conservation of momentum.

Illustration by Tom Bunk in Section 4 of Chapter 3 of *Active Physics*

Image courtesy of It's About Time Publishing.

In the last section, students design a device on the outside of a cart to absorb energy during a collision to assist in reducing the net force acting on passengers inside the vehicle. Students use probes to measure the velocity of the vehicle and the force acting on the vehicle during impact, and then describe the relationship between impulse ($F\Delta t$) and change in momentum ($m\Delta v$).

The class will also decide on the criteria for success for evaluating the safety system devised by each team, including the design, the prototype, and the oral presentation and written report. By having students learn to set the criteria for their own projects and create a grading rubric that is a consensus of the entire class, they become more responsible for pushing themselves and their team partners to excellence.

The 7E Model of Instruction

All the physics concepts are introduced using the 7E Instructional Model (Eisenkraft, 2003), which requires that students have a hands-on, minds-on experience before being told about the way physicists structure the knowledge. The 7E model is an extension of the well-known 5E Instructional Model (Bybee, 1997; Bybee & Landes, 1990), and is briefly described as follows:

Engage: The engage component in the 7E model is intended to capture students' attention, get students thinking about the subject matter, and stimulate thinking.

Elicit: Before introducing any subject, it is crucial to elicit students' current understanding so as to better understand how they perceive the world and to adjust the lesson to meet their needs. The elicit component helps students access prior knowledge and assists teachers in finding out what students already know.

Explore: The explore phase of the Instructional Model provides an opportunity for students to observe, record data, isolate variables, design and plan experiments, create graphs, interpret results, develop hypotheses, and organize their findings.

Explain: Students are introduced to models, laws, and theories during the explain phase of the learning cycle. Then students summarize results in terms of these new theories and models.

Elaborate: The elaborate phase of the learning cycle provides an opportunity for students to apply their knowledge to new domains, which may include raising new questions and hypotheses to explore.

Extend: The addition of the extend phase to the elaborate phase is intended to explicitly remind teachers of the importance for students to experience at least one transfer of learning. Teachers need to make sure that knowledge is applied in a new context and is not limited to simple elaboration.

Evaluate: The evaluate phase of the learning cycle continues to include both formative and summative evaluations of student learning. It takes place during all components of the 7E model and is not limited to a quiz after the lesson.

"Section 2: Newton's First Law of Motion: Life and Death before and after Seat Belts" can serve as an example of the format and 7E Instructional Model. Each section begins with an illustration (drawn by Mad magazine artist Tom Bunk and sure to entertain students). The students are asked, "What do you see?" This is intended to *engage* the students as well as to *elicit* their prior understandings. This is followed by a "What do you think?" question where, in this case, the students are told that stopping themselves in a car collision with their arms on the dashboard is equivalent to stopping 10 bowling balls coming at them at 50 km/hr (equivalent to approximately 30 mph). They are then asked how a seat belt would have to be different if it were to be used in a race car that goes 300 km/hr (approximately 200 mph). Once again, we are trying to engage the students while also trying to elicit their prior understandings. We do not expect teachers to correct students or to introduce any physics at this point—that will occur later in the section.

Illustration by Tom Bunk in Section 2 of Chapter 3 of *Active Physics*

Image courtesy of It's About Time Publishing.

The students then move on to Investigate, where they will *explore* the physics concept. In the 7E model, the students always explore the concept prior to explaining the results or reading about the corresponding physics principles (i.e., ABC = activity before concept). The Investigate in Section 2 requires students to create a clay figure, place it in a cart, and have the cart move down a ramp into the wall. They observe that the clay figure keeps on moving after the cart has been stopped by the wall and subsequently gets crushed. The students repeat this experiment using a wire as a seat belt. They keep increasing the slant of the track increasing the speed of the cart and noting the damage to the clay figure. They continue their inquiry investigation by exploring different materials as seat belts.

Students then move on to Physics Talk where they learn about Newton's first law. Unlike traditional texts where the authors hope that the students can recall what happened to them when a bus stopped suddenly (and assuming that they have been on a bus and that they can remember accurately), the students in *Active Physics* are reminded of the results of their investigation with the clay figure, and this activity is used as the example to explain Newton's first law. The laboratory investigation is not only used as an aid to understanding physics content but also as an opportunity to level the playing field for all students by providing a common experience through which to describe physics principles (Eisenkraft, 2013).

As part of the Physics Talk—the *explain* in the 7E Instructional Model—students explain their results and teacher and the text introduces the wording of Newton's first law. The physics talk also *elaborates* on Newton's first law by describing how an automobile collision is actually three distinct collisions. The first collision takes place when the car stops but the driver/passenger keeps moving. The second collision is when the seat belt stops the person but the internal organs (including the heart) keep moving. The third collision is when the skeleton of the person stops the internal organs. It is often this third collision that causes the severe injuries. The concept of pressure as the force over a given area is introduced, and the results of the experimental seat belts using a wire, cloth, and other materials are better understood.

Students now return to the "What do you think now?" part of the section, where they are asked once again about how to modify a seat belt for drivers in a race car that travels much, much faster than a passenger automobile. They may also be asked at this time to once again refer to the introductory cartoon and describe "What do you see now?" The purpose of these questions is to ascertain what the students have learned, and the expectation is that students should make a claim and provide evidence for this claim (McNeill & Krajcik, 2012). It also provides an opportunity for students to recognize how their knowledge has increased from this instruction and provide confidence and pride for the student.

The next part of the section, "Reflecting on the Section and the Challenge," reviews the content of this section—Newton's first law—by recounting the investigation, the conclusions, and how this new information will be valuable in developing an improved safety device for a vehicle. Relating the physics to the chapter challenge is the *extend* in the 7E Instructional Model.

The section ends with "Physics to Go" and "Inquiring Further." "Physics to Go" is a set of questions and problems that further *evaluate* the students' understanding of concepts in this section. "Inquiring Further" is another way to *elaborate* on the concepts in the section. In Section 2, the "Inquiring Further" has two options. Students can conduct a poll of individuals and conduct a survey research project to determine attitudes about using seat belts. Alternatively, students can add to their knowledge of pressure by considering how the pressure on a brake pedal is able to provide a large enough force to stop a car.

Student teams complete all components of the 7E model in each section in the chapter as illustrated here for Section 2. In doing so, students learn about energy and work and how this can explain the value of air bags, Newton's second law and how this can provide insights into rear-end collisions, momentum and momentum conservation and the relationship to accident reconstruction, and impulse with changes in momentum to better understand crumple zones in automobiles.

Physics for All

Active Physics is for all students and recognizes that differentiated instruction must provide support for students with learning issues as well as enrichment for highly motivated students. For students with learning issues, teacher support materials for each section (a few days of instruction) is accompanied by a full page describing learning issues specific to this physics content and strategies in the form of augmentations and accommodations for each learning issue. A similar corresponding page provides help for teachers with English language learners. Differentiated instruction should also provide opportunities for further elaborations of physics concepts. This is the rationale for the Active Physics Plus part of each section for highly motivated students. Active Physics Plus introduces more math, more concepts, or more investigations. In Section 2—Newton's first law—the students have the opportunity to learn more about pressure by solving mathematical problems using the equation $P = F/A$. Each Active Physics Plus informs the students of the level of difficulty of the math, concept, or investigation.

Illustration by Tom Bunk in Section 3 of Chapter 3 of *Active Physics*

Image courtesy of It's About Time Publishing.

Essential Questions

Each section also provides students with an opportunity to reflect on science practices, crosscutting concepts, and the nature of science for the physics content. The "Essential Questions" for Section 2 and the general overview of each of these questions demonstrate the value of seeing the physics concepts in a larger context.

- "What does it mean?" Newton's first law is a very important part of physics because it describes how objects move in the absence of forces. Use Newton's first law of motion to explain why a passenger keeps moving when a vehicle stops.

  o "What does it mean?"—which is typical for a physics book—requires students to demonstrate some declarative knowledge (Shavelson, Ruiz-Primo, & Wiley, 2005).

- "How do you know?" What evidence do you have from your experiment that collisions at higher speeds will have a greater effect on the passenger?

  o "How do you know?" links the content to science and engineering practices. We know things in science because we have made observations and/or conducted experiments. There must be empirical evidence for much of our knowledge.

- "Why do you believe?" Laws in physics can be applied to a wide range of situations. Describe what happens to the passengers when a bus stops quickly. How is this an example of Newton's first law?

  o "Why do you believe?" refers to the nature of science and the value of crosscutting concepts. We ask students to consider the new content in each section and remind them that for student physicists to accept this content as true, the physics content should connect with other physics content (e.g., forces and motion). It should also fit with big ideas in science (e.g., crosscutting concepts such as systems), and it should meet physics requirements (e.g., good clear explanation, no more complicated than necessary).

- "Why should you care?" How does what you learned about Newton's fist law of motion in this section help you design a safety device for a collision even though you do not know the exact circumstances of the collision?

  o "Why should you care?" incorporates both relevance and transfer of knowledge. Students can see how their learning of physics connects to the chapter challenge. They are then required to transfer this knowledge to this new domain. Transfer of knowledge is an important part of learning (Bransford, Brown, & Cocking, 2000).

Photo by Jason Harris in Section 2 of Chapter 3 of *Active Physics*

Image courtesy of It's About Time Publishing.

The Engineering Design Cycle

Active Physics' students have three distinct exposures to a modified engineering design cycle (or engineering systems model). Students are invited to see their project through the eyes of an engineering team. They will go through the cycle of Goal, Inputs, Process, Outputs, and Feedback as they develop their project.

- Goal: Define the problem, identify available resources, draft possible solutions, and list constraints to possible actions.
- Inputs: Complete the investigations in each section, and learn new physics concepts and vocabulary.
- Process: Evaluate work to date, compare and contrast methods and ideas, examine possible trade-offs to help reach goals and maximize efforts, create a model from your information, and design experiments to test ideas and the suitability of the model.
- Outputs: Present *Mini-Challenge* and intermediary steps or products, present *Chapter Challenge* based on feedback to Mini-Challenge.
- Feedback: Obtain response from target audience leading to modification of the goal, identify additional constraints, require restarting the input and process stages.

The students' first exposure to the Engineering Cycle is when they are first introduced to the Chapter Challenge and have just set the criteria and rubric for the challenge evaluation. The second time is when the students attempt to complete the Chapter Challenge after completing the first half of the chapter. Completing the Mini-Challenge provides a number of benefits. The need to complete a Mini-Challenge removes some of the mystery that surrounds the Chapter Challenge while at the same time student teams become aware of the complexity of the Chapter Challenge. The Mini-Challenge provides practice for the student teams in a low stakes environment in comparison to the Chapter Challenge for which they will be graded.

Engineering design is also found at the section level. For example, in the electricity chapter where students have to design an appliance package for a home with limited electrical power and energy, smaller projects involve students in creating models of a fuse and optimizing the production of hot water. These activities provide additional experience in developing and using models, analyzing systems, and optimizing solutions, which are important elements of engineering that students experience a number of times in *Active Physics*.

Seeing other student teams deliver their Mini-Challenge presentation provides a forum for feedback and an opportunity to see other ideas that may be incorporated in the next iteration—the Chapter Challenge. Finally, when the chapter sections have been completed, each student team returns to the engineering design cycle and uses all the physics content (input) to conceive of a solution to the chapter challenge (process). They then present their project (output) to the class for additional feedback.

Illustration by Tom Bunk in Section 6 Chapter 5 of *Active Physics*

Image courtesy of It's About Time Publishing.

Active Physics and the Next Generation Science Standards

Each Chapter Challenge is unique, and the different parts of the chapters are designed to appeal to students with different interests and different talents. However, all nine chapters in *Active Physics* follow a similar instructional pattern. This section illustrates the overall structure of the course by briefly describing Chapters 5 and 6, and then comparing them with Chapter 3. An overview of all three chapters will also be used to illustrate how *Active Physics* engages students in science and engineering practices as advocated in the *Framework* and NGSS.

Chapter 5: Let Us Entertain You

The Chapter Challenge of Chapter 5: "Let Us Entertain You" is to design a sound and light show to entertain students your age. The sound must come from musical instruments, human voices, or sound makers that the students build. The light show can be produced with a laser or conventional lamps. Both the sound and light parts of the show must illustrate physics principles.

In Section 1, the students connect vibrations and waves to sound by observing the vibration of a plucked string and investigate how the pitch varies with the length of the string. They then explore how the tension of the string affects the vibration rate and the pitch.

In Section 2, the students make waves with coiled springs and observe transverse and longitudinal waves, periodic wave pulses, and standing waves. They investigate the relationship between wave speed and amplitude, the effect of a medium on wave speed, and what happens when waves meet (the principle of superposition). Using standing waves, the students develop the relationship between wave speed, frequency, and velocity.

In Section 3, students return to vibrating strings, interpreting what they observed in Section 1 in terms of standing waves, wavelength, and the frequency of a vibrating string. They then apply the wave equation to human motion, where speed equals stride length times frequency.

In Section 4, the students fill drinking straws and test tubes with water to model wind instruments that use columns of vibrating air to produce sounds. They investigate the relationship of pitch to the length of the vibrating column of air in longitudinal waves and study how diffraction can be used as a method to transmit sound from the vibrating air column to the surroundings.

In Section 5, students investigate how shadows are produced. The rectilinear nature of light rays is used to investigate how to produce the umbra and penumbra shadows of extended light sources.

In Section 6, students explore how plane mirrors reflect light rays. They start by investigating how changing the angle of incidence affects the angle of reflection, and then use their findings to build up a model of how images are formed by plane mirrors.

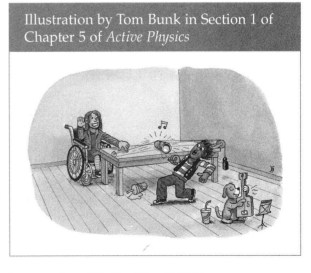

Illustration by Tom Bunk in Section 1 of Chapter 5 of *Active Physics*

Image courtesy of It's About Time Publishing.

In Section 7, the students explore how light reflects from convex and concave mirrors using a laser pointer. They investigate how a convex mirror is able to focus light, and how this property allows convex mirrors to focus light rays to produce real images. Through these activities, they discover the relationship between the distance of the real image from the mirror, the object distance, and the mirrors' focal length. They also discuss virtual images formed by both the convex and concave mirror.

In Section 8, the students use a laser pointer to send a ray of light through an acrylic block to explore how light refracts as it passes from one transparent medium to another. By measuring the angle of incidence and the angle of refraction, they develop the concept of the index of refraction and observe total internal reflection when the angle of incidence reaches the critical angle.

In Section 9, the students develop an understanding of how real images are formed by convex lenses by shining light through a convex lens and locating the image formed at different positions with respect to the light source. By projecting different sizes of images of the light source onto a surface, the students explore how images are formed and used in everyday equipment. They use ray diagrams as a method to predict image size and location and learn about the lens equation.

Finally, in Section 10, the students investigate colored shadows formed by multiple light sources using additive primary colors. By carefully tracing the light rays from different sources, they investigate the colored shadows that are formed and how added light produces different colors. They also investigate the way primary colors are used to create different colors through a subtractive process.

Chapter 6: Electricity for Everyone

The Chapter Challenge of Chapter 6: "Electricity for Everyone" is to design an appliance package for a family that is powered by a wind-driven generator. The constraints are that no part of the package can draw more than 2400 watts (W) of power and the average daily consumption should not exceed 3kilowatt-hours (kWh) of energy. In addition, the students construct a training manual explaining the basic principles of electricity for the family, including a wiring diagram with the locations of outlets and switches.

In Section 1, the students use a simple hand generator, wires, and light bulbs to investigate electric circuits and electrical energy. They learn that that electricity is the result of converting one form or energy into another and investigate the operation of a light bulb.

In Section 2, the students develop a qualitative model of electricity, including how current flows in series and parallel circuits, and how electrical energy is delivered to devices by playing the part of electric charges as they move through a circuit.

In Section 3, the students use their model again to investigate current, resistance, and how electrical energy behaves in series and parallel circuits. In this section, students also learn about fundamental charges.

In Section 4, the students design an experiment to determine the resistance of an unknown resistor and learn the proper use of a voltmeter and ammeter. They set up a series circuit to determine the current for a series of voltages applied to the resistor. They graph the relationship between voltage and current for a resistor to learn about Ohm's law. They then repeat the process for other resistors, and finally for an unknown resistor.

In Section 5, the students create a simple fuse to see how fuses work. The teacher connects a group of appliances to a power strip until a fuse in the circuit blows. The students then calculate the load limit of a household circuit and the watts required by appliances, comparing these to the limits given in the challenge. This also introduces the use of terms and equations for calculating power.

In Section 6, the students assemble a parallel circuit to explore how switches control the flow of electricity through various sections of the circuit. They then use a voltmeter and ammeter to determine the voltage and current for the elements of a parallel circuit, as well as the circuit as a whole. Finally, they mathematically examine voltage, current flow, and total resistance in series and parallel circuits, and in the process learn about circuit diagrams.

Illustration by Tom Bunk in Section 3 of Chapter 6 of *Active Physics*

Image courtesy of It's About Time Publishing.

In Section 7, the students investigate the laws of heat transfer by mixing hot and cold water in different proportions, and learn the concept of specific heat by using hot metal to warm cold water. They then calculate energy transfers between various materials, seeing how well their measurements conform to the law of conservation of energy. They learn the difference between heat and temperature and are introduced to the laws of thermodynamics and entropy.

In Section 8, the students use water heaters to investigate the amount of energy in joules needed to raise the temperature of water, and then calculate the efficiency of different water heaters. They also consider alternate solutions to the need for hot water in a home.

In Section 9, the students conduct an experiment in which they determine and compare the power consumption and efficiency of three systems that could be used to heat water. They collect and analyze data to confirm their response to the challenge in which they recommend appliances for the universal home. They also learn about three methods of heat transfer—convection, conduction, and radiation.

Science and Engineering Practices in *Active Physics*

In *Active Physics,* we provide opportunities for all the science and engineering practices described in the *Framework* and the NGSS throughout the year. These are an integral part of the curriculum at both the chapter level (approximately 1 month of instruction) and the section level (there are between 7 and 10 sections in every chapter and each section requires 2–3 class periods with the physics content). Table 2.1 provides examples of how each of the engineering practices is treated at both the chapter level and the section level for each of three chapters. These chapters were chosen because they represent different domains of physics content—forces, waves, and electricity. Any of the other six chapters could have been chosen instead.

Engineering as a Disciplinary Core Idea

The *Framework* also introduces engineering as a disciplinary core idea. The first core idea has to do with "Engineering Design." *Active Physics* uses engineering design in each chapter and throughout the year. It refers to one engineering design cycle—goal, input, process, output, feedback, goal, . . . —three times in each chapter. Students work on their projects throughout the chapter. They are practicing engineering rather than "trial and error," because each iteration of their design is a result of the application of new physics principles. They design under constraints and try to optimize their solutions. The NGSS specifies the following performance expectations for students to demonstrate their understanding of this core idea:

> HS-ETS1-1. Analyze a major global challenge to specify qualitative and quantitative criteria and constraints for solutions that account for societal needs and wants.

> HS-ETS1-2. Design a solution to a complex real-world problem by breaking it down into smaller, more manageable problems that can be solved through engineering.

> HS-ETS1-3. Evaluate a solution to a complex real-world problem based on prioritized criteria and trade-offs that account for a range of constraints, including cost, safety, reliability, and aesthetics, as well as possible social, cultural, and environmental impacts.

Active Physics provides many opportunities for students to meet the second and third performance expectations. For example, challenges such as creating a light and sound show or devising a sport for NASA that can be played on the moon requires students to design a solution by breaking it into smaller, manageable problems. Both of these and others also meet aspects of HS-ETS1-3 by prioritizing criteria and trade-offs.

However, *Active Physics* may fall short in responding to HS-ETS1-3 in that it does not treat major global challenges. There is a reason for this. When creating *Active Physics*, the decision was made to choose Chapter Challenges that would engage students and for which the science would determine the solution to the challenge. Major global challenges may have aspects of science in their solution, but none of the solutions depend only on science. All major global challenges are dependent on politics, economics, and history. Science plays a role, but it is naïve to think that solutions are solely chosen on the basis of science and engineering principles.

The *Framework* also includes another core idea about the relationships among science, engineering, technology, and society that appears as a pair of crosscutting concepts in the NGSS. The first idea is

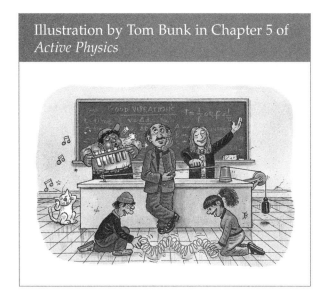

Illustration by Tom Bunk in Chapter 5 of *Active Physics*

Image courtesy of It's About Time Publishing.

that science and engineering are interdependent. Since *Active Physics* is a physics curriculum, it is fairly obvious that the design features and use of engineering practices are always in the context of physics content and scientific practices.

The second idea is that engineering, technology, and science influence society and the natural world. *Active Physics* has chosen to view this influence in terms of challenges that students can best understand and which interest them. Creating a museum display, performing a physics voice overdub for a sporting event, and building a toy using motors are all related to aspect of society as is designing an appliance package for people with limited electricity. What is important to realize is that engineering's impact on society is not restricted to major global issues but appears in everyday solutions to everyday problems.

Illustration by Tom Bunk in Section 5 of Chapter 5 of *Active Physics*

Image courtesy of It's About Time Publishing.

Future Changes to Active Physics

There may be missed opportunities for introducing engineering concepts into *Active Physics* and this may be where the *Framework* and NGSS guide the curriculum development in the next phase. For example, in the chapter where students have to design a light and sound show, in Section 5, they learn about shadows following an inquiry approach to learning. Students have to create shadows, test a physical model of shadow formation against their experimental results, and explore the limitations of the model. The section could have an increased emphasis on engineering concepts by introducing the section with the issue of a stage director who knows the height a shadow must be in the play but does not know the height of the actor that will be casting the shadow. This is an engineering problem that can be solved once students understand how shadows are created.

An additional way of infusing engineering in the shadow lesson would be to have students design a sundial given the latitude. A more complex engineering extension would be to recognize that wind generators cast shadows. The repetitive light/dark because of the rotating blades could disturb homes in the shadow region. Blinking light can also cause epileptic attacks for some individuals. How does one design a wind generator to maximize the electrical production while ensuring that the shadows do not harm people?

Infusing engineering concepts into a physics curriculum must be done with awareness of the time constraints in a physics curriculum. This may allow for the students within the shadow lessons to fully engage in an engineering extension, or it may only permit an exposure to the engineering extension. The exposure can still provide students with a sense of engineering and excite them to the prospect of further engineering study.

Table 2.1 Engineering Practices in Active Physics

Engineering practice	Chapter 3 Safety device	Chapter 5 Light and Sound show	Chapter 6 Appliance package
Asking questions and defining problems			
Chapter level	Design an improved safety device for a car.	Create a light and sound show to entertain your friends.	Create an appliance package for a family with limited electricity.
Section level	What safety device can be effectively used during a rear end collision?	How can we use diffraction to increase the volume of a wind instrument?	Which way of heating water will use the least electricity?
Developing and using models			
Chapter level	Build a model for an improved safety device for a car.	Create a model for a light and sound show.	Create a model for the electrical system in the home powered by a wind generator.
Section level	Build a model of a seat belt.	Build a model of a stringed instrument.	Build a model of a fuse.
Planning and carrying out investigations			
Chapter level	Investigate the effect of different materials on performance of seat belts.	Investigate the effect of string length and tension on sound.	Investigate effect of voltage, current, and resistance, on electrical energy in circuit.
Section level	What are the best materials for a seat belt?	How can you form large images from lenses?	How can you determine what resistors are in a "black box?"
Analyzing and interpreting data			
Chapter level	Why can your safety device not withstand a collision at 10 times the speed?	What is the maximum number of people that can enjoy your light and sound show?	How would your appliance package change if the wind generator was twice as efficient?
Section level	Show the effectiveness of different cushioning for absorbing energy during an accident.	Determine how the size of the shadow varies with the angle of the light source using the ray model of light.	Compare the energy consumption for different ways of heatring water.
Using mathematics and computational thinking			
Chapter level	How much additional cushioning would you need for a car than for a bicycle?	What is the maximum volume of the instruments you built?	How does the appliance package change if the wind generator can only work 6 hours per day?
Section level	What is the maximum impulse your cushion can withstand?	Compare the image size for different lenses.	Which size fuse is needed for your primary circuit?

Constructing explanations and designing solutions			
Chapter level	Show how your safety device meets the defined constraints.	Ensure that your light and sound show meets all the required criteria.	Explain how your appliance package is within the 3 kWh/day and 2400 W maximum allowance of the wind generator.
Section level	Which air bag is best?	How do you choose which wind instrument to build?	When is it best to use parallel circuits in your home appliance package?
Engaging in argument from evidence			
Chapter level	Which safety device is the most effective?	How can different musical instruments all produce the same note?	Demonstrate how the power output of the wind generator will not be exceeded by your appliances.
Section level	Describe how you know that the passenger will be safe for collisions below 2 m/s.	Explain how you know that a longer tube will produce a lower pitch regardless of the material used.	What alternatives exist for limiting the power consumption of your appliances?
Obtaining, evaluating, and communicating information			
Chapter level	Present your safety device to the class and describe why it will protect a passenger.	Present your light and sound show and survey the class regarding its creativity, use of physics principles, and entertainment value.	Create a chart to show how your appliance package meets all the defined requirements.
Section level	Describe how you can be confident that only one car was moving prior to the accident.	Demonstrate three different pitches from your string instruments.	Explain how you can generate electricity from a wind generator.

Conclusion

The *Framework* and NGSS have provided *Active Physics* curriculum developers and teachers with the confidence that the curriculum is on the right track. This should not be a surprise. *Active Physics* was created under a grant from the National Science Foundation and used many of the same resource materials that were utilized in creating the *Framework*. These resource materials included, for example, *Taking Science to School: Learning and Teaching Science in Grades K-8* (Duschl, Schweingruber, & Shouse, 2007), *How People Learn: Brain, Mind, Experience, and School* (Bransford, Brown, & Cocking, 1999), *Tech Talley* (Garmire & Pearson, 2005), America's Lab Report (NRC, 1996), and *Inquiry and the National Science Education Standards* (NRC, 2000).

Active Physics has always tried to bridge the research on how people learn. As it continues to evolve, it will be more explicit about the engineering practices already present in the materials and ensure that students see both the physics facet and the engineering facet as they construct solutions to the chapter challenges.

References

Bransford, J. D., Brown, A. L., & Cocking, R. R. (Eds.). (1999). *How people learn: Brain, mind, experience, and school.* Washington, DC: National Academies Press.

Bybee, R.W. (1997). *Achieving scientific literacy: From purposes to practices.* Portsmouth, NH: Heinemann.

Bybee, R.W., & Landes, N.M. (1990, February). Science for life & living: An elementary school science program from Biological Sciences Curriculum Study. *The American Biology Teacher, 52*(2), 92–98.

Duschl, R. A., Schweingruber, H. A., & Shouse, A. W. (Eds.). (2007). *Taking science to school: Learning and teaching science in grades K-8.* Washington DC: National Academies Press.

Eisenkraft, A. (2003). Expanding the 5E model. *The Science Teacher* 70 (6): 56–59.

Eisenkraft, A. (2009). *Active physics.* Armonk, NY: It's About Time.

Eisenkraft, A. (2013). Closing the Gap. *The Science Teacher* 80 (5): 42–45.

Garmire, E., & Pearson, G. (Eds.). (2005). *Tech tally.* Washington, DC: National Academies Press.

McNeill, K. L., & Krajcik, J. S. (2012). *Supporting grade 5–8 students in constructing explanations in science.* Boston, MA: Pearson.

NGSS Lead States (2013). *Next generation science standards: For states, by states.* Washington, DC: National Academies Press.

NRC (1996). *National Science Education Standards.* Washington, DC: National Academies Press.

NRC (2000). *Inquiry and the national science education standards.* National Research Council (NRC). Washington, DC: National Academies Press.

NRC (2005). *America's Lab Report: Investigations in High School Science.* National Research Council (NRC). Washington, DC: National Academies Press.

NRC (2012). *A Framework for K–12 Science Education: Practices, Crosscutting Concepts, and Core Ideas.* Committee on a Conceptual Framework for New K–12 Science Education Standards. Board on Science Education, Division of Behavioral and Social Sciences and Education, National Research Council (NRC). Washington, DC: National Academies Press.

Shavelson, R. J., Ruiz-Primo, M. A., & Wiley, E. W. (2005). Windows into the mind. *Higher Education, 49*(4), 413–430.

3

Active Chemistry

Amy Fowler Murphy

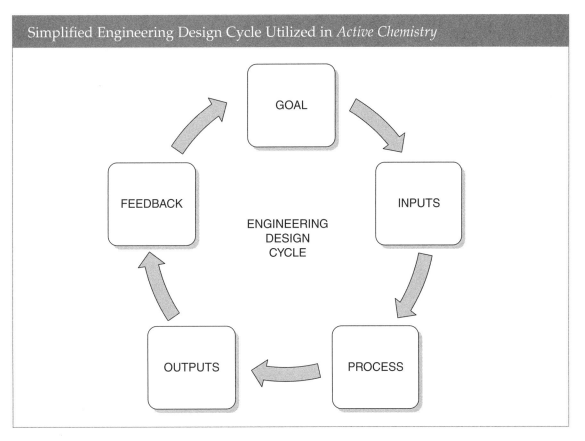

Simplified Engineering Design Cycle Utilized in *Active Chemistry*

GOAL

INPUTS

ENGINEERING
DESIGN
CYCLE

FEEDBACK

OUTPUTS

PROCESS

Image courtesy of It's About Time Publishing.

Developed in association with the American Institute of Chemical Engineers and the National Science Foundation, *Active Chemistry* is a research-based, inquiry-based, and project-based chemistry curriculum designed for a full-year high school chemistry course. While the curriculum contains all the chemistry concepts found in a traditional course, *Active Chemistry* uses a project-based learning model in which a Chapter Challenge engages students in using chemistry to solve problems. Students are introduced to chemistry concepts on a need to know basis, so the sequence of instruction is different from a typical chemistry course. Students also learn to use the Engineering Design Cycle as they deepen their understanding of chemistry.

Active Chemistry revisits important chemistry concepts in several chapters, allowing students to see the concepts in a variety of contexts and at various depths. Each chapter in the curriculum follows a 7E learning cycle as summarized below (adapted from Eisenkraft, 2003):

Engage   Get students interested in the lesson.

Elicit   Identify students' prior knowledge and any misconceptions about the concept.

Explore   Students design/conduct experiments, make observations, and collect data.

Explain   Students share their experimental results, and the teacher introduces concepts to students and helps them make connections to the data they collected.

Elaborate   Students apply knowledge in different ways.

Extend   Students transfer their learning to a new context (the Chapter Challenge).

Evaluate   The teacher uses formative and summative assessments throughout all parts of the lesson.

At the beginning of each chapter, a scenario introduces students to the Chapter Challenge, and they help develop a set of criteria for assessing their final project, which will be a solution to the Chapter Challenge. Students then learn the concepts through a series of sections that also follow a 7E inquiry instructional cycle.

Midway through each chapter, students develop and present a Mini-Challenge. This Mini-Challenge introduces students to the Engineering Design Cycle principles for the chapter and encourages them to set some preliminary goals for their Chapter Challenge. Students use the chemistry content from the beginning of the chapter to prepare a Mini-Challenge presentation, on which they receive feedback. Students then apply this feedback, along with the chemistry content knowledge from the remainder of the chapter, to their Chapter Challenge project. In these projects, students demonstrate their learning in a more formative, authentic way through the application of the Engineering Design Cycle.

Additional information about the *Active Chemistry* program, including an opportunity to review the curriculum and professional development opportunities, can be found online at http://its-about-time.com/index.php.

What *Active Chemistry* Students Do

Each chapter is divided into several sections, beginning with the Chapter Scenario. For example, in the "Artist as Chemist" chapter, the Chapter Scenario involves students in thinking about what art is and who determines what makes something art. Students also think about how the changes in materials and technologies have changed what art has looked like over time.

Next, students review Your Challenge, which describes their challenge to create a work of art that represents themselves and their culture using both artistic techniques and chemistry concepts. The challenge also requires students to demonstrate the techniques used to make their work of art and create a museum placard or pamphlet explaining the chemistry involved.

Students then consider the Criteria for Success used to grade their artwork, demonstration, and museum display. The teacher guides students to work within their groups and as a whole class to create a grading rubric that includes a list of criteria and their point values. Having students participate in the rubric development is important because it gives them ownership in the Chapter Challenge process. This also allows the rubric to contain language the students can understand.

Next, students review how the phases of the Engineering Design Cycle relate to the process of creating their works of art. Finally, the teacher elicits students' prior knowledge through a review of the Chem Corner section, which previews some of the basic chemistry concepts and skills that will be presented in the chapter. Following this introduction, the students explore the chemistry concepts in the first five sections of "Artist as Chemist." These sections provide students with enough chemistry content and art connections to complete the chapter Mini-Challenge, using the Engineering Design Cycle. For "Artist as Chemist," students must prepare a sketch of their artwork, describe it to the class, and create a preview of their museum placard or pamphlet.

Once students explore the chemistry concepts in the remaining three sections in "Artist as Chemist," they review the chapter content in a section called Chem You Learned. This explains the chemistry concepts students could apply to their artwork. Students then elaborate on these concepts through the Chem Connections to Other Sciences, which describes how the areas of biology, physics, and Earth Science relate to the chemistry concepts. The Extending the Connection and Chem at Work pages allow students to extend their understanding of some of chemistry concepts they learned to new contexts.

At the end of the "Artist as Chemist" chapter, students evaluate their learning through a more traditional Chem Practice Test. However, the application of the Engineering Design Cycle (shown below) during the Chapter Challenge provides a more authentic form of assessment.

Goal	Define the problem, identify available resources, draft potential solutions, and list constraints to possible actions.
Inputs	Complete the investigations of each section, and learn new chemistry concepts and vocabulary.
Process	Evaluate work to date, compare and contrast methods and ideas, examine possible trade-offs to help reach goals and maximize efforts, create a model from your information, and design experiments to test ideas and the suitability of the model.
Outputs	Present Mini-Challenge and intermediary steps or products, and present Chapter Challenge based on feedback to Mini-Challenge.
Feedback	Obtain response from target audience leading to modification of the goal, and identify additional constraints requiring restarting the input and process stages.

For the "Artist as Chemist" chapter, students revisit their goals of creating a work of art that represents themselves, demonstrating the techniques used to create the artwork and producing a museum placard or pamphlet that describes the chemistry concepts behind the art. In addition to the chemistry content from each section of "Artist as Chemist," students use the evaluation from their Mini-Challenge as inputs for their challenge project.

During the process phase of the Engineering Design Cycle, students consider the constraints related to creating their artwork, determine the tasks to complete, and divide the tasks among their group members. Students develop their outputs as a group, which include their artwork, museum display, and demonstration of techniques. Finally, students receive feedback according to the grading rubric developed at the beginning of the "Artist as Chemist" chapter.

Sections Within Chapters

Just as each *Active Chemistry* chapter has an overall structure, as described above, the sections within each chapter also follow a consistent pattern that reflects the 7E inquiry learning cycle. To illustrate what this learning cycle looks like in an *Active Chemistry* section, consider the activities from the Physical Properties of Metals section, which is part of the "Artist as Chemist" chapter. In this section, students discover what an alloy is, make a brass-coated penny, and determine how the properties of a metal change when it is made into an alloy. Concepts from this section include the electron-sea model, cations, malleability, alloys, different types of steel, and applications of alloys in the world of art. Here's how the 7Es play out in this section.

Engage and Elicit. Students view a cartoon related to the section (see illustration below), record what they see in their *Active Chemistry* logs, and share their thoughts with the class in response to the question: "What do you see?" This part of the class serves both to engage students in the activity and to elicit their current thinking.

To learn more about the students' current knowledge of metals, they are asked to respond to the questions under the heading What Do You Think? In this section, students are asked: "How can the physical properties of metals be modified?" and "What properties of metals make them useful as works of art or tools for creating art?" The students write their answers in their *Active Chemistry* logs and share their ideas with their groups and the class.

What Do You See?

Image courtesy of It's About Time Publishing.

Explore. Students explore the properties of metals through an investigation in which they heat a penny to create brass. They then manipulate steel bobby pins using heat to modify its properties. They record their observations in their *Active Chemistry* logs.

Explain. Under the heading Chem Talk, students define several Chem Words and read about some important chemistry concepts related to their investigation. The students define several terms and read about some important chemistry concepts. They also answer several Checking Up questions in their *Active Chemistry* logs.

Elaborate. In What Do You Think Now? students revisit their answers to the earlier questions in light of what they learned. Students then answer some additional Chem to Go questions, and respond to the following Chem Essential Questions, in their *Active Chemistry* log.

> *What does it mean?* Students describe their observations of the modified metal properties at the macro, nano, and symbolic levels.
>
> *How do you know?* Students explain how they were able to see the different properties of steel.
>
> *Why do you believe?* Students provide examples of alloys they use in an average day.
>
> *Why should I care?* Students consider how they could incorporate metal or an alloy into their Chapter Challenge.

Extend. *Reflecting on the Section and the Challenge.* Students think about how materials used for sculptures have changed over time and how the chemistry related to those changes could be used for their *Chapter Challenge* project.
   Preparing for the Chapter Challenge. Students make a small metal sculpture and describe the properties that allowed them to make their sculpture in their *Active Chemistry* logs. An additional extension activity is *Inquiring Further*, in which students research how alloys, such as pewter and solder, have changed over time because of health concerns and/or the differences between soldering and welding. They record their research in their *Active Chemistry* logs.

Evaluate. Formative assessment takes place throughout the learning cycle. Having students record their thoughts and activities in their *Active Chemistry* log throughout the section activities documents their thinking and enhances their written communication skills. The logs also allow teachers to provide ongoing feedback to students of all ability levels.

Students commemorated 9/11/2001 in this "Artist as Chemist" Chapter Challenge project. They manipulated steel bobby pins to represent the Twin Towers and used brass pennies as decoration.

   The 7E cycle of activities provides students with the chemistry concepts they will use to complete the Chapter Challenge project at the end of each chapter. As students finish the section activities in each chapter, they reflect on how the chemistry concepts they learned apply to their Mini-Challenge and Chapter Challenge projects. For the "Artist as Chemist" chapter, students create a work of art for their challenge project. The figure at right shows how one student team incorporated the concepts of metals and alloys from the Physical Properties of Metals section into their art.

Active Chemistry and the NGSS Performance Expectations

The NGSS (NGSS Lead States, 2013a) use performance expectations as a means of clarifying not only what all students should know but also how they should be able to use their

Image courtesy of Dr. Amy Fowler Murphy.

knowledge in combination with science and engineering practices and crosscutting ideas. There are 25 performance expectations for high school students in the physical science domain (HS-PS), 12 of which apply to a high school chemistry course. (See Appendix K of the NGSS, pages 128–129, for how performance expectations can be distributed among the traditional high school courses of biology, chemistry, and physics.) In addition, the NGSS contain four performance expectations for high school in the engineering, technology, and applications of science domain (HS-ETS). The following discussion highlights how the *Active Chemistry* curriculum addresses the majority of these performance expectations.

HS-PS1-1. In this performance expectation, students "use the periodic table as a model to predict the relative properties of elements based on the patterns of electrons in the outermost energy level of atoms" (NGSS Lead States, 2013a, p. 91). Students address this performance expectation several times in the "Fun With the Periodic Table" chapter. In Section 5, Line Spectra and Electron Jumps, students first view the visible light spectrum of hydrogen. Students then interpret changes in electron energies in a hydrogen atom to explain where the colors of visible light come from. In Section 6, Ionization Energy and Orbitals, students observe the visible light spectra of additional elements and compare their observations to the previous section. Next, students graphically analyze the periodic trends of first and second ionization energy. Then students compare the structure of the periodic table with the arrangement of electrons into energy levels and sublevels in the atom. In Section 7, Noble Gases as the Key to Chemical Behavior, students first determine the electron arrangement for the noble gas elements. Students then relate the positions of elements on the periodic table, their electron arrangements, and their distances from the noble gases to their chemical properties.

HS-PS1-2. This performance expectation asks students to "construct and revise an explanation for the outcome of a simple chemical reaction based on the outermost electron states of atoms, trends in the periodic table, and knowledge of the patterns of chemical properties" (NGSS Lead States, 2013a, p. 91). Students also address this performance expectation in the "Fun With the Periodic Table" chapter. In Section 8, The Octet Rule and Bonding, students relate patterns in ionization energies to patterns in electron arrangement. Students then use their knowledge of electron arrangements to predict formulas for compounds formed by two elements.

HS-PS1-3. In this performance expectation, students "plan and conduct an investigation to gather evidence to compare the structure of substances at the bulk scale to infer the strength of electrical forces between particles" (NGSS Lead States, 2013a, p. 91). In "Ideal Toy" Section 2, Intermolecular Forces in Solids, Liquids, and Gases, students examine the molecular shapes and sizes of several diatomic elements and organic compounds. Students then determine how the shapes and sizes of the molecules determine the melting and boiling points of these substances. Students could then design an experiment to test their findings.

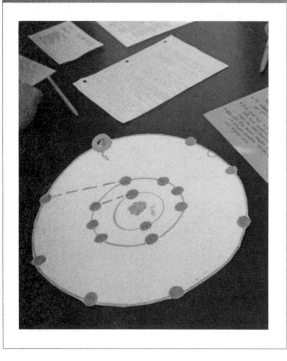

In this game, developed for the "Fun With the Periodic Table" Chapter Challenge, students created a model of the electron arrangement in an atom for their game board.

Image courtesy of Dr. Amy Fowler Murphy.

HS-PS1-4. This performance expectation requires students to "develop a model to illustrate that the release or absorption of energy from a chemical reaction system depends upon the changes in total bond energy" (NGSS Lead States, 2013a, p. 91). Students address this performance expectation in the "Chemical Dominoes" chapter. In Section 7, Enthalpy: Exothermic and Endothermic Reactions, students first use the heat pack from a military MRE (meal ready-to-eat) to examine the extremely exothermic reaction between magnesium and water. Students then learn that chemical reactions occur when bonds in the reactants break and new bonds in the products form. They also learn that breaking bonds is an endothermic process, while forming bonds is an exothermic process. Finally, students model the exothermic reaction through calculating the total change in enthalpy and drawing an energy diagram.

HS-PS1-5. In this performance expectation, students "apply scientific principles and evidence to provide an explanation about the effects of changing temperature or concentration of the reacting particles on the rate at which a reaction occurs" (NGSS Lead States, 2013a, p. 91). In the "Cool Chemistry Show" chapter, students address this performance expectation in Section 6, Factors in Reaction Rates. Students first examine how the reaction rate changes when different concentrations of vinegar react with magnesium metal and different concentrations of hydrochloric acid react with zinc metal. Next, students use a tea bag to determine how hot water and cold water affect the reaction rate of a tea bag and an antacid tablet. Students then investigate how a catalyst affects the decomposition of hydrogen peroxide. Finally, students change the size of the antacid tablet to determine how particle size and surface area affect reaction rates. Students use their observations from these experiments to explain how reaction rates of chemical reactions can be increased.

HS-PS1-7. This performance expectation asks students to "use mathematical representations to support the claim that atoms, and therefore mass, are conserved during a chemical reaction" (NGSS Lead States, 2013a, p. 91). This performance expectation emphasizes a concept that is spiraled throughout the *Active Chemistry* curriculum. Students first examine this performance expectation in Section 3, Atomic Theory and Atomic Mass in the "Fun With the Periodic Table" chapter, when they investigate atomic masses and the law of definite proportions. Students revisit the performance expectation in "Chemical Dominoes" Section 2, Balancing Chemical Equations, where they explain the purpose of a balanced chemical equation model and relate balanced equations to the law of conservation of matter. In "Ideal Toy" Section 5, Types of Reactions and Gas Production, students again investigate the law of conservation of mass through observing synthesis, decomposition, single-replacement, and double-replacement reactions and representing those reactions in balanced chemical equations. Students also observe these four types of chemical reactions and their balanced chemical equations in Cool Chemistry Show Section 4, Reaction Types and Chemical Equations. Students investigate a fifth type of reaction in "Cookin' Chem" Section 2, Combustion Reactions and Hydrocarbons, when they discover the products of a combustion reaction and balance combustion equations. The last experience that helps students meet this performance expectation is during Section 4, Solubility and Qualitative Analysis: White Powders in the CSI Chemistry chapter. Students use the law of conservation of matter to help them identify several unknown substances.

HS-PS1-8. In this performance expectation, students "develop models to illustrate the changes in the composition of the nucleus of the atom and the energy released during the processes of fission, fusion, and radioactive decay" (NGSS Lead States, 2013a, p. 91). In "Fun With the Periodic Table" Section 9, Nuclear Forces, students investigate the composition of the atom's nucleus and use isotope symbols to model the different isotopes of

This piece of art from the "Artist as Chemist" Chapter Challenge exhibited the students' love of pizza. The manipulated steel bobby pins represented shredded cheese, and the brass alloy pennies represented the pepperoni.

Image courtesy of Dr. Amy Fowler Murphy.

elements. Students then use isotope symbols to model alpha, beta, and gamma decay in a decay equation. Students also model fission and fusion reactions in their decay equations.

HS-PS2-6. This performance expectation requires students to "communicate scientific and technical information about why the molecular-level structure is important in the functioning of designed materials" (NGSS Lead States, 2013a, p. 94). Students examine the molecular-level structure at the end of every chapter section through the Chem Essential Questions, but doing so does not fully meet the requirements of this PE. However, students do meet the complete PE numerous times throughout the *Active Chemistry* curriculum. For example, in the Physical Properties of Metals section in "Artist as Chemist" chapter, students learn about the properties of metals and metal alloys through the manipulation of bobby pins, which contain a steel alloy made of iron and carbon. Students first observe the properties of the unaltered steel, which is difficult to bend and springs back into its original shape. Next students heat the steel to red-hot and cool it slowly.

This "annealing" process squeezes the carbon atoms out of the steel's crystal structure, which makes the steel easy to bend and retain a new shape. Students then heat the annealed steel to red-hot and cool it quickly. This "hardening" process traps the carbon atoms in the steel's crystal structure, making it less malleable and more brittle than the annealed steel. Finally, students slowly heat the hardened steel without making it red-hot. This "tempering" process makes the steel hardened yet more malleable by easing the bonds between the iron and carbon atoms in the steel's crystal structure. Through their observations and notes in their *Active Chemistry* log, and their artwork placard, students communicate how the changes to the atoms in the steel structure affect its properties and functioning.

Students also address this PE in the following *Active Chemistry* chapter sections:

- Polymers: Natural and Synthetic in "Movie Special Effects";
- Chemical Properties of Metals in "Artist as Chemist";
- Entropy and Enthalpy: Changes in Rubber Bands in "Chemical Dominoes";
- Properties of Polymers and Plastics in "Ideal Toy";
- Denaturation: How Do Proteins in Foods Change in "Cookin' Chem"; and
- Modeling Organic Molecules: Soap in "Cookin' Chem."

HS-PS3-1 and HS-PS3-4. In performance expectation HS-PS3-1, students "create a computational model to calculate the change in the energy of one component in a system when the change in energy of the other component(s) and energy flows in and out of the system are known" (NGSS Lead States, 2013a, p. 97). Performance expectation HS-PS3-4 requires students to "plan and conduct an investigation to provide evidence that the transfer of thermal energy when two components of different temperature are combined within a closed system results in a more uniform energy distribution among the components in the system (NGSS Lead States, 2013a, p. 97). Students address both of these performance expectations in Section 6, Calorimetry and Specific Heat Capacity of the "Cookin' Chem" chapter. In this section, students experimentally determine the specific heat capacity of various substances used in cookware, such as tin, iron, copper, aluminum, and stainless steel. Students first use the heat equation ($Q = mc\Delta T$) as their computational model to determine the heat absorbed by the water in the system. Since the heat gained by the water is equal to the heat lost by the substance tested, students then rearrange the heat equation to determine the specific heat of their substance.

HS-PS3-3. This performance expectation asks students to "design, build, and refine a device that works within given constraints to convert one form of energy into another form of energy." The clarification statement for this PE notes that the "emphasis is on both qualitative and quantitative evaluations of devices. Examples of devices could include Rube Goldberg devices, wind turbines, solar cells, solar ovens, and generators" (NGSS Lead States, 2013a, p. 97). Students meet this performance expectation by completing the Chapter Challenge in the "Chemical Dominoes" chapter, which requires them to build a Rube Goldberg device using a series of physical and chemical changes that result in the lighting of a light emitting diode, or LED. As shown in the photos below, students use a variety of energy conversions in their Rube Goldberg devices.

HS-ETS1-1. For this engineering performance expectation, students "analyze a major global challenge to specify qualitative and quantitative criteria and constraints for solutions that account for societal needs and wants" (NGSS Lead States, 2013a, p. 129). Students consider criteria and constraints during every Chapter Challenge project, but

Electrical energy allows the hot plate to heat up, which provides thermal energy to the club soda. The club soda heats up and releases carbon dioxide gas, which blows up the balloon. This provides kinetic energy to move the lever, marbles, and string on a pulley. The string causes the water in the bottle to pour into the magnesium in the green FRH (flameless ration heater) bag, which produces thermal energy to melt some ice. Once the ice melts, kinetic energy causes the lever to move, which knocks over a piece of wood and drops the battery to complete the circuit. The complete circuit starts the chemical reaction in the electrochemical cell, which produces electrical energy to light the LED.

a

b

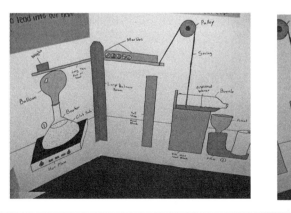
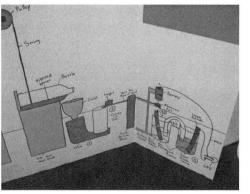

Images courtesy of Dr. Amy Fowler Murphy.

this alone does not address the entire PE. According to the National Research Council (NRC), major global challenges include "generating sufficient energy, preventing and treating diseases, maintaining supplies of clean water and food, and solving the problems of global environmental change" (NRC, 2012, p. 9). The NRC also notes that engineering can mean "any engagement in a systematic practice of design to achieve solutions to particular human problems" (NRC, 2012, p. 11). Based on this definition, one could argue that as more jobs demand employees that can "learn, reason, think creatively, make decisions, and solve problems" (NRC, 1996, p. 1), the need for engaging students in their science education with a research-based, inquiry-based, and project-based curriculum such as *Active Chemistry* is also a major human issue.

HS-ETS1-2 and HS-ETS1-3. These performance expectations ask students to "design a solution to a complex real-world problem by breaking it down into smaller, more manageable problems that can be solved through engineering" and "evaluate a solution to a complex real-world problem based on prioritized criteria and trade-offs that account for a range of constraints, including cost, safety, reliability, and aesthetics, as well as possible social, cultural, and environmental impacts" (NGSS Lead States, 2013a, p. 91). As previously discussed, students complete Mini-Challenge and Chapter Challenge projects during each *Active Chemistry* chapter and utilize a simplified Engineering Design Cycle to complete these projects. The use of this Engineering Design Cycle in *Active Chemistry* addresses both the HS-ETS1-2 and HS-ETS1-3 performance expectations.

Summary

The three dimensions of Science and Engineering Practices, Disciplinary Core Ideas, and Crosscutting Concepts from the *Framework* combine to form the performance expectations found in the NGSS. These NGSS performance expectations explain "what" students need to understand in order to "leave school better grounded in scientific knowledge and practices—and with a greater interest in further learning in science—than when instruction 'covers' multiple pieces of information that are memorized and soon forgotten once the test is over" (NRC, 2012, p. 33). This chapter demonstrates "how" teachers can engage high school chemistry students in these performance expectations through the inquiry-based lessons and project-based assessments of the *Active Chemistry* curriculum.

References

Eisenkraft, A. (2003). Expanding the 5E model. *The Science Teacher, 70* (6), 56–59.

Eisenkraft, A. (2011), *Active Chemistry: Project-Based Inquiry Approach, Student Edition* (2nd Ed.). Mount Kisco, NY: It's About Time.

NGSS Lead States. (2013a). *Next generation science standards: For States, by states, volume 1: The standards.* Washington, DC: National Academies Press.

NGSS Lead States. (2013b). *Next generation science standards: For states, by states, Volume 2: The appendices.* Washington, DC: National Academies Press.

NRC. (1996). *National science education standards.* Washington, DC: National Academies Press.

NRC. (2012). *A framework for K–12 science education: Practices, crosscutting concepts, and core ideas.* Washington, DC: National Academies Press.

Engineering the Future

Science, Technology, and the Design Process[1]

Cary I. Sneider

Portland State University, Portland, OR

Students become deeply engaged in their own design projects.

Image by Cary Sneider, courtesy of Museum of Science, Boston.

*E*ngineering the Future: Science, Technology, and the Design Process *is a full-year course designed to introduce students to the world of technology and engineering, as a first step in becoming technologically literate citizens. Through this course's practical real-world connections, students have an opportunity to see how science, technology, mathematics, and engineering (STEM) are part of their everyday world, and why it is important for* every citizen *to be technologically and scientifically literate.*

Engineering the Future is currently published by Its About Time www.its-about-time .com/etf/. One of the best ways to learn more about *Engineering the Future* is to access the videos about the course on the Museum of Science website (http://legacy.mos.org/etf/), where you can see what it looks like in the classroom and hear what teachers and students have to say.

Goals

Engineering the Future: Science, Technology, and the Design Process, was designed using a "backward design process," described in the book *Understanding by Design* (Wiggins & McTighe, 1998). In broad stokes, this approach begins by defining the goals of the course—what we want students to know and be able to do as a result of instruction. The next step is to decide what evidence we would accept that students have indeed reached those goals and, finally, to develop and test an instructional sequence that will enable students to reach the goals and provide evidence that they have done so.

Although *Engineering the Future* (ETF) was developed before publication of *A Framework for K–12 Science Education* (NRC, 2012), the goals of the course are very closely aligned with the vision of the *Framework*. And as shown later in this chapter, the course can also enable teachers to help their students achieve many of the performance expectations in the NGSS (NGSS Lead States, 2013). That correspondence between the goals of *Engineering the Future* (ETF) and the vision of the *Framework* is illustrated below.

ETF Goal 1. Students will develop a deep and rich understanding of the term *technology.* Students learn that the technologies we take for granted—TVs and DVDs, refrigerators and furnaces, the food on our dinner plates, cars and power plants—were created by people through "the engineering design process."

"We broadly use the term technology to include all types of human-made systems and processes—not in the limited sense often used in schools that equates technology with modern computational and communications devices. Technologies result when engineers apply their understanding of the natural world and of human behavior to design ways to satisfy human needs and wants" (NRC, 2012, pp. 11–12).

ETF Goal 2. Students will develop their abilities to use the engineering design process. Students take on the role of engineers and apply the engineering design process to define and solve problems by inventing and improving products, processes, and systems.

"From a teaching and learning point of view, it is the iterative cycle of design that offers the greatest potential for applying science knowledge in the classroom and engaging in engineering practices" (pp. 201–202). "We are convinced that engagement in the practices of engineering design is as much a part of learning science as engagement in the practices of science" (NRC, 2012, p. 12).

ETF Goal 3. Students will understand the complementary relationships among science, mathematics, technology, and engineering. By learning about the work of practicing engineers, students get an "insider's view" of how engineers apply mathematical skills and scientific knowledge to solve problems and meet human needs and desires.

The inclusion of core ideas related to engineering, technology, and applications of science reflects an increasing emphasis at the national level on considering connections among science, technology, engineering, and mathematics. It is also informed by a recent report from the NRC on engineering education in K–12, which highlights the linkages—which go both ways—between learning science and learning engineering. "Just as new science enables or sometimes demands new technologies, new technologies enable new scientific investigations, allowing scientists to probe realms and handle quantities of data previously inaccessible to them" (NRC, 2012, p. 32).

ETF Goal 4. Students will understand how advances in technology affect human society, and how human society determines which new technologies will be developed. Students learn through a variety of examples how everyone is affected by changes in technology and how people influence future technological development by the choices they make as workers, consumers, and citizens.

The second ETS core idea calls for students to explore, as its name implies, the Links Among Engineering, Technology, Science, and Society, which is one of thirteen core ideas in the *Framework*. "The applications of science knowledge and practices to engineering, as well as to such areas as medicine and agriculture, have contributed to the technologies and the systems that support them that serve people today. . . . In turn, society influences science and engineering. Societal decisions, which may be shaped by a variety of economic, political, and cultural factors, establish goals and priorities for technologies' improvement or replacement" (NRC, 2012, p. 202).

ETF Goal 5. Students will be able to apply fundamental concepts about energy to a wide variety of problems. The concept of energy is fundamental to all the sciences, but it is also challenging to learn. So as to build a useful mental model of energy, students will learn to apply the same energy principles to thermal, fluid, and electrical systems.

"The ability to examine, characterize, and model the transfers and cycles of matter and energy is a tool that students can use across virtually all areas of science and engineering. And studying the *interactions* between matter and energy supports students in developing increasingly sophisticated conceptions of their role in any system. However, for this development to occur there needs to be a common use of language about energy and matter across the disciplines in science instruction" (NRC, 2012, p. 95).

The Projects

The course is divided into four sections, called Projects, each of which takes about eight weeks to complete. On the following pages are descriptions of the four projects. Most of the students' time will be spent working on these projects, while some time will be spent discussing the chapters in the readers. As you'll see on the following pages, the readings about actual engineers and other professionals are intimately related to the students' lab activities, both by illuminating some of the core ideas in science that students encounter in the lab and by illustrating how professionals use the scientific ideas in their work to engineer technologies to meet people's needs.

Project 1: Design the Best Organizer in the World

Project 1 begins with a video of an industrial design team at work reinventing the grocery cart. Then students undertake their first project—to design a better cell phone holder. The purpose of the activity is for the students to find out how important it is to first understand people's needs and to translate that information into criteria and constraints to identify a successful design. Once the students design their cell phone holder, they calculate how it could be produced cost effectively, using geometry (to cut material so as to reduce waste) and algebra (to compare different packaging options). The cell phone holder activity also provides an introduction to the engineering design process. During Project 1, the students also learn how to make engineering drawings, a skill that they will use throughout the course.

During the next design challenge, the students work in teams to conduct marketing surveys to find out what kinds of organizers people would like to purchase. The concept of an *organizer* also helps students recognize the vast array of technologies that exist in the world around them. Student teams design, draw, and construct models of their organizer concepts, build a prototype for testing with the intended audience, and redesign their organizers for efficient manufacturing.

The organizers provide an introduction to the next project, about designing sustainable cities of the future. In an important sense, cities are vast organizers of human activities. Different kinds of buildings enable different functions to take place. Individual buildings are also organized internally and the city as a whole is laid out according to a zoning plan. All these decisions take into account human needs, just as the students did when designing their organizers.

Sample Readings for Project 1

In Chapter 1, Amy Smith, an engineering instructor at MIT explains how she works with her students to design tools that improve lives half a world away. The image at left shows Ms. Smith with her invention, a labor-saving machine that enables people in developing countries to mill grain using a device that does not require electricity and that can be repaired easily. In addition to discussing the importance that Ms. Smith places on the tremendous difference that good engineering can make in people's lives, the chapter introduces how technology surrounds us and helps define us as human beings.

In Chapter 3, Jamy Drouillard, an aeronautical engineering student at MIT who grew up in Haiti describes the process that he and other students use to design entirely new types of flying vehicles. Other chapters in Project 1 include a description by one of Amy Smith's students of a trip to Haiti to design a safe cooking fuel, a technician who uses computer aided design (CAD), an electrical engineer at the design firm IDEO, an automotive engineer who brought a woman's perspective to the design of Ford vans, an athletic shoe designer

Creating the organizer in Project 1 requires calculations and measurements.

Image by Cary Sneider, courtesy of Museum of Science, Boston.

who discusses how prototypes are tested, and a manufacturing engineer who developed affordable ways to provide eyeglasses to people who otherwise could not afford them.

Project 2: Design a Building of the Future

Project 2 introduces students to the problems of urban sprawl and how city planners, architects, and engineers are solving these problems by applying a set of concepts they call *new urbanism*. Students are challenged to work in teams to design a structure based on these concepts; but first they need to learn how to design structures that will bear heavy loads, how to test materials that have the properties needed in different parts of the structure, and how to design a building that minimizes the amount of energy needed to maintain a comfortable temperature. Each of the activities in this unit engages students in developing the knowledge and skills they need to complete the project challenge.

Sample Readings for Project 2

By reading the text, students learn how real-life designers draw on mathematics and science to design structures and systems that will stand the test of time, promote the health and well-being of residents, and preserve more of the natural world. For example, in Chapter 10, city planner Peter Park identifies the elements of a successful city and explains how city planners use zoning laws to control population density so it is high enough to allow for open space and parks but not so high that people feel crowded. The students use similar calculations to plan their own structures, making sure they provide the space needed so residents are not too crowded and also that the building does not take up more space than is necessary.

In Chapter 11, field engineer Kirk Elwell explores the various forces and loads that a structure must be designed to withstand as he describes the design and construction of a major Boston bridge. Although he designs bridges and not houses, the process he uses to calculate maximum loads for the bridge is the same that students use when calculating maximum loads for the floors in the buildings they are designing.

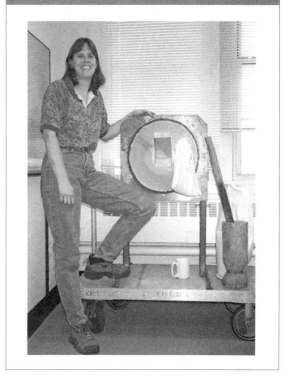

Amy Smith, an engineering instructor at MIT, with one of her inventions: an easily repaired device to mill grain

Image by Kristin Joyce, courtesy of Lemelson MIT Program.

Students are ready to measure the load that their structure can safely carry.

Image courtesy of Museum of Science, Boston.

Lauren Stencel, a college student, helping design and construct an energy-independent building

Image by Donna Foster, courtesy of Ms. Stencil.

To expand the students' horizons, Chapter 12 describes how structural engineer Bill Baker applies concepts of geometry to design the Burj Dubai (now called the Burj Khalifa), the tallest man-made structure in the world. Although the students are designing much smaller buildings, they can still take advantage of some of the structural design ideas used in the world's tallest buildings.

The next few chapters describe the daily work of engineers who design more conventional projects. For example, in Chapter 13, Prity Rungta is a construction manager in Toronto, Canada. She describes how she organizes and manages the work of dozens of architects, engineers, electricians, plumbers, and builders to construct a house on time and on budget. In Chapter 14, Cathy Bazan-Arias explains how her work as a soil engineer can save thousands of dollars by making sure a project rests on solid ground before it starts. In Chapter 15, Chris Benedict describes how to design a building so that it is energy efficient, introducing the activities on insulation that the students undertake later in the project.

The project ends with the story of Lauren Stencel, a college student pictured here, who describes her experience constructing an energy-independent building on the Mall in Washington, DC.

Project 3: Improve a Patented Boat Design

Project 3 invites students to build a "putt-putt boat" that is powered by a thermal/fluid engine. The challenge is to apply fundamental concepts of energy to understand how the boat works and then redesign it. Lab teams work together in a series of activities to learn how energy is transferred through the boat system, from a candle that provides energy input, to the jets of water that propel the boat forward. These experiments involve the behavior of compressible gases and noncompressible fluids, conduction of thermal energy, and the concept of resistance to fluid flow in pipes. As students build knowledge of the science behind the putt-putt boat, they take on the role of working engineers and produce a patent application to communicate their ideas.

Sample Readings for Project 3

Although a putt-putt boat is much simpler in design than the Alvin Submarine that can dive three miles deep to explore life on the ocean bottom, certain design principles are the same. In Chapter 17, Bob Brown, who is both a designer and pilot of the Alvin Submarine at the Woods Hole Oceanographic Institute, explains two key ideas common to both the Alvin and putt-putt boats: he compressibility of fluids and pressure.

The putt-putt boat engine that the students analyze and build works by propelling jets of hot water and vapor out of the back of the boat. The principle is the same as a jet engine and a rocket. Mass ejected in one direction propels the vehicle in the opposite direction. Aeronautical engineer Aprille Ericsson, pictured below, explains this principle in Chapter 18, in the context of a NASA mission to Mars that she is working on that will return a sample of Martian soil to Earth.

Other chapters tell the story of Josh Tickell, a biodiesel engineer who converted his van to operate on used cooking oil; Chris Langenfeld, who helped develop an engine developed to drive a mechanical wheelchair; Rebecca Steinmann, a nuclear engineer; and Lisa Bina, who designs sewage systems. All these are related to the putt-putt boat challenge.

Project 4: Electricity and Communication Systems

Project 4 begins with a project to build a circuit to control a scoreboard for ball games and to create a binary code to illuminate each numeral. They then conduct a variety of activities to learn about the basics of circuit electricity. The students can then build on a firm foundation and explore various communications systems using microphones, speakers, laser diodes, and fiber optics. Students also learn about electrical power systems and why some systems work better than others for different applications. Throughout the project, the students design and test circuits to solve specific problems, from detecting rodents in the basement to controlling two fans so they run at variable speeds.

Sample Readings for Project 4

The primary focus in this project is on electrical energy and communications, and it begins with the story of David Clark in Chapter 24, who is considered one of the "fathers" of the Internet, since he was on the team of engineers who designed it. Chapter 25 is about a software engineer who develops speech recognition software for computers. These two chapters provide real-world connections to the first activity in Project 4, in which students develop binary codes to represent numbers and then build a circuit to display the numbers.

Chapter 26 tells the story of Nanette Halliburton, an electrical engineer whose job with Cisco Systems, Inc. is to evaluate equipment that converts electrical signals into light signals for transmission via optical cables. Ms. Halliburton explains how fiber optics works to transmit information thousands of miles from city to city, and why they are replacing copper cables nationwide.

Students testing their boat.

Image courtesy of Museum of Science, Boston.

Aeronautical engineer Aprille Ericsson at work.

Image courtesy of Ms. Ericsson.

Students working with snap circuits

Image by Cary Sneider, courtesy of Museum of Science, Boston.

To round out the sequence of chapters on electronic communications, in Chapter 27, Alex Hills tells how he developed a radio communications system for small villages in Alaska, where he developed ideas that eventually led to the development of Wi-Fi that now connects nearly everyone to the Internet.

Chapter 28, by Joel Rosenberg, one of the writers of *Engineering the Future*, recounts his own background and explains how he struggled with the best ways of communicating core ideas of electricity in Project 4.

The remaining chapters in the unit concern the various ways that are used today to produce electrical energy to power modern civilization, from home lighting and appliances to heavy industry. These tell the story of Song-Sik Kim, who works on methods to produce electricity from coal with fewer pollutants; Ken McAuliffe, who maintains electrical systems at a large science museum; Christine Bordonaro, who develops solar panels; and Jim Gordon, who develops large wind energy projects.

Focus on Energy

The vision of the *Framework* is that engineering should not be taught separately from science. Instead, science and engineering are to be closely integrated. In *Engineering the*

Electrical engineer, Nanettte Haliburton

Image courtesy of Ms. Halliburton.

Future (ETF), this guideline is consistent with a decision that we made in the earliest stages of developing the course—to focus on a single very rich set of concepts in science that would thread throughout the course. As we discuss in the context of each of the projects, energy is by no means the only science concept that students learn; but it does provide a coherent theme throughout the course that helps the students see the conceptual unity that underlies different engineering subjects, and different science disciplines.

> *The ability to examine, characterize, and model the transfers and cycles of matter and energy is a tool that students can use across virtually all areas of science and engineering* (NRC, 2012, p. 95).

Energy, as a transformative concept that transcends entire fields, is difficult to learn, in part because it is used in very different ways in different disciplines. In biology, it's important to understand how organisms obtain and transform energy for life processes, and how energy flows through ecosystems and food webs. In Earth and space science, students learn that energy from the Sun drives wind and ocean currents, and that thermal energy inside the Earth moves continents and causes volcanic eruptions and earthquakes. In physics, the law of energy conservation is one of the most important ideas that students are expected to learn and apply in solving an endless variety of problems. And our daily use of electricity and fuel keeps hundreds of thousands of engineers employed designing more efficient ways to generate energy and reduce our impact on the environment. In this course, we focus on energy for several reasons:

- Energy offers a useful set of ideas for understanding the world around us.
- Energy is a foundation concept in all fields of science and engineering.
- Energy concepts are difficult for students to learn, and misconceptions about it are widespread.

There are many reasons why many students have misconceptions about energy. In everyday life, we use the term *energy* loosely to describe how we feel, or how hard we work. In science, the term is more precisely defined, but sometimes the definitions are confusing, and even contradictory. In physics, for example, energy is sometimes defined as "the capacity to do work." However, students also learn that in energy transformations some energy is lost to the environment in the form of heat that *cannot* be used to do work. In chemistry and biology, students learn about energy in different contexts and only rarely see the similarity of energy concepts across the two disciplines. In this course, we avoid the problem of finding a consistent definition of energy by focusing instead on the following energy principles that are most helpful in analyzing and designing engineered systems but that are also useful in science:

1. Energy is like a substance in that it can flow from one place to another; but it is not a substance.

2. The rate at which energy flows is directly proportional to a difference in temperature, pressure, or electrical potential. In other words, "difference drives change."

3. Energy input is required to maintain a difference in temperature, pressure, or electrical potential. This idea is summarized as "It takes a difference to make a difference."

4. The rate at which energy flows is inversely proportional to resistance.

If students are to benefit from learning about energy early in their high school experience, they need to learn it in a way that they can apply it readily in new situations. This is the idea of *transfer* of learning. Educational research strongly indicates that transfer will occur more readily if the concept to be taught is presented in different contexts; and if students are guided in recognizing how a concept learned in one context can be abstracted and applied in different contexts (Bransford, Brown, & Cocking, 1999, Chapter 3). Those abstract concepts are the energy principles listed above, which students apply in different contexts during the course. For example, here's how students encounter the second principle "differences drive change" in three different contexts:

Temperature differences drive change. In Project 2, students are asked to design an energy-efficient building. An important consideration in doing so is to minimize the loss of thermal energy through walls by increasing the resistance using insulation. However, no matter how well it is insulated, maintaining a difference between indoor and outdoor temperatures requires the input of energy using a furnace or air conditioner.

Pressure differences drive change. In Project 3, students use inquiry to figure out how an engine transfers chemical energy in fuel to kinetic energy to drive a vehicle or other device. They also learn how kinetic energy can be modified through pneumatic and hydraulic systems, making possible such achievements as helping a single individual lift a truck. They also explore how pipes of various sizes and shapes resist the flow of energy through pipes.

Electric potential differences drive change. In Project 4, students are guided in designing circuits, and in measuring current, voltage, and resistance. Through activities, they see that the flow of electrical energy increases if there is a greater electrical potential difference (measured in volts) and decreases if there is a greater resistance (measured in ohms). Students explicitly connect their lab results to the same principle of energy flow that they used in Projects 2 and 3.

Connections to the NGSS

According to the NGSS, the core ideas and practices of engineering design come together at the high school level, when students apply the skills that they've developed over the years to issues of global proportions.

> "At the high school level students are expected to engage with major global issues at the interface of science, technology, society and the environment, and to bring to bear the kinds of analytical and strategic thinking that prior training and increased maturity make possible. As in prior levels, these capabilities can be thought of in three stages—defining the problem, developing possible solutions, and improving designs" (NGSS Lead States, 2013, p. 290).

The stories of engineers in the Reader related to Project 1 help students make connections between the activities they are doing in the lab and real world global problems, such as Amy Smith's invention to help people in developing nations process grain, or Saul Griffith's inventions that are providing affordable eyeglasses to children in Kenya, so they can learn to read.

The other core idea in Project 1 is the engineering design process, which is described by engineering student Jamy Drouillard in Chapter 3. Although it is a more detailed description than that provided in the NGSS, it can be organized according to the three phases of design described in the NGSS as follows:

The major global challenge that students address in Project 2 is how to design cities so as to preserve quality of life as our population grows. They break down the problem and tackle a manageable piece: to design a multi-use structure that provides living and working spaces to minimize the distance people must travel to work. The students evaluate their structures using a rubric that takes into account their definition of the problem, the adequacy of the structural design for supporting the maximum loads the building will experience, the quality of scale drawings, and design for energy efficiency.

In addition to the core ideas of engineering design, a major focus of Project 2 is on transfer of thermal energy through the walls of the house. The activities involve calculations of thermal transfer and investigations to compare the effects of different amounts and types of insulating materials. These activities will help prepare students to meet performance expectations in the physical sciences.

Table 4.1 Engineering Design in the NGSS and in Engineering the Future	
Engineering Design in the NGSS	**Jamy Drouillard's Engineering Design Process**
A. **Define the Problem:** Identify situations that people want to change, and define them as problems with criteria and constraints.	1. **Define the Problem** in terms of criteria and constraints. 2. **Research the problem** so as to better understand it, and to find out how others may have solved it.
B. **Develop and Test Possible Solutions:** Work as a team to brainstorm ideas. Compare and synthesize ideas. Convey possible solutions through visual or physical representations, and conduct tests to see if they meet the design criteria and constraints.	3. **Develop possible solutions** by working as a team and playing with flying toys to get ideas. 4. **Choose the best solution** by considering each idea in terms of the criteria and constraints of the problem. 5. **Create a prototype**, or working model.
C. **Optimize the Design:** Compare solutions, test, and evaluate them, making improvements to achieve the best possible design.	6. **Test and evaluate the prototype**, then improve it based on the tests. 7. **Communicate the solution** after we think we've got a good design. 8. **Redesign** the solution to work out the bugs and develop the best possible design.

Project 3 provides opportunities for students to design, build, and refine a device—a putt-putt boat—that converts chemical potential energy to kinetic energy. This activity is an excellent match to performance expectations related to the transfer of energy.

Project 4 is primarily concerned with the function of electric circuits. After providing guided experiences in basic concepts, students are challenged to develop circuits that carry out additional functions. These are creative real-world design projects that can be accomplished in a number of different ways, so they enable students to meet the engineering design performance expectations described above, as well as the performance expectation related to devices that convert energy from one form to another.

These connections to the performance expectations in the NGSS are shown in Table 4.2.

Instructional Materials

Instructional materials and laboratory equipment can be thought of as the tools that will enable teachers to help their students accomplish the goals of *Engineering the Future* and understand the ways that they will engineer the world of tomorrow. Printed materials include an Engineer's Notebook and a Textbook for each student and a Teacher Guide.

The Engineer's Notebook guides students in their day-to-day activities. It provides detailed instructions and data sheets for design challenges and supporting activities, as well as rubrics so that students will understand how their work will be evaluated. The Notebook is divided into four booklets for the four major projects of the course. Each booklet is punched so it can be inserted into a 3-hole binder. The pages are perforated so

Table 4.2 Connections to Performance Expectations from the NGSS

	Project 1	Project 2	Project 3	Project 4
HS-ETS1-1. Analyze a major global challenge to specify qualitative and quantitative criteria and constraints for solutions that account for societal needs and wants.	✓	✓	✓	✓
HS-ETS1-2. Design a solution to a complex real-world problem by breaking it down into smaller, more manageable problems that can be solved through engineering.	✓	✓	✓	✓
HS-ETS1-3. Evaluate a solution to a complex real-world problem based on prioritized criteria and trade-offs that account for a range of constraints, including cost, safety, reliability, and aesthetics, as well as possible social, cultural, and environmental impacts.	✓	✓	✓	✓
HS-PS2-1. Analyze data to support the claim that Newton's second law of motion describes the mathematical relationship among the net force on a macroscopic object, its mass, and its acceleration.			✓	
MS-PS2-2. Plan an investigation to provide evidence that the change in an object's motion depends on the sum of the forces on the object and the mass of the object.			✓	
HS-PS2-5. Plan and conduct an investigation to provide evidence that an electric current can produce a magnetic field and that a changing magnetic field can produce an electric current.				✓
HS-PS2-6. Communicate scientific and technical information about why the molecular-level structure is important in the functioning of designed materials.		✓		
HS-PS3-1. Create a computational model to calculate the change in the energy of one component in a system when the change in energy of the other component(s) and energy flows in and out of the system are known.		✓		
HS-PS3-3. Design, build, and refine a device that works within given constraints to convert one form of energy into another form of energy.		✓	✓	
HS-PS3-4. Plan and conduct an investigation to provide evidence that the transfer of thermal energy when two components of different temperature are combined within a closed system results in a more uniform energy distribution among the components in the system (second law of thermodynamics).	✓			
MS-PS3-5. Construct, use, and present arguments to support the claim that when the motion energy of an object changes, energy is transferred to or from the object.		✓		✓

that a task can be neatly torn out, stapled, and given to the teacher for assessment, then returned to the students' binder.

The textbook is written from the viewpoint of practicing engineers. Men and women from various ethnic and cultural backgrounds tell what it's like to practice their profession, and how they came to do what they do. These first-person stories were written to help students learn important concepts that relate to their own design projects, and also to learn how the activities they are doing in class relate to applications in the real world. These include such diverse applications as engineering tools to improve life for people living in developing countries, designing and building energy efficient homes, creating spectacular bridges and livable cities, capturing the wind to produce electricity, and developing methods for making today's coal-fired power plants more environmentally friendly.

Engineering the Future provides a wide variety of experiences that lead to increased technological literacy and a variety of possible career paths.

Image by Cary Sneider.

Assessment Tools include the following:

- **In-class Assessments.** The Task Guidelines suggest ways to lead discussions and examine student work to help you determine how well students are learning, and make appropriate course corrections.
- **Project Rubrics.** Rubrics for assessing individual and team performance on creative engineering design tasks are included in the Engineer's Notebook so that students can see how their work will be evaluated.
- **End-of-Project Tests.** The Teacher Guide includes four Project Tests, which you can administer to your students after each quarter of the course to assess their understanding. The tests can also be given before and after each project if evidence of annual student growth is required.

Laboratory Equipment and Supplies include some common science lab supplies, such as syringes, thermometers, and electrical components, and also materials that are more frequently found in art rooms or woodshops, such as cardboard and glue. Although certain high-tech equipment such as computers with CAD software and 3-D printers could be used in conjunction with this course, high-tech equipment is not essential. We estimate that supplies to teach the course the first time for two or three classes (sharing equipment) would cost no more than about $2,000, and a few hundred dollars per year for consumables. These costs are well within the budget of most science departments and considerably less expensive than other engineering high school programs.

Where Does This Course Fit in the High School Curriculum?

Engineering the Future is NOT intended to provide training in specific vocations. It *IS* meant to help *all* students—whether they eventually choose to attend a university, another tertiary education institution, or enter the world of work—better understand the designed world and the wide variety of career paths that a person might take in designing, manufacturing, maintaining, or using technologies.

For some students, the course will open career interests that would otherwise have lain dormant, until it is too late for them to enroll in elective science and math courses, and gain entry to technical studies at a college or university. Consequently, the intended placement of this course is in the first year of a high school student's career.

Alternatively, *Engineering the Future* can serve as a capstone course for high school juniors or seniors so that students can apply to practical situations all that they learned in high school, ranging from science and math, to history, social studies, communication—even art and music. You may also use this course to provide an excellent introduction to the field of engineering for students who are considering technical careers.

A few middle school teachers have adapted the course to their school's 8th-grade curriculum, especially Project 1 that introduces engineering design without the more challenging science and math concepts found in Projects 2, 3, and 4.

Who should teach this course?

The most important qualification for teaching *Engineering the Future* is a desire to foster students' creative talents and analytical skills. Other valuable qualifications include the ability to lead discussions that encourage students to question their assumptions and consider new ideas as well as to help students work effectively in teams to brainstorm ideas, make decisions, and to build and test prototypes.

Regarding educational background and professional licensure, teachers who have a state license to teach technology/engineering in grades 6–12 are already fully qualified (under No Child Left Behind legislation) to teach this course. However, we envision that licensed physics and mathematics teachers will not find it difficult to learn the additional skills they will need to teach this course.

Which department has responsibility for this course?

Engineering the Future is designed for *all* students, not just those in an accelerated program to become engineers, or for students in vocational tracks. Because it has a strong science laboratory component, most schools include it in their science department, along with chemistry, physics, and biology. However, it could also be included in the technology department. Some schools have even changed the name of their science departments to "Science and Engineering" to recognize the value of integrating these two fields. While any of these solutions is feasible, it will be important to choose the solution that best supports acceptance of the new course by students, parents, and guidance counselors and best demonstrates the integration in math, science, technology and engineering (STEM).

Whatever "home department" is chosen for *Engineering the Future*, the course should not be considered in isolation but as one step in a sequence of courses that students take as they progress through high school. When students complete this course, they will have a broader understanding of the wide variety of technical careers that are open to them. Some students may wish to take more courses in science or math or more specialized courses in technical fields. However, not all students will wish to become involved in science and technology as careers. By providing alternative sequences, students will have opportunities to choose pathways that are consistent with their current interests and desires while keeping open their options for the future.

The Importance of Teamwork

Our extensive interviews with engineers have confirmed that good engineering requires a team effort. Therefore it is vitally important for students to learn to work effectively in teams. There is some tension between the encouragement of teamwork and independent work, given the need for teachers to assign individual grades for students. The tension is considerably reduced if expectations are clearly presented to the students for each activity. Suggestions for how to do this will be offered at various points in the Teacher Guide and built into the Engineer's Notebook.

Future Improvements

Now that the NGSS has been published, we will look for opportunities to modify the course so that it better aligns with the new standards. Following are the ideas currently under consideration:

Connect more explicitly to crosscutting concepts. Each of the design projects in Project 1—the cell phone holder and organizer—involve creating an object whose form matches its desired function. And the section on engineering drawing is all about scale factors. These are natural connections to the crosscutting concepts of *Structure and function,* and *Scale, proportion, and quantity.* We can be more explicit about these connections throughout the curriculum.

Engage the students more deeply in thinking about global issues. Although most of the chapters in the student reader focus on major global issues, and the students are led to see the connections between their laboratory work and how to approach major real-world problems, the project activities do not engage the students in researching global issues. Consequently, we plan to develop an end-of-project activity in which they will choose a global challenge and be provided with guidelines for how to apply what they've learned in the unit to define the problem in terms of criteria and constraints, identify aspects that could be addressed using an engineering design process, and evaluate efforts planned or underway to solve some of these problems.

Project 2 focuses on structural and thermal engineering. There are strong connections to the NGSS with regard to science concepts in these areas, although they could be strengthened further and made more explicit.

At present, Project 3 focuses on the propulsion mechanism of the putt-putt boat. It makes sense to maintain this focus since core concepts related to energy provide coherence to the entire course. However, it is possible to add one or more activities in which the students observe, measure, and analyze data on the boat's motion through the water. This can easily be done with a digital video camera, already standard equipment for computers and many cell phones.

The NGSS places very strong emphasis on electric and magnetic fields and their interactions with matter. Although Project 4 is concerned with circuits, and a number of chapters concern energy and power generation, the activities could be modified to include further work on generators and motors and how they work to be more consistent with the NGSS. These core ideas can help students understand the function of essential technologies in our nation's infrastructure. Whether electrical power is generated by flowing water, burning oil, coal or natural gas, or heating water with radioactive materials in a nuclear power plant, in each case the power is generated by the interaction of electrical and magnetic fields.

Conclusion

Engineering the Future was developed at the Museum of Science in Boston as one of several projects to support teachers in Massachusetts, which was one of the first states to include engineering and technology in its science standards. Since the NGSS weaves engineering even more deeply into the fabric of science instruction, the course will be relevant to teachers in the many additional states where the NGSS has been adopted, or at least under consideration.

Perhaps the most important feature of *Engineering the Future* that lends itself to supporting the new standards is how closely it ties engineering design with the applications of science and mathematics. That is especially true of the physical sciences, specifically core ideas related to energy, forces, and motion. Nonetheless, as we've indicated above, it is not a perfect match. In the next year or two the developers, working with the publisher, will be improving the course to that is an even closer fit to the NGSS.

References

Bransford, J, D., Brown, A. L., & Cocking, R. R. (Eds.). (1999). *How people learn: Brain, mind, experience, and school*. Washington, DC: National Academies Press.

NCTL. (2008). *Teacher guide, engineering the future: Science, technology, and the design process*. Mt. Kisco, NY: It's About Time.

NGSS Lead States. (2013). *Next generation science standards: For states, by states, volume 1: The standards*. Washington, DC: National Academies Press.

NRC. (2012). *A framework for K–12 science education: Practices, crosscutting concepts, and core ideas*. Washington, DC: National Academies Press.

Wiggins, G., & McTighe, J. (1998). *Understanding by design*. Alexandria, VA: ASCD.

Endnote

1. Portions of this chapter were adapted with permission from the *Teacher Guide for EtF* (NCTL, 2008).

5

Engineer Your World

Engineering Design and Problem Solving

Cheryl L. Farmer

The University of Texas at Austin

Student engaged in a robotics activity

Image by Alan Downey.

*E*ngineer Your World is a year-long high school engineering curriculum for students who want to learn more about engineering and its role in shaping our world. Developed by University of Texas faculty and NASA engineers working in collaboration with experienced secondary teachers and curriculum developers, this hands-on course engages students in authentic engineering practices in a project-based environment. By scaffolding student learning over a series of socially relevant design challenges, the curriculum engages students in the story of engineering as they develop design skills and engineering habits of mind.

Engineer Your World is available from the UTeach*Engineering* program at The University of Texas at Austin, which anticipates offering a dual enrollment version of the course beginning in 2015–2016. UTeach*Engineering* is also planning to develop a computationally intensive second-year course that will teach computing in the context of engineering design challenges and that will enable Advanced Placement® credit in Computer Science Principles. For more information, please visit www. EngineerYourWorld.org.

How the Curriculum Was Developed

Engineer Your World was developed by a collaborative team of university faculty from engineering and education colleges, practicing engineers, and experienced secondary teachers and curriculum developers. This team applied the engineering design process to curriculum development while adhering to well-established principles of successful curriculum design. The team began by defining a set of student learning objectives for the course. Next, thinking of the course as a tapestry into which learning objectives should be woven, the team developed a framework for how and when each element should be introduced and reinforced throughout the year. Finally, the team selected design challenge topics to fit the framework and, for each unit, created a detailed scope and sequence prior to developing a full set of instructional materials.

While the curriculum development team adopted as a guiding philosophy the framework of challenge-based instruction, in which student learning is motivated within the broader context of a problem or challenge, members found that this approach failed to provide sufficient guidance for detailed curriculum development work. The team "resolved this challenge by adapting design approaches found in the learning sciences and science education research to create a set of principles to guide [the curriculum development] work" (Berland, Allen, Crawford, Farmer, & Guerra, 2012, p. 3). The most important of these principles are

1. Wherever possible, students construct their own knowledge and understanding;

2. The curriculum employs a standardized engineering design process as an instructional framework;

3. Students are engaged in meaningful (if simplified) versions of the practices of engineers;

4. Student work is contextualized within STEM design challenges that can only be completed through the purposeful application of engineering principles and

relevant science and mathematics concepts, and students experience these principles and concepts as necessary for the successful completion of the projects; and

5. All STEM design challenges have multiple successful solutions.

Examples of the ways in which these principles are manifest throughout the curriculum are presented in the discussion of the design challenges later in this chapter.

Student Learning Goals

Because the development of the *Engineer Your World* curriculum predated any nationally agreed-upon standards for secondary engineering education, the curriculum design team began by developing a detailed list of student learning objectives. These were eventually organized into three categories: engineering applications, engineering process, and engineering skills and habits of mind.

Teachers and engineers engaged in aerial imaging project during professional development

Image by Alan Downey.

Engineering Applications. Students explore engineering's societal impact by learning about past accomplishments; current and future challenges; and the interplay between science, technology, customer needs and evolving designs. Students also learn about engineering disciplines and careers, the multidisciplinary nature of practice, and professional codes and standards to which engineers adhere.

Engineering Process. The acquisition of engineering design skills is central to the *Engineer Your World* course experience. All units employ a standardized engineering design process (shown on the next page) so that the process becomes ritualized for students. This enables students to focus their efforts in each unit on learning and applying engineering skills and habits of mind to solve the immediate challenge at hand.

Engineering Skills and Habits of Mind. *Engineer Your World* seeks to equip students with the skills and habits of mind that engineers use to address and solve design challenges. These may be categorized under the headings of

- Systems Thinking—Systems thinking is a set of habits or practices based on the belief that the parts of a system can best be understood in the context of relationships with each other and with other systems rather than in isolation. Emphasis is placed on a top-down perspective, the system environment, and critical interfaces.
- System Understanding and Quantification—Students learn to characterize systems using quantitative techniques that are common in the practice of engineering.

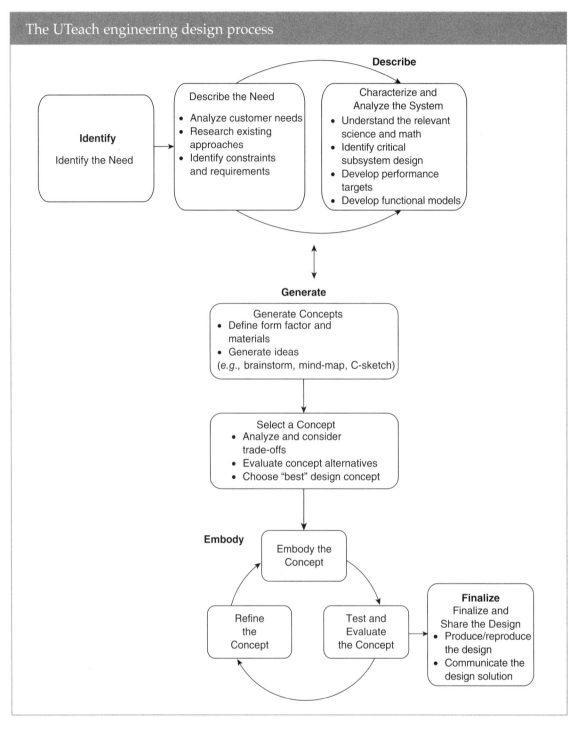

Graphic by Erik Zumalt.

- Creativity—Engineers think creatively within well-defined constructs. Students gain experience with structured concept generation and selection techniques employed by engineers.
- Verification—Engineers must verify that their selected concept satisfies the design constraints, requirements, and customer needs.

- Communication—Students practice good communication skills and learn unique aspects of how engineers document and present design ideas and analytical results. Emphasis is placed on creating clear, detailed, precise, and complete documentation.
- Collaboration—Students learn the importance of working on multidisciplinary teams and understanding the roles of team members. Emphasis is placed on understanding team dynamics and developing strategies for successful collaboration regardless of team composition.
- Common Engineering Tools and Techniques—Students learn to use common tools and techniques that engineers employ to approach and solve problems and to manage projects. These include electronic hardware, software tools, measurement tools, and concepts from multiple STEM disciplines as well as techniques for project scheduling, cost management and risk analysis.

Once the student learning goals had been defined, the course development team benchmarked them against a number of established sources, including *Engineering in K–12 Education* (Katehi, Pearson, & Feder, 2009); *Standards for Technology Literacy* (ITEEA, 2007); *Benchmarks for Science Literacy* (AAAS, 2008); *National Science Education Standards* (NRC, 1996); *A Framework for K–12 Science Education* (NRC, 2012); *Changing the Conversation* (NAE, 2008); and ABET criteria for accrediting post-secondary engineering programs (ABET, 2012). The results of this benchmarking activity are reported in *Engineer Your World: An Innovative Approach to Developing a High School Engineering Design Course* (Farmer, Allen, Berland, Crawford, Guerra, 2012).

The Projects

The *Engineer Your World* curriculum comprises an opening week of materials that introduce the field of engineering and establish class norms and five long (six-week) design challenges interspersed with short (week-long) explorations. Students spend approximately 80% of their time engaged in hands-on work; the remaining time is divided between research, documentation, direct instruction, presentation preparation, and delivery, and similar activities.

Opening Week: The Importance of Teamwork and Communication

Effective teamwork and communication are essential to success in engineering. The first week of *Engineer Your World* is dedicated to exploring what these terms mean in engineering and to establishing class norms. The preponderance of students' work throughout the year will be completed in teams of between two and nine students. While all team members will share responsibility for a team's design and final documentation, which will be graded as team products using a rubric, individual students will be responsible for documenting their work in engineering notebooks and for completing assessments as homework, in-class work or quizzes. Expectations for grading are established with students on the first day of the course.

Challenge 1: Design a Pinhole Camera for Artists With Disabilities

In Design Challenge 1, students discover the design process as they create pinhole cameras to meet the special requirements of artists with disabilities. Core engineering skills acquired include analyzing/interpreting requirements, generating concepts, embodying design, verifying performance, and creating technical documentation.

Design Challenge 1 opens with a short discussion about modern cameras that anchors the unit in students' everyday lives. Students experience the *camera obscura* phenomenon (i.e., light travels through a small hole and projects an image onto a surface inside a box or room that is otherwise completely dark) and discuss what societal want or need might have combined with this technology to lead to the invention of the film-based camera and, eventually, modern digital imagery.

After receiving the design challenge statement, students begin by exploring how customer needs impact design decisions. A fictional customer, who runs an arts program for people with disabilities, has been interviewed and the results have been turned into a list of user needs and a basic description of how the user will interact with the camera. Students analyze these needs and actions to develop quantitative specifications.

Once the specifications are clear, students use a structured sequence of techniques to generate ideas. After brainstorming individually and in pairs, then creating a mind map from the results, and eventually using the mind map as inspiration for concept sketching, students participate in a gallery walk with their classmates to gather additional feedback about their ideas. Once all feedback has been considered, teams select a concept, build a prototype, develop a test plan, and test their cameras. Each team then evaluates its camera's performance against a rubric, documents its design for manufacturing purposes, and creates user instructions.

Curriculum Design Principles in Action. The curriculum development team's background in constructivist theory is evident in Design Challenge 1. The challenge is

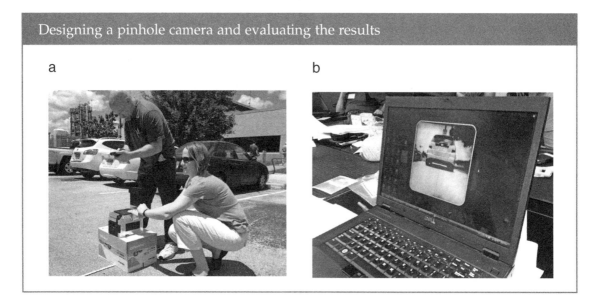

Designing a pinhole camera and evaluating the results

a

b

Images by Alan Downey.

designed to enable students to construct their own under-standing of the engineering design process. Rather than present a step-by-step engineering design process for students to follow, the *Engineer Your World* teacher guides students through the design process and asks students to name each step as it is completed. At the end of the unit, once students have constructed the design process as they understand it, the teacher reveals the "official" *Engineer Your World* design process and facilitates a class discussion comparing the two processes. As a result of constructing the process themselves, students develop a sense of owner-ship over the process that they will use to solve the design challenges in the remainder of the course.

Creating a New Narrative of Engineering. Design Challenge 1 requires that students consider principles of universal design, alluding to engineers' ability to design solutions that improve people's lives. The unit project, which requires that students explore the evolution of imag-ery in its social/historical context, makes clear that engi-neers design products to meet customer wants and needs, and that engineered solutions evolve in response to chang-ing societal wants and needs.

Connections to the NGSS. Design Challenge 1 focuses on the engineering design process, which is the core engineer-ing idea in the NGSS. The challenge also requires students to use most of the eight NGSS-defined science and engi-

Using a model to determine what will happen to a taller building during an earthquake

Image by Alan Downey.

neering practices, including developing and using a model (Practice 2) to inform their design; planning and carrying out an investigation (Practice 3) to test their prototype; using mathematical thinking (Practice 5) to determine design dimensions and exposure times; constructing a design solution (Practice 6); and obtaining, evaluating and commu-nicating information (Practice 8) through manufacturing specifications and user instruc-tions. Finally, the challenge touches on the crosscutting concepts of scale and proportion (Concept 3) and structure and function (Concept 7).

Challenge 2: Design a Safer Building for an Earthquake-Prone Region

In Design Challenge 2, students test and redesign structures for human safety and earth-quake resistance while learning about instrumentation and experimentation, data acqui-sition and analysis, modeling, design modification, and data representation for decision making.

In this challenge, students are asked to redesign an apartment building in an earth-quake-prone region of northeast India to be both taller and safer. Students begin by read-ing and interpreting interview statements from four stakeholders: an engineering firm overseeing redesign, the owner of the building and land, the local government, and residents of the current building. From these interview statements, the students create a single customer-needs statement, piece together general requirements and constraints for the design, and define metrics for safety.

Students plan and conduct experiments in which they use a small earthquake simulator (shaker table) and software to collect acceleration data for two building heights with and without a roof load. They use basic statistical methods to analyze the resulting class data set and use data representations to defend assertions about which of the initial building designs are safe.

Next, students research existing design solutions for quake-resistant structures and brainstorm their own ideas for variables or features that might be changed to improve building design. The class aggregates these ideas and decides which concepts to test, generating another set of data. Based on these results, students generate final design concepts using the structured techniques that they learned in the previous design challenge. They score various concepts and use a structured discussion of the data to select one concept to embody.

Once students have selected a concept, they plan for final design construction by creating drawings, developing a materials list, and dividing responsibilities among team members. Each team constructs its selected design and conducts a final round of tests. All teams compare the metrics for their prototypes against the baseline data and previously reported class data to determine which designs are optimal. Finally, students create a technical report for the project customers.

Curriculum Design Principles in Action. Constructed such that the "design of experiments" activity is essential and useful to students, Design Challenge 2 typifies the way in which the curriculum engages students in meaningful versions of the practices of engineers. It also requires the purposeful application of such STEM concepts as standard deviation, periodic signals, and resonance.

Creating a New Narrative of Engineering. Design Challenge 2 is presented as an opportunity for engineers to improve human lives, a message that resonates exceptionally well with young people. The potential of engineering to enhance human health and well-being is reinforced by a unit project that allows students to examine the role of engineers in developing public policy.

Connections to the NGSS. Like all design challenges in *Engineer Your World*, Design Challenge 2 employs the engineering design process that is the core engineering idea in the NGSS. The challenge also requires students to use all eight of the NGSS-defined science and engineering practices by defining the problem (Practice 1) from a set of interview documents; developing and using models (Practice 2) to generate test data; planning and carrying out an investigation (Practice 3) through their design of experiments; analyzing and interpreting data (Practice 4) using appropriate statistical methods; using mathematical and computational thinking (Practice 5) in the employment of digital tools for collecting, analyzing, and graphing data; constructing a design solution (Practice 6); engaging in argument from evidence (Practice 7) to evaluate competing design solutions; and obtaining, evaluating, and communicating information (Practice 8) through the investigation of existing solutions as well as in the preparation of a technical report. Finally, the challenge touches on the crosscutting concepts of cause and effect (Concept 2), scale and proportion (Concept 3), systems and system models (Concept 4), and structure and function (Concept 6).

Design Challenge 3: Redesign a Human-Powered Flashlight

In Design Challenge 3, students explore the functionality of common objects and think like the engineers who designed them. This unit emphasizes product design, interpreting customer needs, developing design constraints, and understanding patents and intellectual property.

This challenge asks students to reverse engineer and suggest design improvements to a human-powered flashlight. The class begins by using a structured approach to developing interview questions that students then use to gather customer statements. From these statements, the students develop design requirements, performance metrics, and design specifications.

Focusing on product function rather than form, students perform multiple levels of functional modeling and attempt to predict the previous designers' decisions. Teams then disassemble the flashlight to see how their predictions compare with reality and reassemble the product to identify construction inefficiencies. Through this process, students generate a rich set of redesign ideas that they compile to generate concepts using the same structured methods that they have employed in the previous two units.

Once students have completed the concept generation phase of the design process, the teacher leads a discussion in which students analyze their previous experiences in selecting concepts without structured methods or with ill-structured methods. This motivates the introduction of a standard concept selection method for engineering, the Pugh chart. Finally, once a concept has been selected, students are asked to "embody" their chosen design in a technical drawing and report to their manager.

Curriculum Design Principles in Action. The delayed introduction of a structured technique for concept selection in Design Challenge 3 is a manifestation of the curriculum development team's commitment to ensuring that students experience the desired STEM

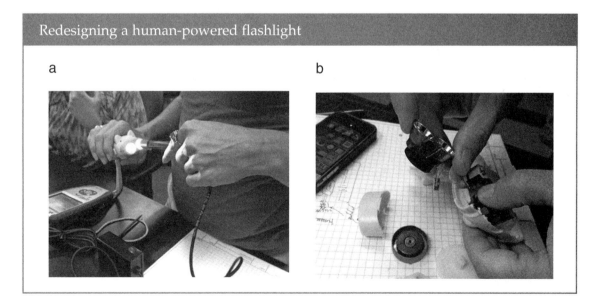

Redesigning a human-powered flashlight

a

b

Images by Alan Downey.

content, tools, and techniques as necessary for successful completion of the design projects. While students learn structured techniques for concept generation in Design Challenge 1 and use them again in Design Challenge 2, they are given only vague instructions for selecting among those concepts. In Design Challenge 3, the teacher elicits student descriptions of frustration with the absence of structure in that process and uses this frustration to motivate the introduction of a structured concept selection technique.

Creating a New Narrative of Engineering. Design Challenge 3 makes obvious the influence of engineers on the objects of our everyday lives.

Connections to the NGSS. Like all design challenges in *Engineer Your World*, Design Challenge 3 employs the engineering design process that is the core engineering idea in the NGSS. The challenge also requires students to use most of the eight NGSS-defined science and engineering practices, including developing and using models (Practice 2) to describe product functionality; carrying out an investigation (Practice 3) to better understand product functionality; analyzing and interpreting data (Practice 4) using appropriate statistical methods; using mathematical and computational thinking (Practice 5) to represent relationships between data; engaging in argument from evidence (Practice 7) to support their proposed redesign solution; and obtaining, evaluating, and communicating information (Practice 8) through a technical drawing and report. Finally, the challenge touches on the crosscutting concepts of cause and effect (Concept 2), systems and system models (Concept 4), energy and matter (Concept 5), and structure and function (Concept 6).

Design Challenge 4: Design and Deploy an Aerial Imaging System

In Design Challenge 4, students design and deploy an aerial imaging system to learn about system decomposition, project management, concept selection, risk analysis, and ethics and safety.

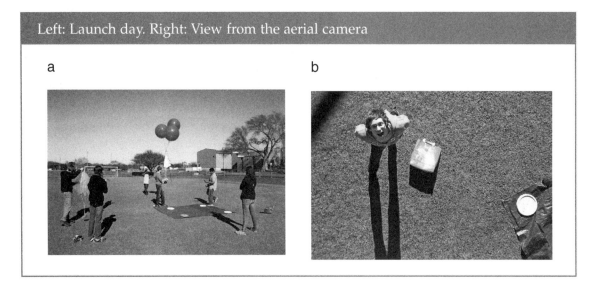

Left: Launch day. Right: View from the aerial camera

a   b

Images by Audrea Moyers.

This challenge begins with a discussion of the human benefits of remote sensing technology before presenting students with the design challenge: "Work in teams to design and build a reusable system that can remotely capture pictures of a target during descent from a specified height." A class discussion encourages students to deconstruct this statement to discover that the challenge comprises not a single problem but several interrelated problems that make up a *system*.

Students work in teams to explore the constraints and requirements of the challenge, decompose the system into subsystems, and map the requirements to functions and parts required of the system. Teams assign members to subsystem teams and specify which subsystem teams are responsible for which data collection activities. They then develop and execute teaming agreements, learn about team engineering notebooks, and develop a basic project schedule.

Next teams divide into their subsystem teams. Each subsystem team then applies the design process to their subsystem, analyzing the subsystem requirements and constraints before generating concepts. These subsystem teams are required to maintain close communication to ensure that their concepts will work together in an integrated system. After employing a weighted decision matrix to select a concept, each subsystem team analyzes the risk of failure of its chosen design using a technique known as a Failure Modes and Effects Analysis before embodying the subsystem concepts to prepare for integration.

When system teams reconvene to prepare for launch, they begin by developing a launch plan known as a Concept of Operations and performing a system-level Failure Modes and Effects Analysis. Finally, the team executes a test launch, makes refinements as necessary, and executes a final launch. The teams reflect on their design experiences and prepare a presentation summarizing their work.

Curriculum Design Principles in Action. Design Challenge 4 exemplifies the use of the standardized engineering design process as an instructional framework. The system-level team works through the first three steps of the design process to understand the system prior to its decomposition. Next each subsystem-level team begins the design process anew, applying it only to their subsystem. Finally, the teams reconvene to integrate their designs and resume the design process at the step where they had previously left off. This nested use of a single engineering design process exemplifies how the standardized process supports students while adapting to fit each new challenge.

Design Challenge 4 also engages students in the authentic practices of professional engineers as they negotiate responsibilities within one large system-level team and among smaller subsystem-level teams. Many of the tools and techniques employed in this unit, including the Failure Modes and Effects Analysis and the Concept of Operations, are commonly used in engineering practice.

Creating a New Narrative of Engineering. Design Challenge 4 illustrates how engineers work collaboratively in teams to solve complex design challenges.

Connections to the NGSS. Design Challenge 4 employs the engineering design process that is the core engineering idea in the NGSS at both the system level and at each of the subsystem levels. The challenge also requires students to use many of the eight NGSS-defined science and engineering practices, including asking questions and defining problems (Practice 1), particularly as they explore subsystem functionality; developing and using models (Practice 2) to test subsystem design solutions; planning and carrying out an investigation (Practice 3) to identify possible failure points and improve their designs;

constructing explanations and design solutions (Practice 6); engaging in argument from evidence (Practice 7) to evaluate different design solutions; and obtaining, evaluating, and communicating information (Practice 8) through a technical presentation. Finally, the challenge treats the crosscutting concept of systems and system models (Concept 4) deeply and touches on structure and function (Concept 6).

Design Challenge 5: Design a Robotics Challenge

In Design Challenge 5, students learn to program a prebuilt robot and employ their newfound knowledge to develop a robotics challenge for their classmates to solve. This final unit extends the concept of a *system* that was introduced in Design Challenge 4 as students learn about automation, control, and programming.

Students first complete programming mini-challenges to explore the functionality of the robot and to expand their knowledge of coding in a text-based integrated development environment. They then extend their understanding of functional modeling to include flowcharts and control algorithms as they learn to use open- and closed-loop functions. Finally, each team creates its own robotics challenge, proves that its challenge is solvable by developing and demonstrating effective code, and poses the challenge for another team to solve.

Curriculum Design Principles in Action. Design Challenge 5 typifies the way in which student work is contextualized within a STEM design challenge. The mathematics presented in the unit is necessary to understand and predict the behavior of a turning vehicle, while programming techniques such as loops, feedback, and logical switches are required for proper vehicle control. The challenge of creating their own design challenge can be successfully completed by students in a number of ways, but all these require knowledge and application of these STEM topics.

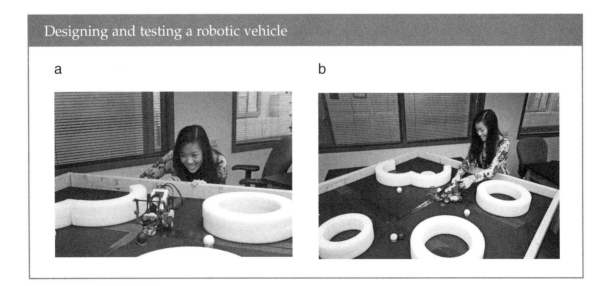

Designing and testing a robotic vehicle

a   b

Images by Alan Downey.

Creating a New Narrative of Engineering. Design Challenge 5 includes a research assignment that engages students in a consideration of how automation and control opens new frontiers by allowing engineers to solve challenges in extreme environments where we cannot or would not want to send humans.

Connections to the NGSS. Like all design challenges in *Engineer Your World*, Design Challenge 5 once again employs the engineering design process that is the core engineering idea in the NGSS. The challenge also requires students to use many of the eight NGSS-defined science and engineering practices, including asking questions and defining problems (Practice 1), particularly to create their own challenges; planning and carrying out an investigation (Practice 3) to identify possible failure points and improve their designs; analyzing and interpreting data (Practice 4) and using mathematical and computational thinking (Practice 5) to develop and improve control programming; constructing design solutions (Practice 6); engaging in argument from evidence (Practice 7) to evaluate different design solutions; and obtaining, evaluating, and communicating information (Practice 8) through a demonstration and presentation. Finally, the challenge touches on the crosscutting concepts of patterns (Concept 1), systems and system models (Concept 4), and structure and function (Concept 6).

Explorations: Discovering Engineering Fields and Professions

Interspersed with the long design challenges described above, the short (one-week) explorations serve three purposes: to change the pace of instruction, to serve as "bridge" activities between units, and to offer students the opportunity to explore engineering fields and professions not otherwise covered in the course.

A Brief Change of Pace. In contrast to the long design challenges, which require students to complete at least one full iteration of the engineering design process, explorations engage students in a relatively simple hands-on activity related to a particular engineering field or profession. This change of pace offers students and teachers a "break" after each long design challenge and allows them to refocus their energies in preparation for the upcoming challenge.

A Bridge Between Units. Each exploration has been designed to introduce a concept that will be important in the design challenge that follows. For instance, *Understanding Data: Designing Coffee* affords students the opportunity to practice tools and techniques for gathering, analyzing, and representing data in preparation for *Designing With Data: Safer Buildings* in which they will analyze large data sets. Similarly, *Programming: Electronic Music* introduces students to programming a microcontroller so that they will be prepared to control their automated system in *Systems Engineering: Aerial Imaging* and to tackle the automation and control tasks in *Control Systems: Robotics*.

An Opportunity to Explore Engineering Fields and Professions. The curriculum designers believe that it is important that students explore as many engineering disciplines as possible. For this reason, each design challenge requires that students complete a parallel study of fields and professions related to the topic of that challenge. Similarly, each exploration is related to a particular field of engineering and requires that students research current topics and career opportunities in that field. In this way, the curriculum enables students to explore mechanical engineering, chemical engineering, civil engineering, electrical engineering, and aerospace engineering, as well as the roles of universal design and automation and control in modern engineering professions.

Instructional Materials

The instructional materials for *Engineer Your World* include detailed lesson plans, student assessment tools, and laboratory equipment and supplies. The course materials are currently available to teachers through an adapted application of the Canvas learning management system, which will be expanded to include student access in 2015–2016. This new system will enhance teaching and learning in *Engineer Your World* classrooms through features, including online student engineering notebooks, additional teacher and student resources, project extensions to support enhanced science and mathematics learning, and advanced analytics for assessing student learning.

Lesson plans provide teachers with the information that they need to understand the lesson materials, prepare for classroom instruction, and teach the lesson. Presentation materials for each lesson currently include an editable PowerPoint file that teachers can use for instruction, as well as an annotated document with teaching notes for those slides. Student handouts and other instructional materials are provided where they add value to instruction, although most student work is documented in engineering notebooks. Finally, teacher reference materials provide additional background where it may be of use.

Student assessment tools include both formal and informal assessments of individual and group work, project rubrics, end-of-unit report guidelines, and peer and self-assessments.

- **Individual student assessments** are provided alongside suggested responses and grading guidelines so that teachers can check for student understanding of important concepts and learning objectives. Where student understanding is lacking, teachers can adjust instruction to reinforce learning.
- **Project rubrics** are presented or developed at a strategic point in each unit, usually immediately before teams begin to generate design concepts. This delayed introduction is intended to maximize students' opportunities to construct their own understanding of each challenge early in the process while still ensuring that teams generate ideas with the full knowledge of how their designs will be judged. Although the curricular materials include default rubrics, teachers are encouraged to view these rubrics as guidelines and to engage their students in developing class rubrics that reflect students' understanding of the challenge at hand.
- **End-of-unit report guidelines**, like project rubrics, are intended to serve as teacher guidelines for a class discussion of what should be included in each final report.
- **Peer assessments** allow students to provide their teammates with feedback on their contributions to the overall team performance.
- **Self-assessments** encourage students to reflect on the feedback from their peers and to identify opportunities for growth. These instruments are typically administered at the end of each unit, although they may also be used during a unit to help "unstick" struggling teams.

Laboratory equipment and supplies include both common science lab supplies and specialized equipment. The full cost of equipment, materials, and supplies required to teach one 24-student section of *Engineer Your World* is under $4000.The consumable cost, which also represents the marginal cost of adding an additional 24-student section of the course, is below $500 per year. These costs represent considerably less expense than is associated with other high school engineering programs.

Integrating EYW into Your High School

What Types of Schools Offer *Engineer Your World*? *Engineer Your World* is taught successfully in STEM schools, engineering academies, college preparatory schools, and comprehensive high schools; in single-gender and mixed-gender schools; in public and private schools; and in urban, suburban, and rural schools.

Where Does *Engineer Your World* **Fit in the High School Curriculum?** Some schools offer *Engineer Your World* as a foundational course to students in 9th and 10th grade, either to provide a context for future STEM learning or as an introductory course in an engineering sequence. Others offer *Engineer Your World* as a capstone course for students in 11th and 12th grade, allowing them to apply the knowledge they have acquired throughout their high school careers. In many cases, the course is "cross listed" as both a science and a technology course. In all cases, it is important that the course be considered as part of a sequence of student learning.

Who Should Teach *Engineer Your World*? Successful teachers of *Engineer Your World* share four characteristics: (1) an interest in fostering students' ability to develop new skills and a new approach to problem solving; (2) comfort with the uncertainty inherent in engineering design, where multiple "correct" solutions exist for any given challenge; (3) a willingness to play the "guide on the side" role that enables successful project-based instruction; and (4) a background in one or more STEM fields.

The educational backgrounds and teaching certifications of *Engineer Your World* teachers vary widely. The typical teacher of this course holds a BS degree in a STEM field, and many hold MA or MS degrees in either a STEM field or STEM education. Some have worked as engineers, while others have never taken an engineering course prior to joining the program. Almost all *Engineer Your World* teachers hold a certification to teach a secondary STEM subject, and many are certified to teach in career and technical education programs. Teaching experience of *Engineer Your World* educators varies from 1–36 years. Most teachers of the course have taught or currently teach physics or engineering, while others have experience in chemistry or mathematics classrooms. This variety of teacher backgrounds is accounted for in the professional development and ongoing support programs offered by the *Engineer Your World* team.

What Type of Student Should Enroll in *Engineer Your World*? *Engineer Your World* is intended to introduce *all* students to what engineering is, what engineers do, and the role that engineers play in shaping the world around us. Students who complete the course will be more STEM-literate citizens and voters, regardless of their professional aspirations and decisions. Some students will enter the course with no knowledge of or interest in engineering as a profession, and some will change their minds as a result of the course. Most students who take the course with an interest in pursuing engineering degrees will retain that intention after the course, although a few will decide that engineering is not for them. The important thing is not that all *Engineer Your World* alumni pursue engineering but that these students make *informed decisions* about their educational futures.

Engineer Your World is suitable for all students and is, in some schools, a required course. Some schools offer the course for "honors" credit by requiring an optional portfolio that aligns with emerging standards for Advanced Placement® in engineering. Others target their recruitment to focus on students who have not excelled in more "traditional" science classrooms with an abundance of seat work, believing that such students may excel in a hands-on, project-based environment. A few schools offer *Engineer Your World* in a "stacked" classroom with the "honors" and "nonhonors" students working in mixed teams; in these cases, the honors students simply complete the additional work required for the portfolio.

It is likely that *Engineer Your World* will be available for dual enrollment through The University of Texas beginning in 2015–2016. This version of the course will be appropriate for all students who are interested in earning university credit and capable of completing the course work, including assessments. Additionally, *Engineer Your World* will remain aligned with emerging Advanced Placement® standards so that students who complete the one-year course will be prepared to submit successful portfolios once that program comes online. Finally, UTeach*Engineering* is planning to develop a computationally intensive second-year course that will teach computing in the context of engineering design challenges and will enable Advanced Placement® credit in Computer Science Principles.

Conclusion

Engineer Your World was developed at The University of Texas at Austin as part of the National Science Foundation-funded UTeach*Engineering* program, which seeks to support teachers of secondary engineering through a combination of curriculum development activities, teacher professional development and support programs, and degree programs for current and future teachers. Although the course was developed in response to an opportunity in Texas, where engineering design and problem solving may be offered for a fourth-year science credit, the curriculum developers have always considered a variety of state and national standards for technology and engineering education. As a result of this the course is, as demonstrated in this chapter, well-placed to support schools in the implementation of the NGSS.

For more information about *Engineer Your World*, please visit our website at www.EngineerYourWorld.org.

Acknowledgments

The work described in this chapter was made possible by a grant from the National Science Foundation (Award DUE-0831811). Support was also provided by NASA through an Intergovernmental Personnel Act agreement.

While the *Engineer Your World* curriculum development team included many talented individuals, special recognition is due to the core team that included, in addition to the authors, Mr. Miguel Alanis, The University of Texas at Austin; Mr. Jesse DeWald, The University of Texas at Austin; Ms. Gretchen Edelmon, National Instruments; Ms. Lisa

Guerra, NASA; Ms. Martha Lee, The University of Texas at Austin; Ms. Rachel McGowan, The University of Texas at Austin; and Ms. Mariel Robles, The University of Texas at Austin. Special thanks are also extended to the many practicing educators who have taught *Engineer Your World* and whose feedback continues to shape the course.

References

AAAS. (1993, 2008). *Benchmarks for science literacy.* Project 2061. New York: Oxford University Press. Retrieved from: www.project2061.org/publications/bsl/online/index.php

ABET. (2012). *Criteria for accrediting engineering programs, 2012–2013.* Retrieved from: www.abet.org/engineering-criteria-2012–2013/

Berland, L., Allen, D., Crawford, R., Farmer, C., & Guerra, L. (2012). *Learning sciences guided high school engineering curriculum development.* American Society for Engineering Education: AC 2012–4186. Retrieved from: http://www.asee.org/public/conferences/8/papers/4186/view

Farmer, C., Allen, D., Berland, L., Crawford, R., & Guerra, L. (2012, June). *Engineer your world: An innovative approach to developing a high school engineering design course.* Paper presented at American Society for Engineering Education Annual Conference, San Antonio, Texas. Retrieved from: http://www.asee.org/public/conferences/8/papers/3949/view

ITEEA. (2000, 2005, 2007). *Standards for technological literacy: Content for the study of technology.* Reston, VA: Author.

Katehi, L., Pearson, G., & Feder, M. (Eds.). (2009). *Engineering in K–12 education: Understanding the status and improving the prospects.* Washington, DC: National Academies Press.

NAE. (2008). *Changing the conversation: Messages for improving public understanding of engineering.* Washington, DC: National Academies Press.

NRC. (1996). *National science education standards.* Washington, DC: National Academies Press.

NRC. (2012). *A framework for K-12 science education: Practices, crosscutting concepts, and core ideas.* Washington, DC: National Academies Press.

6

Global Systems Science

Alan Gould

Lawrence Hall of Science

University of California, Berkeley

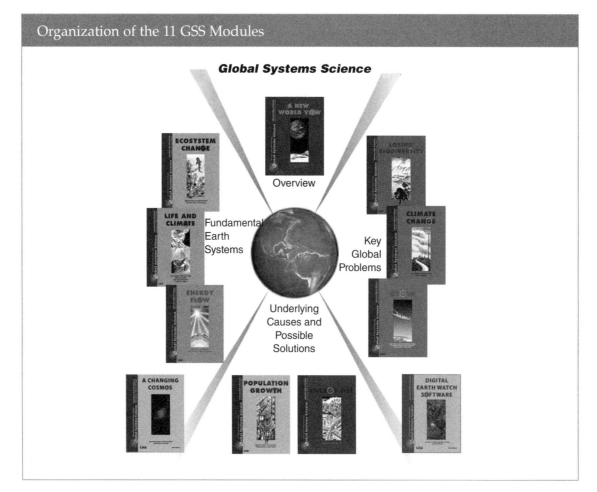

Overview

Global Systems Science (GSS) is a set of curriculum materials for high school teachers and students that is centered on critical societal issues of global concern, such as ecosystem change, losing biodiversity, climate change, and energy use, all which require science for full understanding and thoughtful intelligent engineering for solutions. GSS is a full-year interdisciplinary, integrated course but is also intentionally modularized to easily be used in existing high school biology, physics, chemistry, Earth science, or social studies courses to better support the NGSS.

The materials include 11 modules with teacher guides and "Digital Earth Watch" (DEW) software. They emphasize how scientists and engineers from a wide variety of fields work together to understand significant problems of global impact. GSS is adaptable for high school teachers and students from grades 9–12. The following chart shows the 11 GSS modules:

Introductory module focusing on the theme of systems

- A New World View

Modules for understanding causes of key environmental problems

- Changing Climate
- Ozone
- Losing Biodiversity

Modules for understanding fundamental Earth systems

- Life and Climate
- Ecosystem Change
- Energy Flow

Modules focusing on possible solutions to key environmental problems

- Energy Use
- Population Growth

Modules focusing on analysis of digital images of Earth and space

- ABCs of Digital Earth Watch Software
- A Changing Cosmos

GSS was created at the Lawrence Hall of Science, University of California, Berkeley, by a collaborative team of teachers, scientists, and curriculum developers. The series reflects both the cutting edge of modern interdisciplinary science and the practical realities of the classroom. The modules are available at www.globalsystemsscience.org.

Purpose

In the race-for-space era of the 1950s and 1960s, the primary purpose of science education in the United States was to produce more scientists and engineers. Since then, the geopolitical and economic landscape has changed. While it is still important to attract bright minds to science and engineering fields, it is now recognized that it is essential for everyone, regardless of vocation, to understand the key ideas in science, technology, engineering, and mathematics (STEM). This general level of understanding, called "science literacy" (Bybee, 1997), is needed to address challenges in everyday life in our increasingly technological world. It is also essential for voters, who will be faced with decisions that require scientific ways of thinking. The collective judgment of our people will determine how we manage shared resources such as air, water, and national forests. (NRC, 1996, p. 11). In summary, the purpose of the GSS series is for *all students* to become STEM literate.

The purpose of the Next Generation Science Standards (NGSS Lead States, 2013) is to specify what all students should know and be able to do by the time they graduate from each level of our educational system. As illustrated in Table 1 at the end of this chapter, the Global Systems Science series directly addresses 30% of the high school performance expectations in the NGSS so that GSS can be used as an integrated science course or combined with other high school science courses, as part of a three-year sequence to prepare students to meet 100% of the performance expectations in the NGSS.

Learning Goals

In GSS, the "big ideas" of science are stressed, such as the concept of interacting systems and the coevolution of the atmosphere and life. Moreover, the importance of engineering is emphasized through the goal of a sustainable world and the important role that individuals play in both impacting and protecting our vulnerable global environment. Each module focuses on a different aspect of environmental change.

GSS aims for students to

- Learn actively.
- Perform investigations in the classroom and at home.
- Read and discuss historical background materials.
- Hear from or read about a selection of scientists, both men and women, from a variety of ethnic and educational backgrounds.
- Consider the economic, political, and ethical issues, as well as the scientific concepts and findings associated with each problem area.
- Make intelligent, informed decisions that can translate into personal actions, such as conserving energy and recycling.
- Be thoughtful, environmentally aware consumers.
- Prepare for their role as voting citizens in a modern industrialized society.

Collectively, the GSS modules constitute a unique combination of studies in the natural and social sciences along with engineering through which high school students may view the environmental issues that they are confronting or will confront within their lifetimes. In the remainder of this chapter, we briefly describe nine of the modules that constitute a core integrated GSS course.

A New World View

The introductory module, A New World View, invites students to take a systems view of their home planet and introduces four key ideas that thread through the entire course:

1. The Earth has tremendously diverse environments, yet it is a single planet that we all call "home."

2. We can better understand the Earth if we think of it in terms of systems.

3. Everything is connected to everything else.

4. The goal of global studies is to find out what we can do to sustain life on Planet Earth—now and in the generations to come. This is the place where engineering plays a vital role.

A New World View illustrates these ideas with a story of land use in the Pacific Northwest. Early chapters summarize the history of human impacts, from Native Americans changing forest ecosystems with fire to the clear-cutting of forests by European immigrants in the 19th century, ending with a controversy in the 1990s over the decision by a California holding company to clear-cut a grove of old growth redwoods that sparked major demonstrations by concerned citizens.

A simplistic environmentalist version of this story would have been to honor the majesty of the forests and their importance for wildlife (the spotted owl), then vilify the timber company and financier who intended to log the forest for financial gain. Instead, GSS presents multiple sides of the story, quoting from several environmental groups, from the lumber company's office of public affairs, and from politicians' efforts at forging a compromise.

On the side of the lumber interests, the module points out that a person has a right to cut down trees on their own property, and that the lumber company had already donated large tracts of land with ancient redwoods to be used as state and national forests and supported a variety of conservation programs to preserve wildlife. Also presented is the viewpoint of the lumber workers who have to provide for their families, and interviews with wood scientists who explain that replacing old-growth trees with faster growing forests helps remove carbon dioxide from the atmosphere, thus reducing global warming.

California Senator Dianne Feinstein and then-President Bill Clinton proposed resolving the dilemma by purchasing the land and incorporating it into the state or national park system. The story ends with a ballot initiative that gave California voters the chance to decide if state funds should be used to preserve the ancient trees. The students are asked to decide what advice they would give to the citizens of California.

Cary Sneider, a former Director of the GSS project, commented on this approach in his article "Activism or Education?" (Sneider, 2000). The activist approach is to oversimplify environmental issues by highlighting commercial and societal practices that negatively impact the environment and advocate a specific action: Stop the bad behavior! But environmental issues are exceedingly complex and can be valuable in programs aimed at improving science literacy, but only if presented so as to engage people's thinking. In other words, the purpose of education is to help them learn *how* to think, not to tell them *what* to think. From an ethical standpoint, we believe that students should practice critical thinking skills and be empowered to make their own choices, since that is the essence of a democracy.

In other parts of the module, students take a "virtual field trip" to an old-growth forest in southern Washington state, where they "ride" a canopy crane to observe the seasonal changes in the forest and meet a number of people with various professions who are studying the forest to learn as much as possible about its role in the global ecosystem.

The students also undertake their own laboratory investigation of how to sustain life inside a terrarium and use DEW software to analyze images of Earth from space to observe the effects of deforestation in North and South America. (The GSS module ABCs of Digital Earth Watch Software provides background and pointers for using the software.) It is a technological approach to understanding a problem we face—a first step in solving the problem.

Next we provide a detailed description of the Energy Use module, which provides a "window" into the scientific process, societal engineering challenges, and the need for citizens to understand scientific issues to make intelligent, informed decisions that will affect the quality of life for future generations.

Energy Use

Energy Use begins by inviting students to take an inventory of the ways that they use electricity. By "following the wires" back to a power plant and from there to a grid of all power plants in the country, students begin to grasp the vast infrastructure that supports our way of life. Through laboratory experiments, they learn the basic principles on which electrical devices work; and through a brief history, they learn how our national energy policy came to be. They also learn about the huge amounts of fossil fuels burned for transportation, home heating, and industry on a daily basis and the small fraction of that energy that is actually put to use.

In the last portion of the unit, students conduct simple experiments in which they discover that conservation might allow us to maintain our current standard of living while saving billions of dollars and reducing our impact on the environment. They also explore new technologies for satisfying the energy needs of a growing human population while keeping the impact of energy use to a minimum. Following is a chapter-by-chapter summary of the GSS Energy Use module.

Chapter 1. Using Energy, *Investigation 1.1. Recent History*—To establish historical context for current problems in modern society's energy use, students interview an older relative or other elder to find out how various tasks requiring energy were accomplished long ago (e.g., cooking, communication, transportation, heating, entertainment, business, or vacations).

Chapter 2. Energy Basics, *Investigation 2.1. Create Electricity*—Students manipulate magnets and coils of wire and observe the responses to their actions on an electric meter. The challenge is to arrange and rearrange magnets and wires to generate as much electrical output as possible.

This activity can be extended to a more sophisticated engineering challenge: create a real electric generator by designing the most efficient coil of wire to spin in a magnetic field.

Generating Electricity

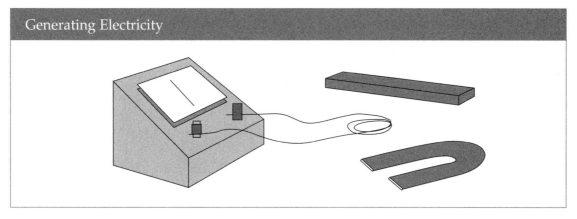

Investigation 2.2. Electric Motor—Students build an electric motor, which is a generator that functions in reverse. That is, a generator transforms kinetic energy into electrical energy, while a motor transforms electrical energy into kinetic energy.

Starting with a simple electric motor made with the same parts used in Investigation 2.1, with the addition of a battery, some paper clips, and thumbtacks, students can progress to more complex challenges to create the most efficient motor possible. Later in this module, when the students explore societal transportation problems they will see that an efficient electric motor can be a vital element in electric vehicles that are much more efficient than fossil-fueled vehicles, and have fewer problems with exhaust and pollution.

Investigation 2.3. Transformations—To make energy transformations "real life," students practice recognizing various forms of energy (Heat Energy, Gravitational Energy, Electrical Energy, Light Energy, Chemical Energy, Potential Energy, Kinetic Energy, Nuclear Energy).

Building an Electric Motor

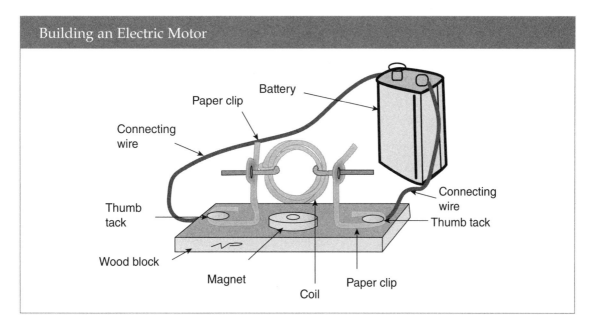

How does a skateboarder transform energy from one form to another?

The students are given a series of "action sentences" and for each one, they write down the starting and ending form(s) of energy:

- A skateboarder rolls down a hill.
- A car fills up at a gas station and drives across country.
- An electric guitarist plays a D-flat minor chord at a rock concert.
- A group of people go to the top of the Empire State Building in an elevator.
- A fan runs on batteries.
- A flashlight shines down a dark tunnel.
- A building is demolished with carefully placed sticks of dynamite.

Students make up similar energy transformation action sentences to challenge fellow students to identify which form of energy changes into which other form of energy.

Chapter 3. Fossil Fuels, *Investigation 3.1. How Much Energy?*—Using joule as a standard unit, students practice finding the equivalent in other types of energy units: therm, barrel of oil, ton of coal, a whole coal train, oil tanker, quad, a candy bar.

Chapter 4. Power Plant, *Investigation 4.1. Home Heating*—Which of three proposed options is the best way to heat a home: (1) Have gas delivered to your home and burn it in a furnace; (2) Have the utility company burn gas and deliver electricity your home's electric heater; or (3) Pipe hot water from a power plant's condenser to your home?

Investigation 4.2. Future Power—Students investigate critical societal questions: How much do we depend on fossil fuels? How will that relationship change in 50 or 100 years? What energy sources would be best for developing nations to consider and implement?

Chapter 5. America Plugged In, *Investigation 5.1. Circuit Breakers*—After reading about the nation's system of electrical energy grids, students find the fuse box or the circuit breaker box in their homes and the meter for reading energy use.

Chapter 6. Energy In Society, *Investigation 6.1. Metering*—Students see how their home electric meter responds to energy use by turning off as many of the electrical appliances as possible, leaving only one on, and then checking the meter to see how much energy is used.

Investigation 6.2. What Are We Paying For?—Determine the costs of various home uses of electricity, learn what our biggest electricity eaters are, and find out where the money goes. This is a crucial step in determining what engineering problems need to be tackled first in a quest to conserve energy use.

Investigation 6.3. Power Failure—Students imagine a major disaster that leaves their town without electric power for a whole week and consider questions such as "How would your life be different each day?" "What conveniences would you do without?" "What energy sources would you use in place of electricity?" Then they write a story about "a week without energy," possibly in the form of a diary or journal, to tell about how their life would be disrupted by the loss of electrical power and how they coped with it.

Chapter 7. Energy for Lighting, *Investigation 7.1. Compare Lights*—Students work in teams to compare, in terms of efficiencies and advertising claims, a collection of various light sources—energy-saver incandescent bulbs, fluorescent bulbs, long-life bulbs, low-cost light bulbs, and specialty lights of all kinds. They decide on a question that requires comparing the brightness of two bulbs (e.g., "Are all 75-watt incandescent bulbs alike?" or "Is a 15-watt compact fluorescent light that is supposed to replace a 60-watt incandescent bulb really just as bright?"). Students answer the question using a clever device: the oil spot photometer.

Investigation 7.2. Life Cycle Cost and Payback Time—The life cycle cost of a light bulb includes the purchase price and the cost of energy use during its entire lifetime. For example, a compact fluorescent bulb lasts 10 times longer than an incandescent bulb but uses way less energy. Buying an energy-efficient light bulb means spending more money at the start, but it also means saving a little money every time you have the light on. Students learn about how the time can come when the energy savings are enough to pay back the extra initial cost of the energy efficient light—the payback time.

Chapter 8. Heating & Cooling, *Investigation 8.1. How Does the Thermos Bottle "Know?"*—Students ponder this question: "If you put something hot in a thermos bottle it stays hot. If you put something cold in a thermos it stays cold. How does the thermos bottle know what it's supposed to do?"

Investigation 8.2. Compute the R-Value of a Material—Students apply the definition of R-Value to answer a number of practical questions.

Investigation 8.3. Refrigerators—Students consider the question of whether or not opening a refrigerator door can actually be a way of cooling down a room in a house. They also explore an actual refrigerator to find features that help "pump" heat from the coils into the air away from the refrigerator.

Chapter 9. Transportation, *Investigation 9.1. Automobile Energy Transformations*—As you drive, you are manipulating at least four types of energy: electrical, chemical, mechanical, and thermal. Students identify energy transformations involved in driving a car.

Electric Meter

Cars transform energy in many different ways

Investigation 9.2. Better Batteries—The "Holy Grail" in electric vehicle design is to develop the lightest and most efficient batteries. Students are challenged to make the most effective cell using simple materials.

Chapter 10. Our Energy Future, *Investigation 10.1. Energy From Sunshine*—Students evaluate two approaches to solar energy: distributed collection at millions of sites versus a solar satellite in Earth orbit.

Investigation 10.2. Payback Time (revisited)—Students compute payback times for various solar energy systems.

Investigation 10.3. Your Vote on Energy Measures—Students analyze six hypothetical pieces of energy legislation and make arguments pro and con for each of them.

Global Environmental Problems

The previous section has focused on the introductory module, A New World View, and Energy Use in some detail to illustrate how Global Systems Science weaves technology and engineering together with science. In the remainder of this chapter, we briefly discuss each of the other GSS modules.

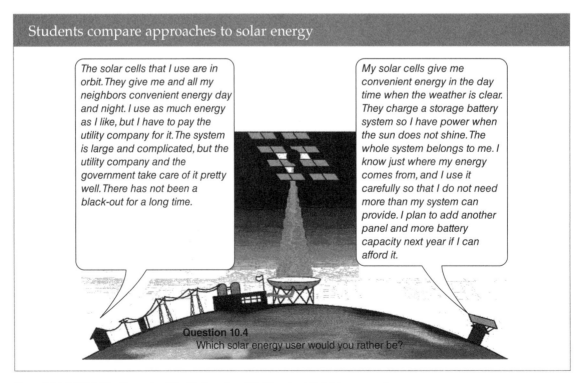

Students compare approaches to solar energy

Three of the GSS modules are concerned with environmental problems, which affect the entire planet: climate change, depletion of the world's ozone layer, and loss of species. These problems are global in nature and each represents a potential threat to life and prosperity on planet Earth. Each illuminates important aspects of the interaction between human activities and Earth systems.

Climate Change

Climate Change addresses the question of how human activities may be changing Earth's climate. It takes students on a "field trip" to Mauna Loa Observatory where they see how scientists have measured carbon dioxide in the Earth's atmosphere since 1957. They graph and interpret data from Mauna Loa and other observatories, which led to the prediction, in 1988, that changes in our atmosphere will cause the entire globe to gradually warm up. They also measure carbon dioxide in the laboratory to find out how much is contained in a sample of human breath and car exhaust.

The module goes on to show how the discoveries at Mauna Loa have been challenged by other scientists in the early 1990s and discuss the consensus of opinion about global climate change that finally emerged in 1995. The module identifies scientific questions, which still remain unanswered, and involves students in thinking about the economic, political, and ethical implications of regulating human activities to reduce the likelihood of global climate change.

Ozone

Ozone is a success story about how people around the globe have cooperated to solve a serious environmental problem. Ozone gas in the upper atmosphere shields our planet from ultraviolet light that is thought to cause skin cancer and cataracts in humans and that may be harmful to a wide variety of plants and animals. The story of how the depletion of ozone came to be recognized and connected to the production of certain chemicals used in refrigerators, air conditioners, and the computer industry demonstrates that science can be an exciting and adventuresome field, and that people in a wide variety of careers often play important roles in scientific discoveries.

The fact that more than 100 countries agreed to phase out the ozone-destroying chemicals clearly shows the connection between science and social action. Since ozone will continue to be depleted for several decades because of chemicals already in the atmosphere, students learn how to protect themselves by monitoring the levels of UV radiation in their community and experimenting with sun block to see if it really offers protection from the ultraviolet rays of the sun.

Losing Biodiversity

Losing Biodiversity is about the endangerment and extinction of entire species of plants and animals throughout the world because of human actions, beginning with the case study of the buffalo. Students learn about the value of biodiversity to humans, from the discovery of new medicines and materials, to the protection of food crops and global systems.

The current loss of biodiversity is put into perspective by involving the students in laboratory work where they see how species can adapt to changing conditions, learn theories about how new species evolve, and study the natural causes of extinctions. Further laboratory work illustrates the vital importance and fragility of soil in supporting entire communities of plants and animals and how soil productivity is impacted by certain agricultural practices. Finally, students consider the history of actions that people around the world have taken to protect endangered species, up to current debates in Congress and international agreements to preserve biodiversity.

Fundamental Earth Systems

The next three modules put global environmental problems into context by focusing on the natural systems within which human activities occur. Such understanding is essential if we are to grapple with key global problems and eventually find ways for humans to prosper and thrive without diminishing the rich diversity of life on Planet Earth.

Life and Climate

Life and Climate is about how our atmosphere and climate came to be as they are today; how life on Earth evolved, and how the evolution of life and climate have affected each other since the Earth was formed. In this module, students find the story of how tiny plants brought oxygen to the Earth's atmosphere, and how changing climates may have brought about the evolution of our human ancestors in Africa 5 million years ago. They construct timelines and find out how we know where to place milestones in the development of life. They learn about the gradual acceptance of tectonic plate theory and how the movement of tectonic plates is now thought to cause the climate changes that affected the evolution of life.

In the laboratory, students experiment with dissolving rocks to explore the long-term carbon cycle that has contributed to the long-term stability of the Earth's climate. In the final chapter, they consider what the Earth's past can tell us about its future.

Ecosystem Change

Ecosystem Change is about the interdependence of all living things and the nonliving environment. It is also about how human activities are changing ecosystems around the world. Through case studies, students learn about the vastly different kinds of ecosystems, or biomes, on our planet. They discover that humans have been changing ecosystems for thousands of years, but that the pace of change has increased with the rapid growth of human populations in the last century. In the laboratory, students investigate the variables that are important in the process of decomposition and relate their findings to the biogeochemical cycles that maintain Earth's biosphere.

Through interviews, students "meet" scientists, such as Samira Omar of Kuwait, who has studied the ecological effects of the Gulf War, and Dr. Dagmar Werner, who has worked to preserve the biodiversity of the rain forests of Central America. They also find out what people in the United States are doing to reduce human impact on ecosystems and consider ways that their own actions can make a difference.

Energy Flow

Energy Flow is about the way energy flows through the atmosphere, oceans, land, and living things. Analyzing the flow of energy is a very useful way to understand Earth systems. For example, through laboratory investigations, students explore the process of convection and see how this process is used to understand earthquakes and volcanoes, global winds, and ocean currents. In other lab activities, the students experiment with the variables that affect water flowing through a bottle and then apply their insights about dynamic equilibrium to understanding how the greenhouse effect is expected to change the Earth's climate.

In the last chapter of Energy Flow, students learn how some of the energy that flows through living systems has been stored, over millions of years, in the form of fossil fuels, and how that energy is being released to power civilization for a few short decades. With this background, your students are asked to think about how the flow of energy through Earth systems affects their daily lives and how life might be different for their children and grandchildren.

Underlying Causes and Possible Solutions

Two aspects of our modern age stand out as possibly the most important underlying causes of global environmental change: (1) the rapidly growing human population and

(2) the ways in which people use natural resources for energy. Earlier in this chapter, we discussed the GSS Energy Use module in some detail. Following is a brief discussion of the Population Growth module. Within both areas, there is reason to hope that intelligent decisions by individuals can reduce the impact of these problems and lead to a habitable world for future generations.

Population Growth

Population Growth addresses a fundamental problem: Even if we can change our habits to use only clean and efficient sources of energy such as solar, wind, and water power, global environmental problems will continue to worsen if the world's population continues to grow at the present rate. Today, there are over 7 billion people on Earth, and the population increases by 1 million every four days. Yet it is difficult for students to see the effects of population growth. They are therefore asked to think about the quality of their own lives as a starting point and to recognize how satisfying their needs take a share of the Earth's resources.

By comparing their own lives with conditions in countries such as China and India, the students will be in a better position to consider what may happen if the human population continues to grow as rapidly as it is today. Through mathematical investigations, students learn about factors that contribute to the rate of population growth and the idea of carrying capacity, which relates an ecosystem to the populations it can sustain. The cultural and religious dimensions of efforts to curb population growth are sensitively discussed, and students are encouraged to form their own opinions about what can and should be done by individuals and by governments to control the growth of the global human population.

Conclusion

We urge you to pay special attention to the left-hand column in Table 6.1. These are the performance expectations from the NGSS that the GSS series are designed to teach. Although performance expectations in the NGSS have been carefully chosen to enable all students to thrive as workers, consumers, and citizens, this particular set of concepts and skills is especially important to help our students understand and solve the global problems that they will encounter as they reach adulthood in a world with an ever-increasing human population and dwindling supplies of arable land, fresh water, and mineral resources.

| **Table 6.1** GSS Alignment With Performance Expectations in the NGSS | | | | | | | | | |

GSS Modules: Performance Expectations	A New World View	Energy Use	Climate Change	Ozone	Losing Biodiversity	Life and Climate	Ecosystem Change	Energy Flow	Population Growth
HS-ETS1-1 Analyze a major global challenge to specify qualitative and quantitative criteria and constraints for solutions that account for societal needs and wants.	✓	✓	✓						
HS-ETS1-2 Design a solution to a complex real-world problem by breaking it down into smaller, more manageable problems that can be solved through engineering.		✓							
HS-ETS1-3 Evaluate a solution to a complex real-world problem based on prioritized criteria and trade-offs that account for a range of constraints, including cost, safety, reliability, and aesthetics, as well as possible social, cultural, and environmental impacts.	✓	✓							
HS-ETS1-4 Use a computer simulation to model the impact of proposed solutions to a complex real-world problem with numerous criteria and constraints on interactions within and between systems relevant to the problem.		✓							
HS-ESS1-1 Develop a model based on evidence to illustrate the life span of the sun and the role of nuclear fusion in the sun's core to release energy that eventually reaches Earth in the form of radiation.								✓	
HS-ESS1-5 Evaluate evidence of the past and current movements of continental and oceanic crust and the theory of plate tectonics to explain the ages of crustal rocks.								✓	

(Continued)

Table 6.1 (Continued)

GSS Modules: Performance Expectations	A New World View	Energy Use	Climate Change	Ozone	Losing Biodiversity	Life and Climate	Ecosystem Change	Energy Flow	Population Growth
HS-ESS2-1 Develop a model to illustrate how Earth's internal and surface processes operate at different spatial and temporal scales to form continental and ocean-floor features.								✓	
HS-ESS2-3 Develop a model based on evidence of Earth's interior to describe the cycling of matter by thermal convection.								✓	
HS-ESS2-4 Use a model to describe how variations in the flow of energy into and out of Earth systems result in changes in climate.			✓			✓			
HS-ESS2-6 Develop a quantitative model to describe the cycling of carbon among the hydrosphere, atmosphere, geosphere, and biosphere.						✓		✓	
HS-ESS2-7 Construct an argument based on evidence about the simultaneous coevolution of Earth systems and life on Earth.						✓			
HS-ESS3-2 Evaluate competing design solutions for developing, managing, and utilizing energy and mineral resources based on cost-benefit ratios.		✓							
HS-ESS3-3 Create a computational simulation to illustrate the relationships among management of natural resources, the sustainability of human populations, and biodiversity.									
HS-ESS3-4 Construct an argument supported by evidence for how increases in human population and per-capita consumption of natural resources impact Earth's systems.		✓							✓
HS-ESS3-5 Analyze geoscience data and the results from global climate models to make an evidence-based forecast of the current rate of global or regional climate change and associated future impacts to Earth systems.			✓						

GSS Modules: Performance Expectations	A New World View	Energy Use	Climate Change	Ozone	Losing Biodiversity	Life and Climate	Ecosystem Change	Energy Flow	Population Growth
HS-ESS3-6 Use a computational representation to illustrate the relationships among Earth systems and how those relationships are being modified due to human activity.									
HS-LS1-5 Use a model to illustrate how photosynthesis transforms light energy into stored chemical energy.							✓		
HS-LS2-1 Use mathematical and/or computational representations to support explanations of factors that affect carrying capacity of ecosystems at different scales.	✓						✓		✓
HS-LS2-2 Use mathematical representations to support and revise explanations based on evidence about factors affecting biodiversity and populations in ecosystems of different scales.	✓				✓		✓		✓
HS-LS2-3 Construct and revise an explanation based on evidence for the cycling of matter and flow of energy in aerobic and anaerobic conditions.	✓								
HS-LS2-4 Use a mathematical representation to support claims for the cycling of matter and flow of energy among organisms in an ecosystem.	✓						✓		
HS-LS2-5 Develop a model to illustrate the role of photosynthesis and cellular respiration in the cycling of carbon among the biosphere, atmosphere, hydrosphere, and geosphere.	✓								
HS-LS2-6 Evaluate the claims, evidence, and reasoning that the complex interactions in ecosystems maintain relatively consistent numbers and types of organisms in stable conditions, but changing conditions may result in a new ecosystem.	✓				✓		✓		✓
HS-LS2-7 Design, evaluate, and refine a solution for reducing the impacts of human activities on the environment and biodiversity.					✓		✓		✓

(Continued)

Table 6.1 (Continued)

GSS Modules: Performance Expectations	A New World View	Energy Use	Climate Change	Ozone	Losing Biodiversity	Life and Climate	Ecosystem Change	Energy Flow	Population Growth
HS-LS3-1 Ask questions to clarify relationships about the role of DNA and chromosomes in coding the instructions for characteristic traits passed from parents to offspring.					✓				
HS-LS3-3 Apply concepts of statistics and probability to explain the variation and distribution of expressed traits in a population.					✓				
HS-PS2-5 Plan and conduct an investigation to provide evidence that an electric current can produce a magnetic field and that a changing magnetic field can produce an electric current.		✓							
HS-PS3-3 Design, build, and refine a device that works within given constraints to convert one form of energy into another form of energy.		✓							
HS-PS3-4 Plan and conduct an investigation to provide evidence that the transfer of thermal energy when two components of different temperature are combined within a closed system results in a more uniform energy distribution among the components in the system (second law of thermodynamics).		✓							
HS-PS3-5 Develop and use a model of two objects interacting through electric or magnetic fields to illustrate the forces between objects and the changes in energy of the objects due to the interaction.		✓							
HS-PS4-4 Evaluate the validity and reliability of claims in published materials of the effects that different frequencies of electromagnetic radiation have when absorbed by matter.				✓					

GSS Modules: Performance Expectations	A New World View	Energy Use	Climate Change	Ozone	Losing Biodiversity	Life and Climate	Ecosystem Change	Energy Flow	Population Growth
HS-PS4-5 Communicate technical information about how some technological devices use the principles of wave behavior and wave interactions with matter to transmit and capture information and energy.				✓					

References

Bybee, Rodger W., *Achieving Scientific Literacy: From Purposes to Practices,*. Portsmouth, NH: Heinemann, 1997.

NGSS Lead States (2013). *Next generation science standards: For states, by states, volume 1: The standards.* Washington, DC: National Academies Press.

NRC. (1996). *National science education standards.* Washington, DC: National Academies Press.

Sneider, C. (2000, July). Activism or education? Implications for achieving science literacy. Presented at the International Geoscience and Remote Sensing Symposium Conference in Honolulu, Hawaii. Retrieved from: http://www.globalsystemsscience.org/resources/sneider

7

Science and Global Issues

Electricity: Global Energy and Power

John Howarth and Janet Bellantoni

Lawrence Hall of Science

University of California, Berkeley, California

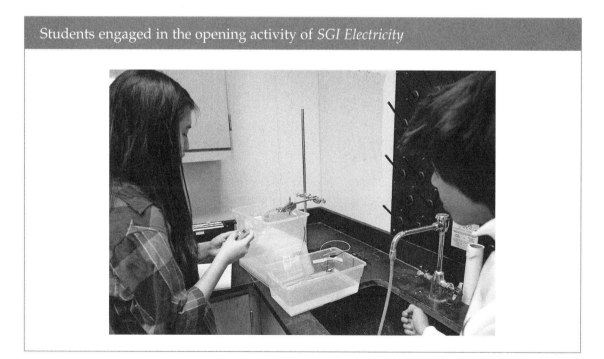

Students engaged in the opening activity of *SGI Electricity*

SEPUP (The Science Education for Public Understanding Program) develops issue-oriented science instructional materials for middle and high school classrooms. SEPUP is a program of the Center for Curriculum Development and Implementation at the University of California, Berkeley's Lawrence Hall of Science. SEPUP courses are developed with the input of scientists and tested by classroom teachers, who teach the curricula in their classrooms and provide feedback for revision of the materials.

Science and Global Issues (SGI) is a two-year high school program that was developed with funding from the National Science Foundation. *SGI* consists of nine units, including a full year of Biology and a semester each of Physics and Chemistry. This chapter will focus on one of the Physics units, *Electricity: Global Energy and Power* (SEPUP, in press).

Lab-Aids, Inc. (www.lab-aids.com) of Ronkonkoma, New York publishes and produces the kits for all SEPUP instructional materials, which include comprehensive courses, individual units from these courses, supplemental modules, and single concept kits.

SEPUP Goals and the Next Generation Science Standards

SEPUP's high school courses are based on SEPUP's philosophy that *all* students deserve an opportunity to learn science and understand how it relates to their present and future lives. SEPUP's instructional materials utilize an instructional model that we call issue-oriented science. The goals for SEPUP's issue-oriented science materials are to

- engage students in the process of learning science,
- encourage students to use scientific evidence to make decisions, and
- help educate tomorrow's citizens about the application of science to everyday life.

SEPUP instructional materials do not advocate a particular position on issues but encourage students to support their views with relevant evidence. SEPUP selects issues that

- require an understanding of important scientific concepts and processes,
- require an application of evidence,
- are interesting and accessible to diverse groups of students, and
- are open-ended and complex enough to foster discussion and debate.

An important part of all SEPUP high school units is the opportunity for students to engage in evidence-based decision making on community and global issues. This is consistent with the emphasis on the use of scientific evidence in the *Next Generation Science Standards*, or NGSS (NGSS Lead States, 2013). Such evidence-based decision making manifests in different ways in the various *SGI* units. For example, in the introductory Sustainability unit, students role-play a diverse group of stakeholders as they discuss a proposal regarding the future of a polluted lake in a fictitious community. These roles include resident, farmer, environmentalist, fertilizer plant owner, wastewater plant manager, land developer, and others. In the culminating activity of the Genetics unit, students summarize data gathered from four scientific studies on a fictitious genetically modified

(GM) variety of soybean. They evaluate and compare the studies and examine the potential benefits and trade-offs of growing this GM organism. Finally, they make an evidence-based recommendation about whether a country that relies heavily on soybean crops should grow the GM soy. Culminating activities in other units include discussing proposals on where to build a nuclear power plant, deciding between different fishery management strategies, and recommending a conservation strategy for a biodiversity hotspot after analyzing the phylogenetic diversity of endemic primates. The activities that precede the culminating activities help students build content knowledge and inquiry skills to make and support these evidence-based decisions.

The SEPUP Instructional Model

The SEPUP instructional model is shown on the next page. To motivate students, a personal or societal issue provides a theme for each SEPUP unit, and students' questions are addressed in the subsequent series of activities. Each activity begins with a challenge, a specific question or goal. To tackle the challenge, students collect evidence in guided or open-ended investigations. They run experiments, collect data, work with models, and work on projects. Reading activities provide background information, extend investigations, and help students build their conceptual knowledge and make connections between concepts and their everyday lives. Throughout the instructional activities, students analyze evidence, from their own investigations and from secondary sources. These activities help them build scientific knowledge and make connections to help them address the central issue. At the end of a unit, students use their evidence and new knowledge in a culminating activity or activities that require them to reach a decision to solve the original problem. Through these activities, they learn how science affects people's lives. This instructional model aligns well with the NGSS, which integrate core ideas with crosscutting concepts and scientific and engineering practices.

The original development of *SGI* was guided by the *National Science Education Standards*, referred to as the NSES (NRC, 1996). In addition to the core science standards in Life, Physical, and Earth and Space Sciences, *Science and Global Issues* includes strong correlations to the standards on Inquiry, Science and Technology, Science in Personal and Social Perspectives, and History and Nature of Science. The NGSS build on the previous work done in developing the NSES but go further in integrating scientific and engineering practices and crosscutting concepts with core conceptual understanding. The NGSS are based on the National Research Council's *A Framework for K–12 Science Education: Practices, Crosscutting Concepts, and Core Ideas*—referred to in this chapter as the NRC *Framework* (NRC, 2012). The engineering design activities in *SGI* align with the principles of the NRC *Framework* in addition to the NSES. Likewise, the emphasis on engaging in argument based on evidence is also an area of common ground between the NSES-based materials and the NRC *Framework*.

The NRC *Framework* identifies four criteria for core ideas and indicates that any core idea should meet *two or more* of these criteria. These criteria have always been important in SEPUP's curriculum design. Note that Criterion 3 refers specifically to relevance and to personal or societal concerns.

1. Have broad importance across multiple sciences or engineering disciplines or be a key organizing principle of a single discipline.

2. Provide a key tool for understanding or investigating more complex ideas and solving problems.

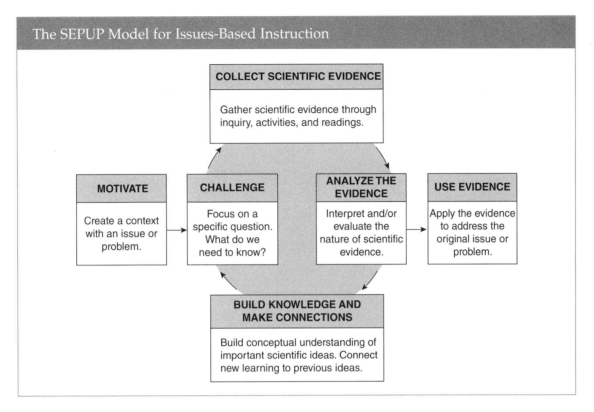

3. Relate to the interests and life experiences of students or be connected to societal or personal concerns that require scientific or technological knowledge.

4. Be teachable and learnable over multiple grades at increasing levels of depth and sophistication. (NRC, 2012, p. 31).

Instructional Materials

Science and Global Issues is a two-year science sequence that includes a full year of biology and a semester each of chemistry and physics. The courses are intended to prepare all students to learn and apply science to their own lives, their local communities, and to the world at large. It is possible to implement *SGI* as one or more complete courses or to select one or more of the nine units to develop customized and coordinated sequences. The shared pedagogy of the units and the common SEPUP assessment system used across the sequence facilitate customization while helping maintain coherence across the units.

Like all SEPUP materials, *SGI* utilizes inquiry-based instructional strategies that give students experience with scientific practices and natural phenomena. The instructional activities follow an inquiry continuum, from guided to open-ended. Guided inquiry is used to introduce students to important ideas and gives them a model for scientific approaches. Open-ended inquiry experiences encourage students to develop their abilities to ask and investigate questions, to understand how to apply scientific principles to new problems, and to think critically about scientific evidence. A variety of activity formats, including hands-on investigations, analysis of data from other sources, use of physical and computer models, discussion of information and evidence gathered from readings, and role-plays and presentations, are intended to meet the needs of students who have different learning styles and to stimulate all students to improve their laboratory, research, reading, writing, and presentation skills. The program consists of printed materials for teacher and student, electronic resources, and laboratory equipment.

Student Materials

The student book contains the activities that make up each unit. Laboratories and investigations, readings, modeling activities, discussions, role-plays, projects, and other types of activities are designed based on the nature of the concepts to be learned. These activities are sequenced in a logical way that allows students to make sense of what they are learning and build their understanding.

Every activity has the following major components:

- An Introduction sets the stage for the activity, often relating it to previous activities. In some cases, this section helps explain a new concept or term.
- The Challenge is a question that helps students focus on the purpose of the activity. The student should be able to answer the challenge question after completing the activity.
- The Procedure, the central part of the SEPUP design for guided inquiry, provides activity directions. These directions, often supplemented by illustrations, support the majority of students in performing activities with minimal assistance from the teacher. This gives the teacher the opportunity to observe and listen to what groups are doing and be available for individualized assistance. Activities may be made more (or less) open-ended at any time by modifying the instructions and the amount of teacher intervention.
- Activity follow up is led with Analysis Questions that probe students' understanding of the content of the activity. Often, the responses to these questions are based on students' own investigations. Some questions call for interaction among students to help deepen their understanding.

Teacher Materials

The Teacher's Edition and Teacher Resources books are designed to assist the teacher with implementing *SGI* in the classroom. The Teacher's Edition takes the teacher through each activity in the student book. It contains information about key content and process skills developed in the activity, materials preparation and distribution, safety, additional background, a teaching summary, detailed teaching suggestions, including assessment strategies and suggested answers to Analysis Questions.

The Teaching Suggestions provide specific and detailed suggestions on how to accomplish the goals of the activity. Suggestions might include possible discussion prompts, student's responses to questions, and key points for following up the activity. The teaching suggestions provide insight into the design and intent of the curriculum and include important tips and information identified by field test teachers as essential for running the activities. Descriptions of embedded SEPUP assessment opportunities are provided with sample exemplar responses.

The Teacher Resources book provides information on all aspects of teaching with SEPUP materials, including tips for successful implementation, advice for working with diverse learners, explanations of each of the many literacy strategies used in the program, and support for using the SEPUP assessment program. Together, the Teacher's Edition and Teacher Resources books fully support the teacher using *Science and Global Issues* in the classroom.

Laboratory Equipment and Supplies

The equipment kit provides the specialty items students and teachers need for the experiences that are central to the program. The kit is designed for typical classroom settings and does not usually require a laboratory. Information is also provided to help the teacher replenish consumable solutions.

The SEPUP Assessment System and the Framework and NGSS

As with all SEPUP units, *SGI* utilizes the SEPUP Assessment System, which provides teachers with tools for both formative and summative assessment of student learning. This research-based system was developed in collaboration with the Berkeley Evaluation and Assessment Research (BEAR) group in the Graduate School of Education at UC, Berkeley (Wilson & Sloane, 2000) and has been cited in nationally-known publications such as *Classroom Assessment and the National Science Education Standards* (NRC, 2001a) and *Knowing What Students Know* (NRC, 2001b).

Many of the assessment tasks are embedded in the program activities, and many engage students in authentic tasks of scientists and engineers, thereby naturally integrating the practices of science and engineering (NRC Framework Dimension 1) with crosscutting concepts (Framework Dimension 2) and core ideas (Framework Dimension 3). The assessment system provides powerful formative feedback that helps teachers monitor what students know and are able to do and adjust instruction accordingly and summative feedback on what students have achieved at the end of each unit. Each unit includes a culminating assessment that engages students in applying concepts and practices to a personal or societal issue or problem, and many units engage students in the engineering design process. The components of the SEPUP assessment system are shown in the diagram on the next page.

The assessment variables of the SEPUP system show good alignment with the NRC Framework. Table 7.1 shows how eight of the SEPUP assessment targets, or student progress variables, relate to the Practices of Science and Engineering (Framework Dimension 1: Practices), Crosscutting Concepts (Framework Dimension 2), and Core Ideas (Framework Dimension 3).

SEPUP and the NGSS Emphasis on Engineering

The NRC *Framework* emphasizes the parallels between the practices of science and engineering. Scientists ask questions, make observations, and collect and analyze data, in an attempt to make sense of the natural world. Similarly, engineers create, test, and redesign

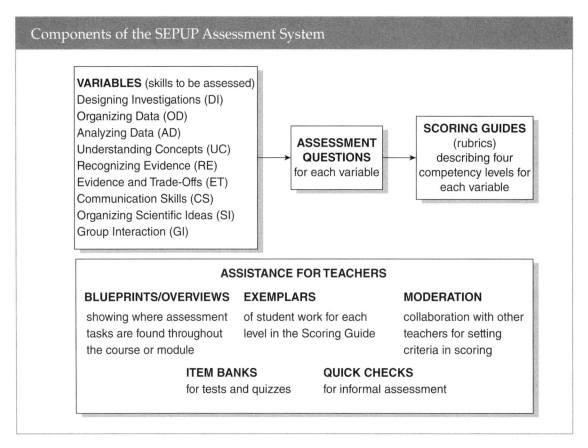

Components of the SEPUP Assessment System

VARIABLES (skills to be assessed)
Designing Investigations (DI)
Organizing Data (OD)
Analyzing Data (AD)
Understanding Concepts (UC)
Recognizing Evidence (RE)
Evidence and Trade-Offs (ET)
Communication Skills (CS)
Organizing Scientific Ideas (SI)
Group Interaction (GI)

ASSESSMENT QUESTIONS for each variable

SCORING GUIDES (rubrics) describing four competency levels for each variable

ASSISTANCE FOR TEACHERS

BLUEPRINTS/OVERVIEWS
showing where assessment tasks are found throughout the course or module

EXEMPLARS
of student work for each level in the Scoring Guide

MODERATION
collaboration with other teachers for setting criteria in scoring

ITEM BANKS
for tests and quizzes

QUICK CHECKS
for informal assessment

Table 7.1 SEPUP Assessment Variables and Practices From the Framework

SEPUP Assessment Variable	Relationship to the Framework
Understanding Concepts	**Practice 2**: Ability to make, use, and evaluate models **Practice 6**: Constructing explanations and designing solutions **Dimension 2**: Ability to connect ideas through crosscutting concepts **Dimension 3**: Core ideas
Designing Investigations (includes Designing Procedures)	**Practice 1**: Asking questions (in science) and defining problems (in engineering) **Practice 3**: Planning investigations **Practice 6**: Constructing explanations and designing solutions
Organizing Data	**Practice 3**: Planning investigations **Practice 8**: Communicating information

SEPUP Assessment Variable	Relationship to the Framework
Analyzing Data	**Practice 4**: Analyzing data **Practice 5**: Using mathematics, information and computer technology, and computational thinking **Practice 7**: Engaging in argument from evidence
Organizing Scientific Ideas	**Practice 8**: Communicating information
Communication Skills	**Practice 8**: Communicating information
Recognizing Evidence	**Practice 4:** Analyzing data **Practice 6:** Constructing explanations and designing solutions **Practice 7:** Engaging in argument from evidence
Evidence and Trade-offs	**Practice 4:** Analyzing data **Practice 7:** Engaging in argument from evidence

as they respond with solutions to human needs. And just as we use scaffolds in the teaching of scientific inquiry to improve student learning and practice, so do we use scaffolds in teaching about engineering for our students. The NRC *Framework* emphasizes three major phases of the engineering design process:

- DESIGN: Creates design, prototype or plan, noting constraints of proposed use
- TEST: Tests design, prototype or plan, collecting qualitative or quantitative data
- REDESIGN: Evaluates prototype, design or plan, suggests further changes as needed

Areas of engineering practice are emphasized in *SGI* by activities that support the initial stages of design, criteria development, and evaluation that precede the full design cycle by having students suggest or evaluate scientific or technological solutions to real-world problems. Others involve students in one or more steps of the design cycle as they build, test, and/or redesign prototypes.

In addition, the NRC *Framework* emphasizes the role of design in solving human problems and of designers in developing criteria for solutions, evaluating solutions, and determining the trade-offs involved in a design or solution. The phases of the engineering design process are reflected in the various specific NGSS that integrate traditional science content with engineering through an engineering practice or disciplinary core idea. The NGSS also include performance expectations in science and engineering, including some expectations that couple engineering practices with disciplinary core ideas in science. *SGI Electricity: Global Energy and Power* directly addresses two engineering-related performance expectations as described later in this chapter.

SGI and Sustainability

Science and Global Issues consists of nine units organized around important global issues related to sustainability. Sustainability refers to the ability of a community to meet its present needs without compromising the ability of future generations to meet their own needs. Sustainable development is one of the most critical issues of our time and requires analysis that takes into account personal, societal, and global perspectives. Understanding the scientific concepts behind some of the major challenges of the 21st century is a prerequisite to informed decision making. Developing scientific literacy in all students involves having students apply this understanding to complex issues that have no simple solutions.

Each unit examines a different sustainability challenge. These range from the control and eradication of diseases to balancing electricity production and consumption and from threats to biodiversity to the use and distribution of natural resources. As students explore potential solutions to specific problems, they consider the environmental, economic, and social impacts of each course of action. This approach is authentic to the way that scientists and engineers work, and SEPUP asks students to begin to think and investigate in such a manner.

Like the other units of *Science and Global Issues*, the electricity unit, *Global Energy and Power* was written to correlate with the NSES. However, this unit also aligns well with the NGSS as shown in Tables 7.2 and 7.3 at the end of this chapter. Table 7.2 shows the correlations to the NGSS Science and Engineering Practices, Disciplinary Core Ideas, and Crosscutting Concepts. Table 7.3 shows potential and existing correlations to the Performance Expectations.

Circuits and Cir-Kits

In the unit, students look at sustainability issues surrounding the generation and consumption of electricity. The first two activities of the unit focus on the efficiency of devices and energy consumption at the personal and community level. In the third activity, the perspective moves from personal to global. In the fourth and fifth activities, students develop an understanding of the advantages and disadvantages of various methods of electricity generation. They learn, for example, that one disadvantage of renewable resources, such as wind and solar, is that they produce an intermittent supply of electricity. It is in this context that the concept of storage of electrical energy is introduced.

In Activity 6, students model one type of storage device by building a circuit that includes a capacitor. This is the first activity in which students use specially designed, modular circuit pieces called Cir-Kits. Electrical components, such as capacitors, meters, motors, and switches, are mounted on the Cir-Kit pieces. Each is also imprinted with the symbol that represents the component. The Cir-Kit pieces connect to a small, four-way hub and since each piece is the same length, this allows students to quickly connect circuits that resemble schematic diagrams. By beginning with creating circuits that look like the schematic diagrams in the instructions, students can gain confidence in their ability to connect circuits and can eventually transfer this understanding to creating more complex circuits or those using wires and loose components. Students use the Cir-Kit modular system to construct varying kinds of circuits in the unit, including series and parallel circuits. This section on current electricity dominates the middle of the unit and culminates with a performance assessment in the form of an engineering design challenge.

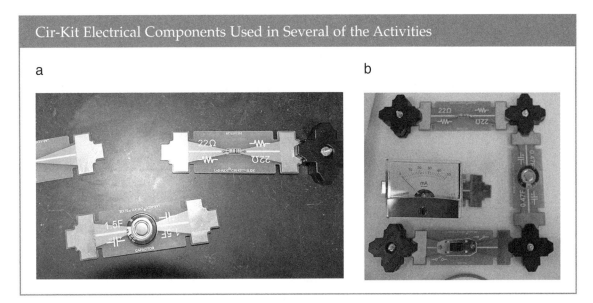

Cir-Kit Electrical Components Used in Several of the Activities

a   b

The Design Challenge

As can be seen from the outline near the end of this chapter, in Activity 15 students are asked to participate in an engineering design challenge where they apply what they have learned about electricity to design and build a circuit that performs a specific function. This Design Challenge is an excellent match for Performance Expectation, HS-PS3-3: "Design, build, and refine a device that works within given constraints to convert one form of energy into another form of energy." The engineering challenge in this activity is framed in the context of a fictitious scenario:

> The community on Plumm Island has suffered a catastrophic natural disaster. Basic services are out, including electricity and running water. Part of the disaster relief effort is to restore the electrical services. You are part of a group of engineers that has been sent to the hospital to restore the hospital to functioning. Time is of the essence, and resources are in short supply. Most urgently, the hospital needs to run cooling fans, air conditioning, lights, and water pumps. This will require you to discuss with your colleagues how best to design a circuit from the available supplies, test your design with a model, and then make modifications based on the results.

With this scenario, two challenges are provided, with groups of four students working on one of the challenges. Having half the class working on one challenge while half works on the other adds richness to the activity by considering two designs instead of one. Each challenge is accompanied by equipment that models each component in the scenario. For example, the emergency backup generator is modeled with D-cell batteries, a UV light for sterilizing water is represented by an LED, and a portable electrical source is represented by a capacitor.

Challenge 1 asks groups to ensure that adequate supplies of water are provided for a hospital that has lost its main source of power. The water must be pumped to the hospital

Students Engaged in the Design Challenge

from a reservoir downhill from the village. Each group has two electric pumps and has to figure out how to connect them to pump at different rates according to a specified ratio. The two pumps must be run on a single circuit, one for drinking and one for sanitation. The drinking water must also be sterilized with a UV light. One pump must be run continuously while the other can be turned on and off.

Challenge 2 involves providing a portable source of electricity (represented by a capacitor) to operate the cooling fans, air conditioning, and lights at the hospital situated in a tropical setting. Air conditioning and lights are needed at night in the hospital. The cooling fans must operate continuously and must produce a specified air flow. The cooling fan and air conditioner are modeled by motors with fan blades.

Both challenges require students to design, build, and test their circuits using Cir-Kit modular pieces. Student understanding of concepts in electricity inform their design choices on components and configurations. For example, they can use their understanding of parallel and series circuits to determine what resistors to incorporate, and what configuration to use, for the desired effect. However, it is through the iterative process of testing, redesign and retesting that they perfect their circuits so that they meet the design requirements. This activity provides an example of how to successfully integrate science content and engineering practice into an NGSS Performance Expectation.

Culminating Activity: Power for an Island

In the final activity of the unit, students return to the fictitious island from the Design Challenge. This activity is well aligned with NGSS Performance Expectation, HS-ETS1-3: "Evaluate a solution to a complex real-world problem based on prioritized criteria and trade-offs that account for a range of constraints, including cost, safety, reliability, and aesthetics, as well as possible social, cultural, and environmental impacts." Again, students are confronted with a scenario:

> In the rebuilding effort after the disaster, the government of Plumm Island has decided to upgrade the electricity infrastructure on the island. The government does not want to simply reconstruct the sections of the electricity network that were destroyed during the earthquake; it wants to plan ahead for future growth. The officials' preliminary evaluations of power sources excluded, for political reasons, nuclear energy and biomass. After further paring down the possibilities, officials have decided to consider only coal, hydroelectric, solar thermal, and wind power.

> The project involves adding capacity to the electrical power system and some new transmission lines. The government of Plumm Island has estimated that over the next 25 years the electricity needs of the increasing population will require at least another 250 MW of generating capacity on the island.

Although the island in the scenario is fictitious, the data that students analyze is realistic. Student recommendations must consider the resources required, the location(s) of the new generating facility (or facilities), the impact on the location and nearby communities, safety, and long-term sustainability. Students work in groups to analyze maps and data from the island before recommending how to generate the additional power that the island needs. Data include the amount of reliable power supplied by each method of generation, the costs associated with construction and operation, consumer cost, and annual emissions of CO_2 equivalents. As students in small groups discuss the possibilities, they examine maps that show the topography of the island, major ecosystems, population centers, and existing electricity grid. Having chosen potential locations, groups calculate the cost of constructing new transmission lines, which in some cases are significant, along with evaluating possible social, cultural, and environmental implications.

Ideas are shared during a class discussion before each student writes a report detailing plans to supply the extra electrical power for the island, citing evidence to support their recommendation, including the environmental, social, and economic implications. They also describe the advantages, disadvantages, and trade-offs of their proposal. A complete outline of the activities in the unit can be found at the end of this chapter.

Future Steps

Science and Global Issues was written to correlate with the NSES and to be consistent with best practices in science teaching. Although the program predates the NGSS, it is clear that there is good alignment with the NGSS and with the vision of *A Framework for K–12 Science Education*. With some adjustments, the alignment can be strengthened. For example, several performance expectations are already partially addressed in various activities in the Electricity unit, as shown in Table 7.3 at the end of this chapter. Some of the activities could be modified so that they more fully address the performance expectations.

The Physics unit on electromagnetic waves and the Chemistry units, "Earth's Resources" and "Fueling the World," are both undergoing revision after national field testing. The timing of the revision of these units will allow even closer alignment with the NGSS. The revised program should be in print by the time this chapter goes to press.

Outline of *SGI Electricity: Global Energy and Power*

Activity 1. Laboratory: Measuring Efficiency. Students investigate the efficiency of electrical energy transformations. They measure the efficiency of a small water pump and consider how much energy is lost in the electrical to mechanical transformation.

Activity 2. Investigation: Personal Energy Use. Students compare the energy and power consumed by, and the cost to run, common electrical household devices. Students also explore the amount of energy their classroom uses, the amount of energy used in everyday situations, and investigate the amount of energy various devices use when turned off.

Activity 3. Talking It Over: Electricity Use Around the World. Students investigate how electrical energy consumption differs between countries around the world. They examine potential correlations between electricity consumption and factors such as the Human Development Index, Gross Domestic Product, population, and carbon dioxide emissions. Students also explore trends in global electrical energy consumption over time.

Activity 4. Reading: Nonrenewable Resources for Electricity. Students learn about the various nonrenewable resources that are used to generate electricity and read about the benefits and trade-offs of using these nonrenewable resources.

Activity 5. Investigation: Renewable Energy. Students observe a solar cell, windmill and hydro generator producing electricity to run a variety of devices. Students then analyze maps and data sets to explore the reasons why different geographic locations rely on different sources of electrical energy.

Activity 6. Laboratory: Storing Electrical Energy. Students investigate capacitors as a way to store intermittent electrical energy from renewable resources. They explore some of the properties of capacitors and the factors that affect how they charge. Schematic diagrams are introduced as a standardized way to depict electrical circuits.

Activity 7. Laboratory: Discharging Capacitors. Students release electrical energy stored in capacitors through a conductor. They graph how the current varies with time and discover the discharge is not linear. From this work, students develop a conceptual understanding of current and how it relates to the flow of charge.

Activity 8. Reading: Electric Fields. Students read about the concept of an electric field and how it relates to the force on a charge. Students learn about the work of Michael Faraday and compare different kinds of fields, including electric, magnetic, and gravitational.

Activity 9. Investigation: Electric Potential Difference. Students use an interactive simulation to investigate electric charges, electric fields, electric potential difference, and the relationships between these concepts. In the simulation, students build electric fields and measure the potential difference between locations.

Activity 10. Laboratory: Voltage in Circuits. Students build circuits and measure the voltage across devices within the circuit. A relationship between the source voltage and the voltage across the devices is determined.

Activity 11. Laboratory: Electrical Resistance. Students investigate electrical resistivity as an intrinsic property of metals and design an experiment to test which characteristics of wires affect resistance. Students then apply this knowledge to the transmission of electrical energy over large distances.

Activity 12. Laboratory: Ohm's Law. Students derive Ohm's Law by graphing current versus voltage for different resistors. The graphs allow students to determine the mathematical relationship between current, voltage, and resistance.

Activity 13. Investigation: Circuit Analogies. Students examine three commonly used analogies for electrical circuits to help visualize the behaviors of circuits. Students investigate the strengths and limitations of each circuit analogy.

Activity 14. Laboratory: Series and Parallel Circuits. Students build and compare series and parallel circuits. They apply what they have discovered about Ohm's Law to analyze the relationship between current, voltage, and resistance in series and parallel connections.

Activity 15. Laboratory: Design Challenge. Students apply what they have learned about circuits to a fictitious scenario of a community recovering from a natural disaster. Students design and test electrical circuits to pump water, clean water, and run cooling systems as a part of vital hospital functions.

Activity 16. Investigation: Electromagnetic Induction. Students investigate magnetic fields and their properties. They discover that current-carrying wires produce magnetic fields and changing magnetic fields near a conductor can induce a current in the conductor. Groups also use a computer simulation to investigate the factors affecting the force on a current-carrying conductor in a magnetic field.

Activity 17. Investigation: Electric Motors and Generators. Students build a simple electric motor to explore how they operate. In addition, they investigate electric generators and how they differ from electric motors. Students then use a computer simulation that provides a visual model for the behavior of electric motors and generators.

Activity 18. Investigation: Transformers. Students explore how transformers use induction to increase and decrease voltages. They also investigate the use of transformers in the national electric grid system.

Activity 19. Reading: The War of Currents. Students read about the development of direct current (DC) and alternating current (AC) systems and the transmission grid in this country. Highlighted is the conflict between the electrical engineers Edison, Westinghouse, and Tesla, and Tesla's invention of the modern transformer.

Activity 20. Investigation: Powering Plumm Island. Students are again presented with a fictitious scenario where they have to upgrade the electrical infrastructure of an island that is rebuilding after a natural disaster. Students use evidence to develop a unique proposal for the island's electrical system and energy resources.

Table 7.2 *SGI Electricity: Global Energy and Power alignment with A Framework for K–12 Science Education* (NRC, 2012)

Activity:	1	2	3	4	5	6	7	8	9	10	11	12	13	14	15	16	17	18	19	20
Dimension 1: Practices																				
Developing and using models									✓				✓			✓				✓
Planning and carrying out investigations						✓								✓	✓	✓	✓	✓		✓
Analyzing and interpreting data	✓	✓	✓	✓	✓	✓	✓	✓		✓	✓	✓	✓	✓		✓	✓	✓		✓
Using mathematics and computational thinking	✓	✓	✓	✓	✓	✓	✓	✓	✓	✓	✓	✓	✓	✓				✓		✓
Constructing explanations and solving problems			✓		✓					✓					✓					✓
Engaging in argument from evidence			✓		✓		✓				✓	✓							✓	✓
Obtaining, evaluating, and communicating evidence	✓	✓	✓		✓	✓	✓		✓	✓		✓	✓	✓	✓	✓				✓
Dimension 2: Crosscutting Concepts																				
Patterns			✓																	
Cause and effect			✓		✓			✓	✓	✓	✓	✓		✓	✓	✓	✓	✓		
Scale, proportion, and quantity	✓		✓	✓		✓		✓	✓		✓	✓		✓						✓
Systems and system Models							✓		✓		✓		✓			✓	✓			
Energy and matter	✓	✓		✓		✓	✓	✓		✓		✓		✓		✓	✓	✓		
Structure and function					✓		✓				✓			✓	✓		✓		✓	
Stability and change			✓				✓	✓	✓						✓					

Activity:	1	2	3	4	5	6	7	8	9	10	11	12	13	14	15	16	17	18	19	20
Dimension 3: Core Ideas																				
PS.3.A: Definitions of Energy	✓	✓	✓	✓	✓	✓	✓	✓	✓	✓	✓	✓	✓	✓	✓	✓	✓	✓	✓	✓
PS.3.B: Conservation of Energy and Energy Transfer	✓			✓		✓	✓	✓	✓	✓	✓				✓	✓	✓	✓		
PS.3.C: Relationship Between Energy and Forces									✓							✓				
PS.3.D: Energy in Chemical processes	✓				✓						✓							✓		
ESS.3.A: Natural Resources			✓	✓	✓															
ESS.3.C: Human Impacts on Earth Systems			✓		✓															
ESS.3.D: Global Climate Change				✓	✓															
ETS.1.A: Defining and Delimiting Engineering problems			✓	✓	✓									✓	✓	✓				✓
ETS.1.B: Developing Possible Solutions			✓	✓												✓			✓	✓
ETS.1.C: Optimizing the Design Solution																				✓

Table 7.3 SGI Electricity: Global Energy and Power Alignment with NGSS Performance Expectations

Activity:	8	15	16	17	20
HS-PS2-4. Use mathematical representations of Newton's Law of Gravitation and Coulomb's Law to describe and predict the gravitational and electrostatic forces between objects.	✓				
HS-PS2-5. Plan and conduct an investigation to provide evidence that an electric current can produce a magnetic field and that a changing magnetic field can produce an electric current.			✓	✓	
HS-PS3-3. Design, build, and refine a device that works within given constraints to convert one form of energy into another form of energy.		✓			
HS-LS2-7. Design, evaluate, and refine a solution for reducing the impacts of human activities on the environment and biodiversity.					✓
HS-ETS1-3. Evaluate a solution to a complex real-world problem based on prioritized criteria and trade-offs that account for a range of constraints, including cost, safety, reliability, and aesthetics, as well as possible social, cultural, and environmental impacts.					✓

References

NGSS Lead States. (2013). *Next generation science standards: For states, by states, volume 1: The standards.* Washington, DC: National Academies Press.

NRC. (1996). *National science education standards.* Washington, DC: National Academies Press.

NRC. (2001a). *Classroom assessment and the national science education standards.* Washington, DC: National Academies Press.

NRC. (2001b). *Knowing what students know: The science and design of educational assessment.* Washington, DC: National Academies Press.

NRC. (2012). *A framework for K–12 science education: Practices, crosscutting concepts, and core ideas.* Washington, DC: National Academies Press.

SEPUP. (In Press). *Science and global issues. Electricity: Global energy and power.* Ronkonkoma NY: Lab-Aids ®, Inc.

Wilson, M., & Sloane, K. (2000). From principles to practice: An embedded assessment system. *Applied Measurement in Education, 13*(2), 181–208.

Engineering by Design High School Courses

Greg Strimel

ITEEA Teacher Effectiveness Coach

Director of K–12 Initiatives

West Virginia University

Students engaged in *Engineering byDesign*™ activities

Image courtesy of *EbD*™ and Greg Strimel. Logo courtesy of ITEEA.

The *Engineering byDesign*™ (or *EbD*™) program is built on the belief that the ingenuity of children is an untapped, unrealized potential that when properly motivated, can lead to the next generation of technologists, innovators, designers, and engineers. Based on this belief, the International Technology and Engineering Educators Association (ITEEA) STEM Center for Teaching and Learning™ has developed the *EbD*™ program as a truly integrative and comprehensive standards-based model STEM program for Grades K–12 to enable all students to achieve technological and engineering literacy.

The importance of technological and engineering literacy for all students has grown in prominence with the recent development of Next Generation Science Standards (NGSS Lead States, 2013a), which includes engineering as a fourth set of core ideas for all students to learn and includes practices of engineering design at the same level as scientific inquiry. And in 2014, the National Assessment of Educational Progress (NAEP), also known as "The Nation's Report Card," has for the first time assessed a large national sample of students on their technological and engineering literacy (NAGB 2012). The results will be reported in 2015.

This chapter will describe what the *EbD*™ program is and how it can be used to infuse and reinforce technology and engineering at the high school level to enable *all students* to achieve technological and engineering literacy. *EbD*™ includes dynamic curriculum materials based on the national *Standards for Technological Literacy* (ITEEA, 2000, 2002, 2007), on-going professional development, and student assessments.

Rationale and Goals

As described in the report *Technically Speaking: Why All Americans Need to Know More About Technology* from the National Academy of Engineering and National Research Council (2002), technological literacy is essential for people living in a modern industrialized nation such as the United States. The report also discusses the benefits of a technologically literate society, which can be defined as a country whose citizens are better prepared to make well-informed decisions on matters that affect or are affected by technology. The National Assessment Governing Board defines technological and engineering literacy as "competence in using, understanding, and evaluating technology, as well as the understanding of technological principles and strategies needed for developing solutions and achieving goals" (NAGB, 2012, p. xi).

Despite the importance of engineering and technological literacy, recent reports indicate that there is a lack of educators with the know-how for effectively designing and teaching the integrated subjects found within technology and engineering. Furthermore, the critical mass of teachers who understand and love science, technology, engineering, and mathematics (STEM) well enough to inspire their students is even fewer. Recognition of this problem is a key part of the report to the President of the United States by the President's Council of Advisors on Science and Technology:

> Teachers are the single most important factor in the K–12 education system, and they are crucial to the strategy of preparing and inspiring students in STEM. Great STEM teachers have at least two attributes: deep content knowledge in STEM and strong pedagogical skills for teaching their students STEM. These two attributes allow great teachers to help students achieve deep understandings of STEM that they can use in their lives and careers. These attributes also enable teachers to excite students about the dynamic nature of STEM fields, motivating them for lifelong

study. Too few of these teachers are in the Nation's classrooms, in part because of a lack of professional respect, the inconsistency of teacher preparation programs, and the salary disparity of teaching relative to other STEM fields (PCAST, 2010, p. 57).

The report goes on to recommend specific steps for recruiting and preparing 100,000 STEM teachers in the next 10 years. The report also notes "there is an urgent need for well-designed courses in technology and engineering, with high-quality instructional materials, particularly in high schools" (PCAST, 2012, p. 46). The *EbD*™ curriculum materials and professional development programs are intended to meet these needs.

The overarching goal of the *EbD*™ program is to provide a standards-based K–12 program that ensures that all students are technologically literate regardless of gender or ethnic origin. Specific goals are to

- Provide clear standards and expectations for increasing student achievement in STEM subjects.
- Provide leadership and support that will provide continuous program improvement.
- Provide a program that constructs learning from a very early age and culminates in a capstone experience that leads students to become the next generation of technologists, innovators, designers, and engineers.
- Restore the status of the United States as a leader in innovation.

Engineering byDesign™ Curriculum & Instruction

EbD™ curricula and instruction are based on a constructivist learning theory. This theory posits that students retain more knowledge when they build an understanding of an idea themselves through linkages to prior knowledge. A constructivist classroom is not a teacher-centered environment where students are reliant on teacher knowledge. Rather, learning is more student-centered. Students partner with the teacher in attaining knowledge.

The lessons are structured with a "6 *E*s learning model" (ITEEA, 2013, adapted from the 5E model by Bybee, 1997, and Bybee & Landes, 1990). Each E is a different portion of the lesson that allows a teacher to conduct their class in a constructivist manner. The 6 Es stand for: Engage, Explore, Explain, Extend, Evaluate, and Enrich. The Engage step is the *hook* of the lesson, intended to grab students' interest. This is generally a media rich or hands-on introduction to the lesson. The Explore section allows students to share and apply what they already know, which provides a level of comfort, while building new connections to content on their own.

Once the students have had a chance to showcase their prior knowledge and create new levels of understanding, the explanation part of the lesson allows for the instructor to clear up any misconceptions or gaps in content knowledge. Then the main part of the lesson revolves around the extension section, which gives the students the chance to apply their new knowledge in an authentic design challenge. The constructivist lesson also provides an evaluation segment that allows the instructor to monitor student progress but more importantly enables the students to assess their own learning throughout the lesson. The ability to assess one's own knowledge is a lifelong learning skill. Last, the lessons include an enrichment section in which the students find a particular topic that intrigues them to take their learning process even further.

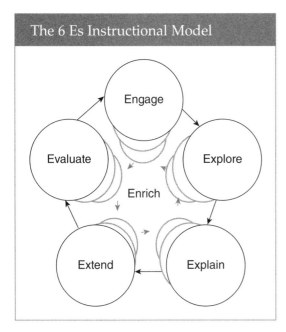

The 6 Es Instructional Model

Image courtesy of ITEEA.

Another important strategy *EbD*™ uses to prepare students for the innovation-driven economy is problem-based learning. The curriculum consists of carefully designed problems that demand acquisition of critical knowledge, problem-solving proficiency, self-directed learning strategies, and team participation skills. A systemic approach to solving problems can prepare students for challenges they may encounter in their lives and careers.

EbD™ is available in the form of web-based, media-rich course guides. These guides provide access to lesson resources that are built directly into the lesson plans themselves. The course guides provide a variety of media to support the teacher in the classroom and to engage the students in the learning process. Additionally, the media-rich course guides are dynamic documents that can continually change based on data collected from student assessment and teacher feedback.

The entire series of *EbD*™ courses are listed in Table 8.1. This chapter will briefly summarize the high school courses.

Table 8.1 The *EbD*™ K–12 Core Sequence

Elementary Materials		
K–2	*EbD*-TEEMS™	1–6 weeks
3–5	*EbD*-TEEMS™ and I³	1–6 weeks
Middle School Courses		
6	Exploring Technology	18 weeks
7	Invention and Innovation	18 weeks
8	Technological Systems	18 weeks
High School Courses		
9	Foundations of Technology	36 weeks
10–12	Technology and Society	36 weeks
10–12	Technological Design	36 weeks
11–12	Advanced Design Applications	36 weeks
11–12	Advanced Technological Applications	36 weeks
11–12	Engineering Design (Capstone Course)	36 weeks

Engineering byDesign™ High School Core Program (Grade 9)

Grade 9: *Foundations of Technology* **is the cornerstone of the high school technology and engineering program.** This course builds on student understanding gained in elementary and middle school courses. The course prepares students to understand and apply technological concepts and processes through group and individual activities that engage students in creating ideas, developing innovations, and engineering practical solutions to real life problems. Foundations of Technology students learn technological content, as well as how to apply science, mathematics, and other school subjects in authentic situations through laboratory and classroom activities.

Students collaborating in the Foundations of Technology course

Image by Greg Strimel.

To illustrate a small portion of the Foundations of Technology course, following is a brief summary of Unit 2, Lesson 1. The big idea of the lesson is "The engineering design process is a systematic, iterative problem-solving method, which produces solutions to meet human, wants and desires."

In the Engagement phase, students view an inspiring Ted Talk (from www.ted.com) by William Kamkawamba entitled "How I Harnessed the Wind." Based on the book by the same name (Kamkawamba & Mealer, 2010), Mr. Kamkawamba tells the inspiring story of how he grew up in Malawi, where his parents could not afford to send him to school, so he explored books in the library and taught himself how to build a wind-powered generator. He used this generator to help irrigate his village's crops and helped solve the terrible famine his village faced. Although he experienced deep poverty and harsh living conditions, he was able to use the engineering design process to help his village with his self-taught skills. His innovative spirit was eventually recognized and he was finally able to study engineering at Dartmouth College in New Hampshire.

Students building trusses from Unit 2, Lesson 1 of the Foundations of Technology course

Image by Greg Strimel.

Next, students explore the engineering design process by arranging its steps through a card sorting activity based on the process William Kamkawamba used to build his wind generator. The teacher then explains the engineering design process with the help of a graphic organizer. During the extension part of the lesson, the students apply what they learned to design and build a crane truss (constructed of triangles) that supports the greatest weight. They then engage in two mathematics-related activities: "Crain Strain Truss Calculations," and "Crain Efficiency."

A student models a "green" home in the Construction Unit of the Advanced Design Applications course

Image by Greg Strimel.

During the lesson the teacher evaluates the students' knowledge, skills, and attitudes using brief constructed response items and performance rubrics for class participation, discussion and design briefs. Finally, the students complete an enrichment activity in which they conduct mathematics calculations to determine the weak points in their crane truss designs, which inform their redesigns.

The course as a whole prepares students for the more specialized technology courses at the high school level, such as Technology and Society, Technological Design, and Engineering Design.

Grades 10–11: *Technology and Society* **builds on the Foundations of Technology course and helps students expand their awareness of technology in their lives, and how invention and innovation have improved the quality of life and extended human capabilities.** The course also helps students develop critical thinking skills through the study of contemporary issues at the interface of science, technology, society and the environment, including not only the beneficial effects of technology but also some of the unanticipated consequences. Students are introduced to structured methods for investigating and addressing these issues and guided in developing defensible opinions and positions.

Grades 10–11: *Technological Design* **engages students in teams to meet engineering design challenges by applying their knowledge of mathematics, science, and design principles.** Students learn professional engineering practices as they research, develop, test, and analyze innovative engineering designs using criteria such as design effectiveness, public safety, human factors, and ethics.

Students engaged in research in the Biotechnologies Unit of the Advanced Technology Program

Image by Greg Strimel.

Grades 11–12: *High School Advanced Technology Program* **builds on the problem-based learning courses for grades 9, 10, and 11 and enables students interested in joining our nation's technical workforce to engage in advanced technology and engineering topics.** The program consists of three courses: Advanced Technical Applications, Advanced Design Application, and Engineering Design Capstone Course. Thanks to a grant from the National Science Foundation, these courses have been designed to articulate with community college courses so that students can earn college credit while still in high school.

Foundations of the Engineering byDesign™ Curriculum

The high school courses described above are part of a coherent *Engineering byDesign™* K–12 sequence that begins in Kindergarten and continues through a high school capstone course. Coherence has been achieved by a deliberate curriculum development process based on two documents: *Standards for Technological Literacy* (ITEEA 2000, 2002, 2007) and the *Advancing Excellence in Technological Literacy Standards* (ITEEA, 2003). The following chart depicts the guide for developing *EbD™* courses and lessons from the standards.

While the *Standards for Technological Literacy* has been the primary organizer for the program content, *EbD™* has purposefully integrated content and practices from the common core state standards, principles of engineering, and is currently infusing the NGSS into its curriculum.

Tables 8.2 and 8.3 provide an overview of the unit titles in each of the high school courses.

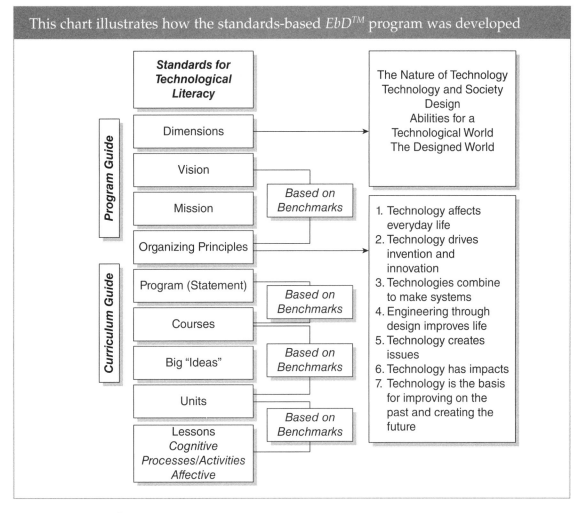

Reprinted courtesy of © ITEEA

Table 8.2 *Engineering byDesign™* High School Core Program

Grade	Course Title and Unit Titles
9	*Foundations of Technology* 1. Technological Innovations & Inventions 2. The Engineering Design Process 3. The Designed World 4. Systems 5. Lunar Plant Growth Chamber (NASA Unit)
10–11	*Technology and Society* 1. Skills for Analyzing Technology & Science Issues 2. The Human Technical Paradox 3. Change by Design 4. Contemporary Issues in Science & Technology 5. Transportation & Space: Reuse and Recycle
10–11	*Technological Design* 1. Systems & Optimization 2. Technology/Society & Ethics 3. Concurrent Engineering 4. Modeling & Problem Solving 5. Design

Table 8.3 *Engineering byDesign™* High School Advanced Technology Program

Grade	Course Title and Unit Titles
10–12	*Advanced Technological Applications* 1. Information & Communication Technologies 2. Agricultural & Related Biotechnologies 3. Entertainment & Recreation Technologies 4. Medical Technologies
10–12	*Advanced Design Applications* 1. Manufacturing Technologies 2. Construction Technologies 3. Power & Energy Technologies 4. Transportation Technologies
12	*Engineering Design* 1. Principles of Design 2. Engineering Resources 3. Engineering Design Process 4. Project Management 5. Project Management—NASA Style

Where Does *EbD*™ Fit in?

EbD™ is designed as a K–12 STEM solution for schools with a focus on achieving technology and engineering literacy for *all* students. This program is not intended to prepare students for a certain vocation, but it does intend to inspire students to explore STEM career options. Therefore, the program focuses on teaching what has been called the "little e" of engineering. The "little e" means striving to teach all students to think like an engineer and to utilize engineering concepts. This is in contrast to the "big E" of engineering, which specifically prepares students for a career in engineering. However if the "little e" is taught correctly it can inspire more students to pursue post-secondary engineering education. This being said, the *EbD*™ program should be taught at every high school and not just in career and technical education centers. All high school students should receive some type of technology and engineering education, especially since they are being assessed on their technological and engineering literacy through the *National Assessment of Educational Progress*.

In most high schools the program fits within the technology and engineering education department. In areas without a technology department, the courses sometimes fall under career and technical education or STEM education departments. The teachers qualified to teach the high school core program are licensed technology teachers. However, in many locations there may be a lack of technology teachers. To solve this issue, *EbD*™ provides professional development for nontechnology teachers to teach these courses.

With the inclusion of engineering and technological content and practices within the NGSS, *EbD*™ can provide resources for science educators. Science teachers should recognize that they are not alone in the effort to teach engineering concepts and practices to all students. Science teachers may not have to incorporate in-depth design and engineering concepts and practices in their classrooms. Instead, science teachers can work with the technology and engineering teachers in their schools to establish a transdisciplinary approach to meeting the NGSS. Science teachers can focus on addressing their scientific content and practices while taking on a role to reinforce engineering design connections within the natural world of science. The technology and engineering teachers can do what they do best and teach engineering design content and practices contained in both standards documents while reinforcing the need for scientific inquiry and its application to the designed world. In an ideal environment, science teachers should work with technology and engineering teachers to ensure that students learn the interdisciplinary nature of engineering design and scientific inquiry, as well as mathematical problem solving.

Students working in a high school technology and engineering production lab

Assessment

A unique feature of the *EbD*™ program is the built-in assessment feature. It provides an assessment system that will monitor the educational growth of the students based on educational standards. The

Image by Greg Strimel.

assessment is broken into three portions: a pre-assessment, design challenge, and post-assessment. The pre- and post-assessments are an online summative assessment of student content knowledge while the design challenge is a hands-on assessment of the student's use of the engineering design process to solve problems. The data collected through this process is accessible at any time and is used by teachers to inform their instruction, as well as the curriculum leadership team to inform professional development and curriculum redesign.

Professional Development

To meet the needs of teachers, students, and administrators, *EbD*™ provides a learning community for continuing professional development in order to increase the effectiveness of its curriculum and student achievement. The learning community consists of both online and face-to face professional development. Teams of Teacher-Effectiveness Coaches, or TECs, are fully prepared to travel to different locations and are available to provide hands-on professional development opportunities to teachers and administrators. TECs can provide a level of comfort with curriculum implementation and materials. Moreover, the *EbD*™ program provides an on-going learning community through *EbDonline*, which connects teachers around the country to ensure consistent curriculum delivery and to supply ongoing professional development for teachers while they are implementing the courses. Through the *EbD*™ professional development, the national consistency of curriculum implementation is broadened and therefore national technological and engineering literacy is increased.

Access to Engineering byDesign™

The *EbD*™ course curricula can be purchased by any individual, school, district, or state for a low price at www.iteea.org. However, schools can become a part of the *EbD*™ school network to access the full benefits of the entire *EbD*™ program and learning community. These benefits include the following:

- Online access to the curriculum and the latest updates.
- Exclusive access to *EbDonline*™ to converse with online facilitators and teachers around the country who are also implementing the same courses.
- Online assessments for the students in their classes—access to real-time student performance data.

To become an *EbD*™ network school, you can download and complete a network agreement at www.iteea.org. Additionally, *EbD*™ has created a consortium of states to serve as leaders in collaborating for higher quality education. Any schools within a consortium state are provided with free access to the *EbD*™ program. The leaders in these states work together to create consistency in the advancement of STEM education. The state leaders implement the *EbD*™ curriculum in their school systems and together evaluate student achievement to make informed decisions in enhancing technological and engineering literacy for all. These state members develop the necessary professional growth opportunities for teachers and propose any needed changes to the curricula. With the increase of states in the consortium, state decisions can become a powerful tool in

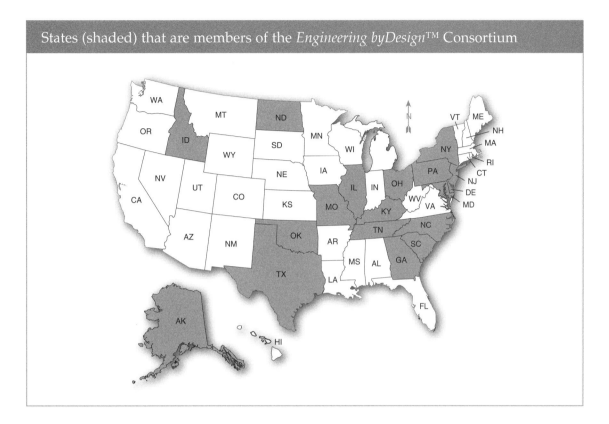

States (shaded) that are members of the *Engineering byDesign*™ Consortium

shaping the future of education and furthering students' technological and engineering literacy. The figure above illustrates the current consortium of states for *EbD*™.

Access to the Engineering byDesign™ Portal

The *EbD*™ network schools and consortium states have access to the curriculum through the *EbD*™ Portal. The *EbD*™ Portal is a cloud-based solution for providing curriculum, assessment, and professional development. Through the portal, teachers can access the dynamic course curriculum and *EbD*™ for on-going professional development. Additionally, teachers can assign and manage student assessments through the portal to make data-driven decisions about their instruction.

Connections to the Next Generation Science Standards

As described in the introduction of this book, *A Framework for K–12 Science Education* (NRC, 2012) includes content in engineering design and technology, as well as engineering practices. The engineering content and practices were combined with crosscutting concepts to develop the engineering design standards included in the NGSS (NGSS Lead States, 2013). The inclusion of engineering and technology in science education is founded on the belief that the United States needs to provide students with the skills necessary to compete in the innovation-driven global economy. This belief mirrors those of the *Standards for Technological Literacy* and *EbD*™ curriculum. Furthermore, the new science framework and standards discuss student understanding of the interconnectedness of science, technology, and engineering through assessing and evaluating the impacts that the designed world can have on the natural world. Understanding this relationship is the foundation of developing technological and engineering literacy, which is the overarching goal of the *EbD™* curriculum. In reviewing the *EbD™* curriculum, clear connections between the courses and NGSS can be seen. Table 8.4 depicts relationships between the NGSS and the high school benchmarks from the *Standards for Technological Literacy*, which are the foundation of the *EbD™* High School curriculum.

Table 8.4 Connections between the *Next Generation Science Standards* and *Standards for Technological Literacy*

Next Generation Science Standards for Engineering Design	Standards for Technological Literacy (STL) High School Benchmarks
HS-ETS1-1 Analyze a major global challenge to specify qualitative and quantitative criteria and constraints for solutions that account for societal needs and wants.	*STL 2 AA*—Requirements involve the identification of the criteria and constraints of a product or system and the determination of how they affect the final design and development. *STL 2 BB*—Optimization is an ongoing process or methodology of designing or making a product and is dependent on criteria and constraints. *STL 6 H*—Different cultures develop their own technologies to satisfy their individual and shared needs, wants, and values. *STL 6 I*—The decision whether to develop a technology is influenced by societal opinions and demands, in addition to corporate cultures. *STL 11 N*—Identify criteria and constraints and determine how these will affect the design process. *STL 13 J*—Collect information and evaluate its quality.
HS-ETS1-2 Design a solution to a complex real-world problem by breaking it down into smaller, more manageable problems that can be solved through engineering.	*STL 8 H*—The design process includes defining a problem, brainstorming, researching and generating ideas, identifying criteria and specifying constraints, exploring possibilities, selecting an approach, developing a design proposal, making a model or prototype, testing and evaluating the design using specifications, refining the design, creating or making it, and communicating processes and results. *STL 9 L*—The process of engineering design takes into account a number of factors. *STL 11 Q*—Develop and produce a product or system using a design process.
HS-ETS1-3 Evaluate a solution to a complex real-world problem based on prioritized criteria and trade-offs that account for a range of constraints, including cost, safety, reliability, and aesthetics as well as possible social, cultural, and environmental impacts.	*STL 5 L*—Decisions regarding the implementation of technologies involve the weighing of trade-offs between predicted positive and negative effects on the environment. *STL 8 K*—Requirements of a design, such as criteria, constraints, and efficiency, sometimes compete with each other. *STL 9 I*—Established design principles are used to evaluate existing designs, to collect data, and to guide the design process. *STL 13 K*—Synthesize data, analyze trends, and draw conclusions regarding the effect of technology on the individual, society, and environment.

Next Generation Science Standards for Engineering Design	Standards for Technological Literacy (STL) High School Benchmarks
	STL 13 L—Use assessment techniques, such as trend analysis and experimentation to make decisions about the future development of technology. *STL 13 M*—Design forecasting techniques to evaluate the results of altering natural systems.
HS-ETS1-4 Use a computer simulation to model the impact of proposed solutions to a complex real-world problem with numerous criteria and constraints on interactions within and between systems relevant to the problem.	*STL 9 K*—A prototype is a working model used to test a design concept by making actual observations and necessary adjustments. *STL 11 O*—Refine a design by using prototypes and modeling to ensure quality, efficiency, and productivity of the final product. *STL 11 P*—Evaluate the design solution using conceptual, physical, and mathematical models at various intervals of the design process in order to check for proper design and to note areas where improvements are needed. *STL 11 R*—Evaluate final solutions and communicate observation, processes, and results of the entire design process, using verbal, graphic, quantitative, virtual, and written means, in addition to three-dimensional models.

Science and engineering practices are a major component of *A Framework for K–12 Science Education* (NRC, 2012). All these practices focus on the importance of students being able to apply content and skills by actually performing in real life contexts. This approach is designed to help increase procedural knowledge while engaging them in learning the topics at hand. These science and engineering practices are required performance expectations for many of the *EbD*™ course activities. Table 8.5 shows the relationship between the Science and Engineering Practices and sample *EbD*™ high school course activities.

Table 8.5 Sample *Engineering byDesign*™ activities that require science and engineering practices

Science and Engineering Practices	EbD High School Course Example Activities
1. Ask questions and define problems	Students will develop a problem statement that is clearly and precisely stated. The problem statement includes the who, what, when, and how the problem will be addressed.
2. Develop and use models	Students will develop conceptual, physical, and mathematical models for a variety of geometric figures.
3. Plan and carry out investigations	Students will conduct market research to develop and finalize a design proposal. Students will create a 5–10 question survey based on their product description. The survey should address the product's use, cost, and how the product can be improved. Include in the survey a product description and any annotated sketches.

(Continued)

Table 8.5 (Continued)

4. Analyze and interpret data	Students will use data analysis software to record data collected during their Crane Strain Extension activity. Students will then analyze the data and determine if a relationship exists between crane boom weight, boom length, boom type and the overall efficiency of the design.
5. Use mathematics and computational thinking	Based on data recorded during crane design testing, students will calculate the efficiency of the design. Students are reminded to make sure all units of measurement are parallel throughout their calculations.
6. Construct explanations and design solutions	Students will apply aesthetic and engineering design principles to design a marshmallow launcher. The launcher must be able to fire from three specific positions for various points. Each team will be given a period of 30 seconds to warm up, prior to a 120-second period to score as many points as possible. Only two marshmallows can be used during any given testing period.
7. Engage in argument from evidence	Students will research two different construction methods and construct a scale model depicting the processes and resources needed for each of the construction types. Students will list the advantages and disadvantages of both construction methods and include a rationale for choosing each construction type.
8. Obtain, evaluate and communicate information	Students will develop an electronic engineering design journal using available technology. Students may use Google Docs, a Wiki, or blog to complete this assignment. Students may also use Word or another technology available locally to complete the assignment.

Table 8.6 Alignment between *Engineering byDesign*™ Process Performance Tasks and Scientific and Engineering Practices in the NGSS

Engineering Design Process Steps	Engineering Design Process Performance Task (EbD™)	S&E Practices for Grades 9–12 (NGSS Lead States, 2013b, Appendix F)
Define the Problem	Develops a problem statement that is clearly and precisely stated. The problem statement includes the who, what, when, and how the problem will be addressed.	**Practice 1 Asking questions (for science) and defining problems (for engineering)** Define a design problem that involves the development of a process or system with interacting components and criteria and constraints that may include social, technical, and/or environmental considerations.
Brainstorm Possible Solutions	Contributes multiple plausible ideas, which are expanded on to show understanding of the concept. All notes are recorded in the Engineering Folio or EDJ.	**Practice 6 Constructing explanations (for science) and designing solutions (for engineering)** Design, evaluate, and/or refine a solution to a complex real-world problem, based on scientific knowledge, student-generated sources of evidence, prioritized criteria, and trade-off considerations.

Engineering Design Process Steps	Engineering Design Process Performance Task (EbD™)	S&E Practices for Grades 9–12 (NGSS Lead States, 2013b, Appendix F)
Research Ideas/ Explore Possibilities	Contributes several plausible ideas and with clearly documented research. Produces accurate conceptual models to show the design concepts with annotated sketches. Notes are recorded in the Engineering Folio or EDJ.	**Practice 8 Obtaining, evaluating, and communicating information** Gather, read, and evaluate scientific and/or technical information from multiple authoritative sources, assessing the evidence and usefulness of each source.
Specify Constraints and Identify Criteria	Clearly identifies the criteria and specifies the constraints as they pertain to the project and their suggested designs. All notes are recorded in the Engineering Folio or EDJ.	**Practice 7 Engaging in argument from evidence** Compare and evaluate competing arguments or design solutions in light of currently accepted explanations, new evidence, limitations (e.g., trade-offs), constraints, and ethical issues.
Consider Alternative Solutions	Did not enter the research phase with a preconceived idea of the final design. Satisfactorily analyzes a variety of possible solutions, based on research and the relationship of those designs to the criteria and constraints. All notes are recorded in the Engineering Folio or EDJ.	**Practice 7 Engaging in argument from evidence** Evaluate competing design solutions to a real-world problem based on scientific ideas and principles, empirical evidence, and/or logical arguments regarding relevant factors (e.g., economic, societal, environmental, ethical considerations).
Select an Approach	Selects a promising solution based on the problem statement, criteria, and constraints as well as evidence collected through research. Uses some type of evaluation method to determine the final design. All notes are recorded in the Engineering Folio or EDJ.	**Practice 6 Constructing explanations (for science) and designing solutions (for engineering)** Construct and revise an explanation based on valid and reliable evidence obtained from a variety of sources (including students' own investigations, models, theories, simulations, peer review) and the assumption that theories and laws that describe the natural world operate today as they did in the past and will continue to do so in the future.
Develop a Written Design Proposal	Design proposal is written technically and precisely and contains the who, what, when, where, and how the solution will be developed as well as how the solution will be evaluated and what tests will be conducted to determine success. Includes annotated sketches, notes, and technical drawings.	**Practice 5 Using mathematics and computational thinking** Use mathematical, computational, and/or algorithmic representations of phenomena or design solutions to describe and/or support claims and/or explanations.

(Continued)

Table 8.6 (Continued)

Engineering Design Process Steps	Engineering Design Process Performance Task (EbD™)	S&E Practices for Grades 9–12 (NGSS Lead States, 2013b, Appendix F)
Make a Model or Prototype	The model or prototype is neatly and precisely developed to meet the problem statement and the given criteria and constraints. A record of the construction process as well as how the design was improved during construction can be found in the Engineering Folio or EDJ.	**Practice 2 Developing and using models** Develop and/or use a model (including mathematical and computational) to generate data to support explanations, predict phenomena, analyze systems, and/or solve problems device, process, or system.
Test and Evaluate	Testing and evaluation processes are clearly defined in the Design Proposal and align to the problem statement. The data collected during evaluation is clearly documented and used to improve the design.	**Practice 2 Developing and using models** Design a test of a model to ascertain its reliability. **Practice 3 Planning and carrying out investigations** Plan and conduct an investigation or test a design solution in a safe and ethical manner, including considerations of environmental, social, and personal impacts. **Practice 4 Analyzing and interpreting data** Analyze data to identify design features or characteristics of the components of a proposed process or system to optimize it relative to criteria for success.
Refine/Improve	Refinements were made from data collected during testing and evaluation. Data-driven decision making is clearly evident and documented. Refinements to the solution are documented, and the solution has improved based on testing.	**Practice 2 Developing and using models** Develop, revise, and/or use a model based on evidence to illustrate and/or predict the relationships between systems or between components of a system. **Practice 5 Using mathematics and computational thinking** Create and/or revise a computational model or simulation of a phenomenon, designed device, process, or system.
Create/ Make Product	Finished solution (product) aligns to the design proposal and reflects the Engineering Design Process and includes evidence of refinement based on testing and evaluation of the design. The solution (product) is well constructed and easily meets the problem statement.	**Practice 6** **Constructing explanations (for science) and designing solutions (for engineering)** Apply scientific ideas, principles, and/or evidence to provide an explanation of phenomena and solve design problems, taking into account possible unanticipated effects.

Engineering Design Process Steps	Engineering Design Process Performance Task (EbD™)	S&E Practices for Grades 9–12 (NGSS Lead States, 2013b, Appendix F)
Communicate Results	Solution is presented accurately and precisely using the Engineering Design Journal. The Engineering Design Process is well documented, with supporting evidence. All information aligns to how the solution meets the problem statement as well as the criteria and constraints. A more formal presentation/showcase was developed to support the solution.	**Practice 7 Engaging in argument from evidence** Construct, use, and/or present an oral and written argument or counterarguments based on data and evidence. **Practice 8 Obtaining, evaluating, and communicating information** Communicate scientific and/or technical information or ideas (e.g., about phenomena and/or the process of development and the design and performance of a proposed process or system) in multiple formats.

These eight practices closely relate to the high school 12-step engineering design process used throughout the *EbD™* curriculum. The curriculum requires students to use the engineering design process to solve the various design problems presented in each course. To successfully solve problems using this process, students must perform all eight of the science and engineering practices. In fact, the *EbD™* high school performance tasks for each step of the design process are similar to the performance tasks of the eight science and engineering practices. The alignment of the engineering design process performance tasks and the eight science and engineering practices can be seen in Table 8.6.

Conclusion

Engineering byDesign™ was developed by the International Technology and Engineering Educator's Association to support a consistent approach for achieving technology and engineering literacy throughout the United States. Now that the NGSS has included the study of engineering and technology into the structure of science education, the *Engineering byDesign™* program is poised to become a powerful, useful, and relevant tool for teachers in the science profession. As described in this chapter, the *Engineering byDesign™* curriculum closely ties with the engineering design and applications of science performance expectations and practices. Therefore, *Engineering byDesign™* truly lends itself to supporting the new science standards. Recently, the *Engineering byDesign™* curriculum leadership committee has developed

Students engaged in hands-on learning

Image by Greg Strimel.

a standards responsibility matrix for the redesign of its various courses. This standards responsibility matrix will help ensure that the curriculum is closely aligned with the NGSS.

To learn more about the *Engineering byDesign*™ program visit http://www.iteea.org/EbD/ebd.htm.

References

Bybee, R. W. (1997). *Achieving scientific literacy: From purposes to practices*. Portsmouth, NH: Heinemann.

Bybee, R. W., & Landes, N. M. (1990, February). Science for life & living: An elementary school science program from Biological Sciences Curriculum Study. *The American Biology Teacher, 52*(2), 92–98.

ITEEA. (2000, 2002, 2007). *Standards for technological literacy: Content for the study of technology*. Reston, VA: Author.

ITEEA. (2003). *Advancing excellence in technological literacy: Student assessment, professional development, and program standards*. Reston, VA: Author.

ITEEA. (2013). *Engineering byDesign: A standards based model program*. Retrieved from: http://www.iteea.org/EbD™/EbD™.htm

Kamkawamba, W., & Mealer, B. (2010). *The boy who harnessed the wind: Creating currents of electricity and hope*. New York: William Morrow.

NAE & NRC. (2002). *Technically speaking: Why all Americans need to know more about technology*. Washington, DC: National Academies Press.

NAGB. (2012). *Technology and engineering literacy framework for the 2014 national assessment of educational progress. Pre-publication Edition*. Washington, DC: Author.

NGSS Lead States (2013a). *Next generation science standards: For states, by states, volume 2: Appendices*. Washington, DC: National Academies Press.

NGSS Lead States (2013b). *Next generation science standards: For states, by states, volume 1: The standards*. Washington, DC: National Academies Press.

NRC (2012). *A framework for K–12 science education: Practices, crosscutting concepts, and core ideas*. Washington, DC: National Academies Press.

PCAST (2010). *Report to the President: Prepare and inspire: K–12 education in science, technology, engineering, and math (STEM) for America's future*. Washington, DC: Government Printing Office.

9

Science by Design

Construct a Boat, Catapult, Glove, and Greenhouse

Lee Pulis

Plymouth, MA

Science by Design combines four projects in a single 376-page book

Image courtesy of NSTA.

143

F ield-tested and revised over multiple school years in cooperation with 48 teachers and hundreds of students in both core academic and technical education courses, *Science by Design* features engaging hands-on team product design challenges as motives to learn science on a need-to-know basis.

Each stand-alone supplemental module is supported by NSTA's sciLINKS initiative, which links science content with instructionally rich Internet sources that have been vetted by science experts and NSTA staff to ensure the links are appropriate and up to date.

Author Perspective

After decades of debate, at its December 1998 convention, the American Vocational Association (AVA) voted to change its name to the Association for Career and Technical Education (ACTE), followed quickly by renaming of affiliated state associations. The change was reflected in the naming of some states' career-oriented student education standards to CTE frameworks, or "standards," in a format of course syllabi. The move was mostly to disassociate from a past stigma of "vocational" and "vocational-technical" education as being less desirable than "academic" preparation. Over the years, vocational courses had become more academic, more challenging, and more technical, and the new name more accurately reflected those changes. Meanwhile, academic courses were thought by some to have become more theoretical, less hands-on, less applied, less practical, less motivating, less universal (particularly to visual and kinetic learners), and overall less effective in preparing graduates for the world of work and employer and national needs.

Also in the late 1990s TERC (an educational research and development center in Cambridge, MA) received funding from the National Science Foundation for *Science by Design*—a research-based development project intended to bridge the gap between high school academic and vocational disciplines by blending both in a common curriculum. Extensively field-tested in both types of courses, this effort reflected the perceived need for students to learn how to integrate science, technology, engineering, and mathematics as practiced in creative and innovative STEM careers. This was deemed critical to international prestige, national security, advancement of knowledge, graduate job placement, business innovation, and the economy.

I clearly recall Dr. Salinger, our NSF Program Officer, visiting and reminding us that what we were developing would be five if not ten years ahead of its time; therefore difficult to find a publisher, because only a small niche existed in the current educational curriculum marketplace for a curriculum that blended science and engineering. At the start of the new millennium in 2000, the National Science Teachers Association's NSTA Press took up the cause and published the series. At the time, NSTA Press renamed the supplements with vocational-sounding "Construct-a- . . ." titles, likely meant to notify their science teacher membership that these materials were meant to add hands-on relevance and motivation into their existing courses. Such titles would also have certain appeal to technology teachers seeking materials sanctioned by academic science, if they somehow became aware of their existence and availability through NSTA. The idea of joint publication by NSTA and the Association of Career and Technical Education (ACTE) was too big a leap. Change takes time.

Now STEM is hot. We have Common Core State Standards stressing research and communications. At the end of the last millennium *Science by Design* authors chose, after much thought and advice, to use the term *technology* broadly to include and encompass the engineering design process that we charted for students. This fit the educational vernacular of the time and hopefully avoided "scaring off" potential teacher-adopters, few of whom would be engineers. Now we have NGSS integrating science inquiry and engineering design processes. There is wide acceptance that non-engineer teachers can and should introduce engineering design process to *all* students. The *Science by Design* series is truly *Engineering Curricula Ready to Go!*, for which the time has come.

My own opinion is that it could be advantageous now for the publisher to restore the original titles the authors believed would best catch the notice of high school teachers in both "tracks" seeking hands-on integrated STEM inquiry via product design. That would mean changing the current titles from prescriptive-sounding ("Construct-a-...") directions to build specific objects. To better represent the actual inquiry-based nature of the materials, the fun and excitement of the engaging discoveries that students make, and the broader applicability of the STEM topics that students encounter, the new titles would read:

- Catapult!
- Great Pumpkin!
- Hot Hands!
- Boat + Speed!

Where to Get It

Compilation (376 pages) published 11/15/2012 by NSTA Press (available in paperback print, e-book, or bundle). ISBN (print): 978-1-936959-48-8.

Science by Design (TERC, 2000, 2013) is a set of four (nominally two-week) curriculum supplements developed at not-for-profit TERC in Cambridge, MA, with funding from two National Science Foundation grants (ESI-9252894 and ESI-9550540). The compilation is published and sold by NSTA Press <www.nsta.org/store/> (The four supplements are also available separately, used, through Amazon and eBay.)

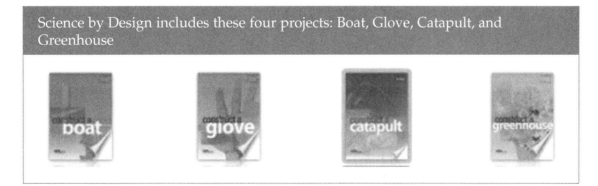

Science by Design includes these four projects: Boat, Glove, Catapult, and Greenhouse

Image courtesy NSTA.

Overview of the Instructional Materials

The four research-based teaching supplements provide team projects designed backward from then-current national standards. They were written both for physics teachers seeking the motivating learn-by-doing approach with strong technology content as well as technology education teachers seeking to add key science content in their hands-on product design-and-build projects. Each supplement is intended for easy implementation in diverse settings (e.g., science labs, math classrooms, or technology shop settings), in ten to twelve 45-minute sessions, or five to six 90-minute blocks.

The Goals of the *Science by Design* materials are to

- Provide standards-based hands-on inquiry experiences for science and math classes;
- Integrate more explicit grade-level math and science for technology classes;
- Demonstrate linkages between the iterative processes of scientific inquiry and technological design (a.k.a., engineering);
- Engage students as members of product research and development teams;
- Facilitate implementation of design challenge learning in diverse existing courses (by standards connections and brief modular format);
- Motivate open-ended discovery (using quick-builds as starting points for deeper problem solving that involves learning on a need-to-know basis); and
- Ensure accessibility to all schools and students by use of readily available low-cost curricula and materials.

The materials are intended for grade levels 9–12, and the earlier the better, assuming that the materials and experiences will motivate students to take more advanced math and science as they progress through high school.

These materials and activities are well suited for both school and after school: science, technology, engineering, and math (STEM) classes or clubs; weekend academies or contests; home school, youth organizations, and summer camp activities.

Construct-a-Boat

Working as members of product research and development (R&D) teams, students investigate the physics of boat performance, using a systems approach and modeling. They explore buoyancy and drag, then redesign a quick-build scale model boat hull to improve acceleration and top speed. They compare parameters of performance for their design to the challenge specifications and baseline data for a quick-build design.

The research activities in this teaching supplement use structured activity sheets to provide a model for identifying variables and organizing the research and measurements that students need for their more open-ended development phase. Students learn about scaling, minimizing surface area, and fluid friction dynamics. In the broadest technological context, they are exploring how boats work, why they float, and how they move through water. Their goal is to redesign a boat hull to achieve the highest top speed and to reach that top speed as quickly as possible after starting. School facilities and cost will influence the criteria and constraints that teachers set, such as whether students will work with wood or polystyrene in fabricating their boat hulls.

Teams communicate their findings and conclusions in a written report and oral presentation. They describe their model boat, its construction, and design improvement factors.

Accommodations are provided for students of varying abilities, including a well-guided extension (Side Road) for advanced students into mathematical systems modeling. They create a chart in order to review how multiple factors (mass, thrust, drag, and acceleration) influence boat speed, identify relationships between variables one-by-one, quantify the chart with their data, and compare calculated values to observations. This facilitates informed iteration in design by allowing students to predict how specific changes in the hull such as mass, area or roughness of the wet gliding surface, and motor force would impact top speed.

Construct-a-Catapult

Students review the following design challenge: "As a member of a product development team, you are to design, build, and document a mechanical launching system that can deliver a small object repeatedly and predictably over a specified range of distances" (TERC, 2013, p. 108).

Key topics in STEM that are encountered as students test their first quick-build catapults ("insta-pults") and then improve designs through team research, development, and testing are:

- applying *inquiry and design processes* to generate challenge solutions,
- quantifying *elasticity* by documenting force/stretch relationships,
- creating *torsion* and converting elastic potential *energy* to kinetic energy to achieve distance or "range" of a projectile,
- using Hooke's Law and principles of gravity to correlate range to applied *force,*
- *calibrating* their prototypes using *frequency distribution* graphs to meet performance specifications such as predictability and reliability, and
- reading about the *history of design* of catapult technologies from circa 400 BCE warfare to present-day pole-vaulting and steam catapults that launch jet planes off aircraft carriers. This activity in particular helps teams consider innovative uses for their designs in the modern marketplace.

This supplement perhaps best employs the principle of providing motivation to learn through activities that are low cost and fun to do. Amidst the chaos of students launching projectiles (such as plastic practice golf balls) with the energy of stretched rubber bands, teams maintain order by working at purposeful data collection. If the weather is warm and dry and wind is calm, catapult testing is a great outdoor activity. If not, clearing some open space in the classroom or setting up a testing arena in a gym or hallway can also provide students a similarly energizing change of pace and infusion of enthusiasm.

The materials required for this project, like the others, are intentionally readily available and low cost, at around seventy dollars for a class of 25 students. The cost lessens for teachers who can find rulers, scrap wood, 3-ring binders, rubber bands, binder clips, pie tins, and screws in a school supply closet, shop, or recycling bin. It's always good to have a bit of budget though, because not everyone wants to go gathering, and having some items on hand, such as two practice golf balls for each team, would be a long shot for most teachers.

The final communication for this project is for teams to write a user manual, a simple set of detailed but clearly understandable and illustrated instructions, for calibration and operation of their prototype catapult. Suggested sections include a team mission statement, system overview, parts and materials specifications, performance specifications, operating instructions, safety measures, firing tips, launching graph, and a section on underlying science. Teams actually exchange prototypes and the final performance tests of each device are then conducted and evaluated based on the quality of the user manual and device in the hands of novice operators. The most successful solution could be defined as the one that can be fired most accurately by another team. Great action and fun! Teachers are encouraged to recruit an audience for the final Challenge Event.

As with all four supplements, at the end of the project, students revisit the same Snapshot of Understanding questions they encountered in the first session, providing comparison of pre- and post-learning answers to assess gains in understanding.

Construct-a-Glove

Without the development of gloves, the productive advance of humans into the coldest regions of the earth, and now space, would not be possible. Again working as members of a product R&D team, students integrate science and technology to investigate basic thermodynamics of heat transfer and insulation in relation to the body's homeothermic processes. Their challenge is to "design an insulated glove system that keeps the tip of your index finger as warm as possible in uncomfortably cold surroundings [ice water], while maintaining dexterity for a specific function" (TERC, 2013, p. 200). After reading the "Insulated Glove Design Brief" students answer the preactivity Snapshot of Understanding questions to record what they already know about homeothermy, heat transfer, and research and development.

Examples of pre-assessment questions are as follows:

1. List as many special purpose kinds of gloves as you can. Place a "T" by those specifically designed to provide thermal protection (e.g., Welding—T).

2. Think of a time when your hands were really cold. What were you trying to do? How did you warm them? Which heat transfer process did you use (e.g., radiation, conduction, convection)?

3. What test(s) could you perform to determine if an animal is "warm-blooded" (homeothermic) or "cold-blooded" (poikilothermic)?

As in all four modules, the Teacher Pages offer rich scaffolding. For Question 2 above, teachers are given the following list of possible special-purpose gloves and encouraged to conduct a class discussion to help students better relate form to function:

. . . staining/painting/waxing, food handling, gardening, dish washing, skiing, driving, diving, golfing, meat cutting, boxing, baseball, hockey, fashion, surgical, wood cutting, mountain biking, cattle roping, chemicals handling, fire fighting, traffic directing, electrical line working, space walking, hunting, archery, ice fishing, mountain climbing.

Next, students review some basics in biology, such as that the ". . . body's many biological sensors can reduce and reflect heat, and even activate evaporative cooling (sweating)" (TERC, 2013, p. 207). This is followed by an analogy to a home heating and cooling system's "on/off switching or speed control of fans and dampers, or pumps and valves"

(TERC, 2013, p. 207). In teams students construct and test a waterproof quick-build insulated glove according to guidelines, using their own selection of insulation materials. They tape a thermometer or temperature probe directly to the tip of the index finger inside the glove and immerse the gloved hand in ice water for four minutes. Temperature is recorded over time, and any evidence of biological feedback (cold-induced vasodilation) is discussed. Based on data reported by all teams and further research and reflection, each team improves their glove design in a second iteration.

Construct-a-Greenhouse

Because of the subject matter this project is best started midway in the Spring semester where Winters are cold. Using two black or white vinyl-clad 3-ring binders, students work as members of development teams to "design and build an environment adaptable to changing heat, light, humidity, and space requirements for the progressive growth stages of a giant pumpkin (or other specified [fruit or] vegetable)" (TERC, 2013, p. 286). A key idea is the transformation and transfer of energy involved in greenhouse technology. Teams discover how physics can enhance plant production. Student research will inevitably lead to discovery and discussion (beyond the published materials) of the related issue of "greenhouse" gases in the atmosphere and its connection to global climate change. Passive solar thermal control is another topical outcome of student research. Depending on student interest and the scope of your objectives, this project might be completed in the span of a couple weeks or spread over several months and extended into summer. Students are assigned to reflect and write continuation recommendations and instructions, which might include transplanting outdoors; competing in a fair or contest; or growing for market, for decoration, or for further learning and enjoyment.

Students investigate the varying environmental conditions required in stages of plant growth from germination to seedling, leaf, stem, root growth, and fruit development. They must repurpose their model greenhouse from originally favoring conversion of incoming light to heat for germination, to optimizing light and controlling heat during growth. Students must consider the whole growth cycle and make design trade-offs in the scaling of volume and surface area, as well as the light transmitting, reflective, and thermal properties of materials, costs, and construction alternatives.

The first quick mini-experiment is to flatten a soda can, paint it black, and set it in an open-top box along with a thermometer. The top opening is covered with clear glass or plastic and sealed to prevent air leaks. This small passive solar collector with no air exchange powerfully demonstrates the conversion of light energy to heat and the basic heat transfer processes of radiation, conduction and convection. When placed in direct sunlight or under a 60-watt bulb, the time versus interior temperature rise is recorded, illustrating the greenhouse effect. This initial "insta-build" construction, data collection, reflection, and reporting is followed by team construction of "quick-build" model greenhouses based on readily available 3-ring binders. Teams follow technical instructions and drawings for the overall structure, introducing modifications based on their research. They again introduce a light source and collect baseline temperature rise data against which the performance of their subsequent design improvements will be assessed.

Students discover from research that when seeds are in the ground, the goal is to optimize transformation of incoming light energy to heat, in order to facilitate germination. However, after the seed has sprouted, reconfiguring the environment to optimize light capture is key to photosynthesis and early growth. Water, oxygen, and temperature are key criteria for germination, while water, carbon dioxide and light are key to supporting photosynthesis. Therefore, team growth optimizing designs need to be transformable to account for changes in limiting factors. Additional factors include thermal mass of materials, prevention of disease, protection from plant pests, and relevant "rules of thumb." Later, the further development of a giant pumpkin requires design considerations allowing for a continual increase of available space (both above and below ground) as well as increasing water demand.

Since the example species, the Atlantic Giant Pumpkin, takes 120–150 days to grow, students have to research factors such as their latitude, altitude, and frost-free days to maximize time and develop a strategy to provide optimized conditions at specific stages in the growth cycle. Teachers must be clear about how long the project will run. If planted in Spring, students may be able to transplant their pumpkins outside at school or home at the end of the school year and provide or arrange for continuing care through the Summer until Fall harvest, to enter a local fair or contest. At the time of publication, there was a prize of $10,000 and a trip to Hawaii for the first person to grow a pumpkin over 1000 pounds. This represented the ultimate real world motivation and proof-of-design performance evaluation. That milestone has now been surpassed. However, if this project extends through summer and is followed by the Construct-a-Catapult challenge in the Fall semester, students might then consider how much they can launch and how far it will go . . . leading to full-scale catapult prototypes tested in a "punkin chucking" contest.

As in actual product R&D work, students integrate scientific inquiry with engineering design process, conducting Internet research, performing experiments, collecting data, analyzing their data with charts and graphs, setting criteria and constraints, making sketches, building, and testing their engineered environment prototype, reflecting on process, and presenting results. Each of these activities produces documentation (and perhaps photographs) plus artifacts for assessment. In addition, ultimately the size and vigor of the growth-enhanced biological specimens can be qualitatively and quantitatively compared among teams.

Copyrighted methods of estimating the weight of a complex irregular fruit with varying diameter and density (of wall thickness versus seed cavity) prior to an actual weigh-off are also explored.

Connections to NGSS (NGSS Lead States, 2013) include gaining insights into the wider "greenhouse effect" on global warming, key design considerations in passive solar construction, and the variations and challenges in worldwide agricultural food production.

A table at the beginning of each module, lists what students do, correlated with standards in science (AAAS, 1993; NRC 1996), technology (ITEEA, 1996), social studies (NCSS, 1997), and mathematics (NCTM, 2000) that were current at time of publication (2000). Updating to correlate with Common Core State Standards in English Language Arts and Mathematics (NGA & CCSSO, 2010) and NGSS (NGSS Lead States 2013) is recommended to assist teacher implementation.

Student activities in each module follow the same general pattern:

- **Activity 1: Design Brief**—At the outset of each of the four modules, students receive a Design Brief, including a measurable product design Challenge; a Scope of Work outlining research topics, development tasks, a specified end-of-project communication format; and a quick Snapshot of Understanding exercise to explore what they already know about the key topics. Associated Teaching Suggestions in various modules typically include criteria for measuring success, materials (constraints), preparation, historical context, proposed homework, and themes or alternative criteria and constraints to tailor the challenge.

- **Activity 2: Quick-Build**—A quick and simple hands-on build-to-specifications activity is used to engage students at the outset and also to provide a common starting point and focus for discussion shared by all students, regardless of gender and prior content knowledge.
- **Activity 3: Research**—A sequence of suggested tasks guides students to work in teams discovering what they need to know via brainstorming, Internet search, identifying variables, conducting experiments, making measurements, and analyzing data they collect.
- **Activity 4: Development**—Teams differentiate the learning experience for members as they develop unique ideas based on a mix of their research conclusions, personal interests, and collective motivation. During this phase of the technological (engineering) design process, teams choose solutions and then build and test them. Personal relevance, competitiveness, and team pride become key factors in the learning experience and outcomes.
- **Activity 5: Communication**—In addition to the team-built test models and portfolio records of data and decision making, each teaching supplement calls for a different format for teams to communicate their final product designs:
- Project report and presentation (Boat)
- User's manual (Catapult)
- Product prospectus and marketing plan (Glove)
- Oral presentation, FAQs, and written instructions (Greenhouse)

Teacher Pages immediately follow each student activity and include an Overview, required Materials (and common hand tools), a checklist for Preparation, detailed Teaching Suggestions, and extension ideas (Side Roads).

Appendix resources include additional activities (Side Roads), Text Reconstruction exercises to actively improve students' science reading skills, Sample Answers to questions arising in student activities, Glossary, and References.

What Students Do

In each of the four stand-alone teaching supplements, students have fun learning by doing, while integrating science, technology, engineering, and mathematics (STEM). They employ an iterative multistep cycle of activities that blends the processes of scientific inquiry and technological, or engineering, design. Realizing and instilling the similarity of such complex processes across many disciplines, as illustrated in Table 1, is perhaps the most lasting outcome for students in later life. This may also be the most comforting aspect for teachers encountering these materials for the first time. Sharing at least some of the columns of this chart with students may be helpful.

Connections to the NGSS

In each of the *Science by Design* modules, students integrate scientific inquiry and (engineering) design process through all eight "practices of science and engineering" described in Next Generation Science Standards (NGSS Lead States, 2013b, Appendix F):

Practice 1: Ask questions and define problems.

Practice 2: Develop and use models.

Table 9.1 Iterative Problem-solving Processes Compared

Scientific Inquiry	Engineering Design	Science by Design R&D	Mathematical Modeling	Creative Writing
Formulate a question	Define a human need	Accept a design challenge	Consider a real problem	Focus on a topic or scenario
Research how others have answered it	Research how others have solved it	Discover key concepts with a quick-build	Research existing models	Pre-write
Brainstorm hypotheses and choose one	Brainstorm solutions and select one	Form teams, brainstorm, and research	Make modeling assumptions	Organize
Conduct an experiment	Create and test a prototype	Identify variables, develop design, & test	Set up a mathematical model	Draft
Modify hypothesis based on results	Redesign solution based on tests	Analyze data and modify design as warranted	Analyze model	Review: get feedback
Draw conclusion, write paper	Finalize design, make drawings	Form and record conclusions	Interpret results and compare with reality	Revise and edit
Submit paper for peer review	Present optimal solution to client	Communicate results in specified format	Deliver conclusions	Publish
Ask a new question	Define a new need	Encounter a new challenge	Identify a new problem	Shift focus

Practice 3: Plan and carry out investigations.

Practice 4: Analyze and interpret data.

Practice 5: Use mathematics and computational thinking.

Practice 6: Construct explanations and design solutions.

Practice 7: Engage in argument from evidence.

Practice 8: Obtain, evaluate and communicate information.

And as shown in Table 2, nine of the twelve Core Ideas in the NGSS are addressed in *Science by Design*.

Enhancement Recommendations

I recommend that *Science by Design* be improved in the following ways, either by revising the materials or by teacher adaptations.

Table 9.2 Series Connections to NGSS

NGSS Core Ideas	Boat	Catapult	Glove	Greenhouse
Physical Science				
Matter and Its Interactions	■	■	■	■
Motion and stability: Forces and interactions	■	■	■	■
Energy	■	■	■	■
Waves and their applications in technologies for information transfer				
Life Science				
From molecules to organisms: Structures and processes			■	
Ecosystems: Interactions, energy, and dynamics			■	■
Heredity: Inheritance and variation of traits			■	■
Biological evolution: Unity and diversity				
Earth and Space Science				
Earth's place in the universe				
Earth's systems	■	■	■	■
Earth and human activity	■	■	■	■
Engineering				
Engineering design	■	■	■	■

- Tag as Engineering; STEM; Low Cost; Construction (Process); Design; High Schools; Mechanics (Physics); Problem Solving; Research Methodology; Resource Materials; Science Activities; Teaching Methods; Technology.
- Update to show standards correlations to CCSS and NGSS.
- Highlight the green technology themes (repurposing, recycling, insulating, renewable energy, local agriculture).
- Change descriptive terminology from edu-speak "modules" and "supplements" to engineering "projects".

Conclusion

As NGSS today intermingles engineering into science instruction, so also does *Science by Design* integrate technology research and development (R&D) with inquiry (emphasizing physical and life sciences). As NSTA Press has recognized by compiling the four supplements with a fresh publication date, *Science by Design* was ahead of its time, and its time has now come.

Science by Design is a STEM engineering curriculum without the "E" word. In districts or states where a stealth implementation plan is needed for engineering, *Science by Design* is perfect. If seeking to adopt curricula specifically to implement NGSS core ideas and practices, simply explain to students (and administrators) that the technology design process is called *engineering*. Similarly, for teachers and students scared by their own perceptions of the "E" word, use of it can be saved until ready. Point out that graduates savvy to team integrative problem solving can seek and find work on engineering projects and for engineering companies without majoring in engineering. Engineering is an integrative team activity open to people with specialty knowledge and skills in all fields encompassed by STEAM (STEM plus the arts, social sciences, and humanities).

References

AAAS. (1993). *Benchmarks for Science Literacy*. Project 2061, American Association for the Advancement of Science (AAAS). New York: Oxford University Press. Retrieved from: www.project2061.org/publications/bsl/online/index.php

ITEEA. (1996). *Advancing excellence in technological literacy: Student assessment, professional development, and program standards*. Reston, VA: Author.

ITEEA. (2000, 2002, 2007). *Standards for technological literacy: Content for the study of technology*. Reston, VA: Author.

NCSS. (1997). *National curriculum standards for social studies*. Silver Spring, MD: Author.

NCTM. (2000). *Principles and standards for school mathematics*. Reston, VA: Author. Retrieved from: http://www.nctm.org/standards/default.aspx?id=58

NGA & CCSSO. (2010). *Common core state standards: Mathematics*. Washington, DC: Author.

NGSS Lead States. (2013). *Next generation science standards: For states, by states, volume 1: The standards*. Washington, DC: National Academies Press.

NRC. (1996). *National Science Education Standards*. National Committee on Science Education Standards and Assessment, Board on Science Education, Division of Behavioral and Social Sciences and Education, National Research Council (NRC). Washington, DC: National Academies Press.

TERC. (2000, 2013). *Science by design*. Arlington, VA: National Science Teachers Association Press.

10

Nature's Designs Applied to Technology

Susan E. Riechert

Department of Ecology & Evolutionary Biology and
Center for Enhancing Education in Mathematics & the Sciences (CEEMS)

University of Tennessee

Follow That Spiral! Exercise 9 from Animal Kingdom Unit of *Biology in a Box* Project

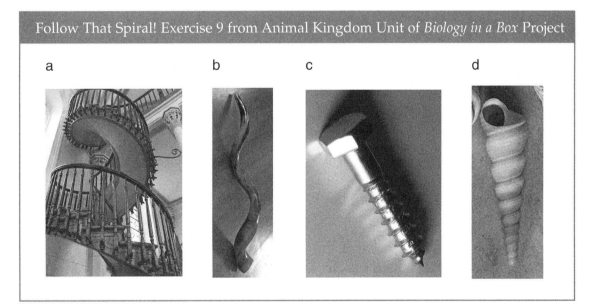

a   b   c   d

All images from Wikipedia Creative Commons, from left to right courtesy of BenFrantzDale, Olve Utne, Bronzaclose, and Tom Meijer.

The STEM (Science, Technology, Engineering, & Mathematics) education initiative has developed out of a desire to increase the number of students who choose to pursue careers in the sciences and mathematics. One of its approaches has been to integrate technology, engineering, and mathematics within science curricula. While physics and chemistry are the sciences most often targeted by this initiative, engineering has long gained insight from biological systems. In recent years, engineers, often in collaboration with biologists, have been explicitly mining nature for structures and processes that might be applied to solving problems and meeting human needs. This area of technology has been variously identified as *biomimetics, biomimicry* and *bio-mimicking*, where *bio* refers to life and *mimicry* to imitate. It has also been called *bionics* (life-like), referring to some function of a system being copied from nature. I prefer to use *biomimetics* as the field and *bio-mimicking* as the process to avoid confusion with the *biomimicry* that occurs in nature.[1]

Examples of Bio-Mimicking

It is not surprising that engineers look to nature for insight into designs that might be applied to solve problems of interest to humans. The structures and processes organisms possess are, after all, the end product of testing through the process of natural selection over extensive periods of time. If a solution exists naturally, one should be able to utilize it in designing products and devices that can be used to inspire an engineering solution.

This is not as simple as it may seem because one has to fully understand the multiple systems that might be involved in the trait of interest. Take, for instance, the recent interest in geckos, small lizards that are unique for their ability to climb slippery surfaces, given their large size. They are, in fact, small as lizards go but very large for an animal capable of moving across a surface upside down, Spider-man like. The toes of the Gecko have inspired the idea for a reusable dry adhesive that can be put down, taken up and reused, just as geckos pick up their feet and put them down again while moving across a slippery substrate (see figure on next page). Close examination of the underside of the gecko toe indicates that it has hundreds of thousands of tiny bristles. These bristles are approximately 5 microns (0.005 mm) in diameter and 100 microns (0.1 mm) in length. When pushed forward onto a surface, the bristles attach, and when pulled back detach, because of their angle and shape. A UC Berkeley team (Chary, Tamelier, & Turner, 2013) report that their silicon-based fibers modeled after gecko bristles successfully attach and detach making a decent dry adhesive, albeit a very small one that does not function as well as nature's model.

Another group (Bartlett et al., 2012) from the University of Massachusetts took a different approach to the same problem of how to produce dry adhesive materials by mimicking the unique climbing abilities of geckos and other animals. The University of Massachusetts researchers point to the fact that some insects can climb with smooth attachment pads that lack the minute bristles seen on gecko toes. This led them to ask: What is it about the structure of the seta (bristle) on a gecko toe and the tarsus (foot) of an insect that gives them adhesive properties? Their investigations led them to conclude that both of these structures are stiff in the direction of load (weight-bearing), while being flexible (conforming) at the tip, permitting them to have maximum area in contact with the surface. These researchers used scale-up theory to calculate the characteristics of a large adhesive pad. They tested their ideas by producing a large pad made of a stiff fabric with fibers in the direction of load. They then poured a layer of rubber onto the fabric to produce a conforming material with maximum area for surface contact. The result was a synthetic adhesive pad capable of holding up a large, wide-screen television, which could

Left to right: The gecko lizard, close-up of its foot showing treads compared to auto tire treads, and an electron micrograph of artificial bristles designed to replicate the gecko's foot

All images from Wikipedia Creative Commons, left to right by ZooFari, Bjørn Christian Tørrissen, Clearly Ambiguous@ flickr, and Yurdumakan, Raravikar, Ajayan, & Dhinojwalar, 2005.

be attached and removed from a vertical surface. The image on the next page shows the pad that they produced, along with a graph on which they have plotted the characteristics of both natural and synthetic adhesive pads.

In this chapter, I discuss the merits of offering high school students examples in which knowledge of the structure and function of organisms has been applied to meet human needs. Students of all ages are fascinated by nature and they certainly are interested in technological applications that affect them. But do they recognize the connection between nature and technology?

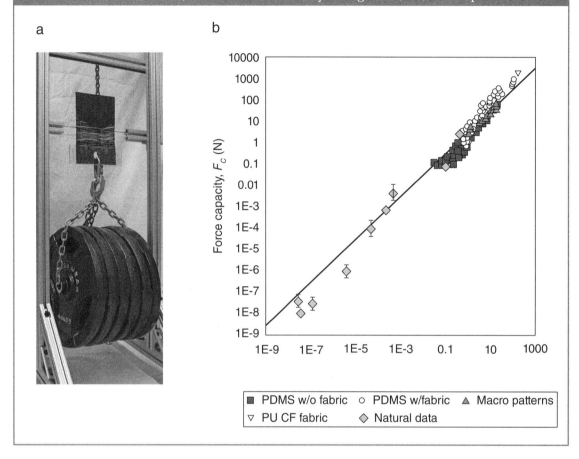

A 100 cm² reversible synthetic adhesive pad (left) was able to hold a hanging mass of 135 kg. The graph (right) shows data from various organisms and synthetic adhesives that led to development of the reversible pad. According to the data, in order for the pad to withstand a high force (Fc), a material must be soft to create adhesive contact area (A) while simultaneously being stiff ($1/C$) when pulled.

Images Courtesy of Michael D. Bartlett, Polymer Science and Engineering Department, University of Massachusetts. (From Bartlett et al., 2012, reproduced under license with John Wiley and Sons.)

Biology in a Box

Too often, grant funds and even educational priorities are focused on the physical sciences and technological application of physics and chemistry. Yet the life sciences have a great deal to offer as well. It is important that our students are educated to function as informed citizens, understanding that we can learn and gain much from outcomes of natural selection on all organisms, even the ones we typically tromp on, given the opportunity to do so. Many examples of this connection can be seen throughout the thematic units of the *Biology in a Box* Project, developed to provide materials and inquiry exercises that match grade level science and mathematics curricula.

I started the *Biology in a Box* project in the early 1990s, recognizing the need for teachers to have materials and inquiry resources in the schools to enhance student learning of the sciences. *Biology in a Box* received primary funding in 1995 as the community outreach project from a Howard Hughes Medical Institute (HHMI) grant to Biology at the

University of Tennessee and has been partnering with NIMBioS, the National Institute in Mathematical & Biological Synthesis, since 2010 in formalizing the mathematics content. The project has expanded greatly from an initial four units placed in the local Knox County school system to 10 thematic units with over 300 math and science exercises aligned to science and mathematics curriculum standards available to K–12 students in 82 partnering school systems throughout the State of Tennessee. The exercises in their entirety with materials lists, math and science standards, alphabetic cross listings, and suggested readings are available in PDF and PowerPoint versions at the project's website (http://biologyinabox.utk.edu).

Making the link between the wonders of the natural world and our copies of them in our everyday world is particularly important for the understanding it offers our students of the process of evolution by natural selection. In the NSES (NRC, 1996), and again in the NGSS (NGSS Lead States, 2013), evolution by natural selection is one of a small number of core ideas that everyone needs to understand to be scientifically literate citizens. Yet it is a difficult concept for teachers to convey, in part because students come in with alternative conceptions of the diversification of life. Bishop and Anderson (1990) report that college entry tests indicate that the majority of graduating high school students fail to gain an understanding of the process of evolution during the course of their K–12 education. I, too, have data supporting this conclusion from 610 students enrolled in my freshmen biodiversity course for science majors. At the beginning of the course, I gave them a diagnostic exam on the subject that tested for comprehension and application. Although the test supplied definitions so that vocabulary was not a barrier, the average score was 22% correct, and the highest score achieved was 36%. Seventy-three honors students in the honors equivalent course taking the same test scored better on average, but the majority of these high achieving students did not have passing scores. The average score was 47% correct, and the highest score was 80%.

Unit 3. Fur, Feathers, Scales: Insulation

Biology in a Box Unit 3, entitled Fur, Feathers, Scales: Insulation, exemplifies how students gain insight into natural selection and evolutionary change while exploring the relationship between animal structure and function on the one hand and man-made products on the other. By examining samples of body coverings from reptiles, birds, and mammals, students learn that these materials, while exhibiting different appearances, are all made of the protein keratin. The move from an aquatic existence to a fully terrestrial one was a major transition for vertebrates. Keratins are structural proteins essential in forming a variety of rigid body coverings, ranging from fur and feathers to fingernails and claws and, along with a pelvic girdle and associated development of the pentadactyl (five digit) limb, made the vertebrate transition from an aquatic environment to land possible.

Changes in keratin proteins further helped (1) free reptiles from necessary association with moist environments that amphibians require to this day; (2) provide mammals (fur) and birds (feathers) insulation to accompany endothermic metabolism; and (3) enable birds to fly with the special keratin adaptations in the form of feathers. The insulation properties of fur in mammals and fluff feathers in birds permitted these vertebrate classes to maintain body temperatures favorable to metabolic functioning in the cooler environments produced by the volcanic building of the land masses that occurred over long spans of geological time. Vandebergh and Bossuyt (2012) report that this rapid increase in the diversity of keratin proteins in tetrapods (four-limbed animals) was due to only two

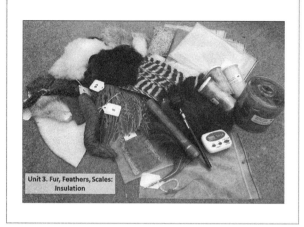

Some of the body-covering samples from Unit 3 Fur, Feathers, and Scales: Insulation

Unit 3. Fur, Feathers, Scales: Insulation

Image courtesy of Susan E. Riechert.

genes that were present in ancestral vertebrates but were changed through duplications and a shift in their functions.

After exploring the variety of fur, feathers, and scales seen in the higher vertebrates, students examine the insulation properties of body coverings in the exercise Insulation Power. They then study the principles of heat exchange in Keeping Warm. Each of these exercises starts with a qualitative examination of the respective problems followed by quantitative measurement of the insulating properties of natural and designed materials with protocols used by professional scientists.

Insulation Power. The insulation power of a material is a function of the amount of still air that it traps and is related to the material's thickness and the density (defined as the number of individual hairs or feathers per unit of surface area). The students begin by predicting the insulation power of different furs based on their physical properties. They do this by measuring the thickness and density of different fur samples and rank order them using a pairwise visual comparison technique. Each member of a team independently takes these measurements on the fur samples supplied in establishing their overall ranking of the fur types and enters the values in a table under the following headings: Fur Type, Density Rank (DR), Fur Thickness (mm), Thickness Rank (TR), Sum Rank (DR + TR), Overall Rank. Teams then combine their individual rankings into a mean score that will correct for the sampling errors individuals may make in their estimates. This ranking provides an index of insulation power based on physical characteristics of the material/fur.

Next the students test their predictions and compare the insulating powers of the furs to man-made materials by measuring the actual insulating performance of different materials. They use plastic mitts, each one filled with a different natural or man-made material between the inner and outer layers in this experiment. The students perform three different sets of trials using these mitts to demonstrate the difference between a qualitative feel test and quantitative measurement:

(1) **The qualitative test** utilizes an individual's sense of feel as well as judgment and memory, as each student compares the feeling experienced in alternately placing their hands inserted in a mitt of one material compared to another placed into a bucket of ice water.

(2) **The quantitative test** involves measuring water from a melting ice cube of standard volume placed in a mitt at room temperature for a given amount of time.

(3) **The rate of temperature change** in a simulated human body is obtained using the same mitts in the most quantitative of the exercises. A body is simulated by a copper pipe, which is capped at the bottom to represent human skin. A dial thermometer is placed into the pipe, which is then filled with warm tap water to represent body fluids. The simulated body is then placed inside the mitt, which is immersed in a bucket of ice water to simulate going outside on a very cold day. The students

observe and graph the change in temperature inside the "body" at regular intervals determined by the class. The experiment is repeated using different materials in between the two layers of the plastic mitts.

Additional materials provided in the unit kit permit students to study several other phenomena, including the effects of an oil spill on the insulation properties of fur, the effects of fluffing fur that animals are able to enact (*goose bumps* in humans), and the comparison of the insulation properties of blubber to other materials. Throughout their examination of insulation power, students are challenged to consider the limitations and survival value of body coverings to the animals that have them so that they appreciate the evolutionary advantage of these adaptations.

Keeping Warm. In this exercise, students apply mathematics to explore the phenomenon of thermal conductivity and its relationship to the R-values of insulation materials used in home and industrial applications. The questions posed here encourage open-ended exploration of the topic of insulation as it relates to animal adaptation to their natural environments versus our uses of insulation materials. For example, there are questions posed about the shedding of fur versus the deposition of body fat, adaptations to the environment in which an animal lives, the loss of heat through windows compared to insulated walls, the effects of sitting in front of a fan versus taking a dip in a swimming pool and the calculation of R-values used in home and industrial applications.

Unit 11. Biomechanics

The field of *mechanics* refers to the effects of applied forces on structures. *Biomechanics* is an interdisciplinary field at the intersection of physics and biology that concerns the effects of forces applied to living structures, including bones and muscles. Bio-mimicking is an application of biomechanics to engineering. An early example of bio-mimicking is Leonardo da Vinci's 16th-century sketches of numerous intricate flying machines. Included among his sketches were gliders, wing-flapping machines, helicopters, and parachutes that clearly were inspired by birds.

In our biomechanics unit, high school students play the roles of engineers, using the principles of biomimetics to draw from living examples to inspire their own designs. There are four groups of exercises in this unit:

From Skeletons to Bridges introduces students to the physcis of bridges and the similarities between bridges and skeletons. They also experiment with fish jaw and bird beak structures, using mechanical pliers that mimic the variety of shapes and forces that fish and birds use to procure food.

Projectile Motion explores the trajectories of falling/dropping on the one hand and of thrown or propelled objects on the other.

Wings, Flying Machines, and Seeds adds the effects of drag to the discussion of projectile motion, pointing to the importance of drag for seed dispersal in the biological world, when designing parachutes in the techological world.

Bioacoustics introduces students to the phenomenon of sound, acoustic communication in animals, and the mechanisms by which it is produced. Students also explore practical technological applications related to the science of sound such as amplification and eavesdropping.

From Skeletons to Bridges provides numerous illustrations of how bones and skeletons respond to patterns of stress with appropriate adaptations just as engineers design such adaptations into the structures that they create. Take, for example, the fact that the human thigh bone consists of a complex framework (truss) of tiny ridges. An engineer and anatomist recognized the similarity in structure between the human thigh bone and the designed truss as a response to the three main types of stress that structures experience: tension, compression, and bending (as shown below).

Student teams examine these three forces by attempting to stretch, compress, and bend thick glue gun sticks. They then apply the understanding they gained from their investigations in designing and constructing bridges using plastic pieces and strands of uncooked spaghetti. The teams compete to see which can design a bridge with the best mass/strength ratio. Following the first competition, students are introduced to the skeletal structure of quadrupeds (animals that walk on all fours) by first examining the articulated skeleton of a rat, provided with the unit kit, and then by examining other

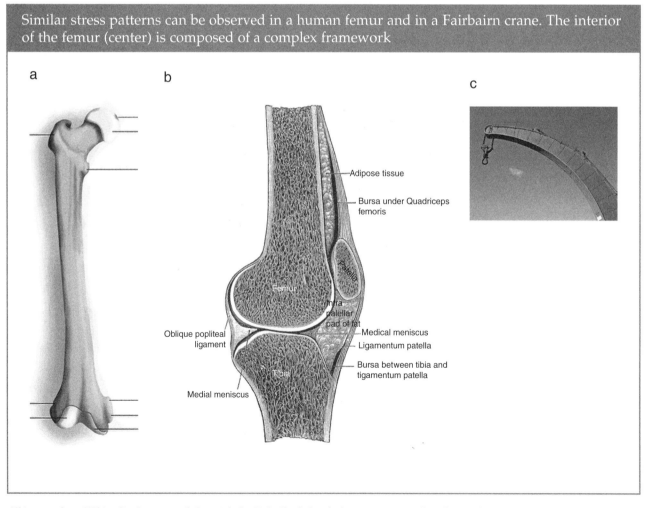

Similar stress patterns can be observed in a human femur and in a Fairbairn crane. The interior of the femur (center) is composed of a complex framework

All images from Wikipedia Commons, left to right by F. Gaillard, *Gray's Anatomy*, 1918, and Andy Dingly.

skeletons they locate on the web. A second bridge-building competition follows, incorporating the inspiration each team has gained from examining the quadruped's spine and supporting limbs. Before leaving bridge building, students are introduced to the bipedal human skeleton, a design compromise, as evidenced by the slight arch present as an evolutionary holdover from our quadrupedal ancestors.

This group of exercises also integrates hands-on use of simple tools with morphological measurements, trigonometry, and biomechanical models to understand functional systems such as the trophic/feeding apparatus of fish (jaws) and of birds (beaks). A pair of pliers is a form of lever that can be used to gain a mechanical advantage in applying a force to an object. Students first experiment with the simplest form of lever, a teeter-totter (wooden ruler in our case) that pivots on a fulcrum. The force is applied downward at one end of the ruler with the load to be raised at the other end. In a pair of pliers, the effort (force) is applied from two directions in the closing of the handles and this serves to grasp and grip objects. Animals need to grip food items to tear, manipulate, and prepare them for consumption. In our exercises, we provide a variety of pairs of pliers and information on various fish and birds, including their food preferences and the shapes of their jaws and beaks (shown below). The goal is to test the tools on simulated food items for their efficiency in

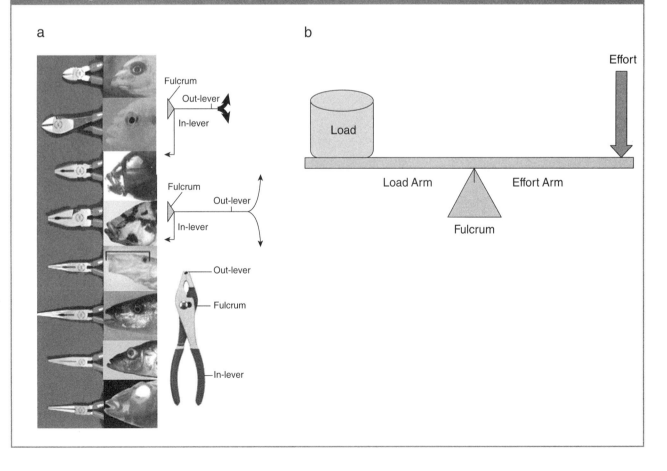

Pliers can be used to mimic jaws and beaks. Above is a simple class one lever showing movement of the load in opposite direction to the force (effort). To the left is an image of different Malawi cichlid jaws compared with different pairs of pliers (double class one levers), illustrating how different jaw configurations generate different forces.

grasping, tearing apart, popping open, and so forth. The food items will vary in type and size, making the challenge quite complex. The goal is to then match each bird and fish with the type of pliers that best mimics the operation of their jaw or beak.

At the end of this exercise, groups of students are encouraged to choose other biological mechanisms and corresponding technologies to investigate. Several examples are provided, including the examination of tree shape as a function of size (tower construction), jumping ability of fleas (springs), process of walking (pendulums), and power generation versus speed in millipede and centipede gaits (gears). Students might also investigate technological advances in the construction of bridges, towers, buildings, skyscrapers, cables, beams, vehicle frames, and airplane body and wing structures, all which follow the basic engineering principles seen in animal skeletons.

Projectile Motion describes what occurs when an object is thrown, launched, or projected. It continues in motion and is influenced only by the downward force of gravity. Projectile motion falls under the discipline of physics known as *kinematics* (the study of motion). The mathematics underlying kinematics includes trigonometry and calculus and math exercises associated with this topic in our Biomechanics Unit, require that students have had some exposure to these math subjects.

Projectile motion has important technological applications in ballistics and is also important in studying organisms. At its simplest, projectile motion is free fall in which the object has only a vertical component. Animals exhibit free fall (i.e., drop off trees, ledges) to escape predators and in the pursuit of prey. The seeds of many tree species exhibit free fall as a mechanism of dispersal from the parent plant. Though less common than free fall, there are animals that launch materials in defense (e.g., horny toads squirt blood from their eyes at predators, monkeys and elephants launch objects) and/or as a prey-capture mechanism (e.g., spitting spiders squirt glue to capture prey items and spitting cobras shoot venom). There are also plant species that use launch as a mechanism of seed dispersal (e.g., jewel weed, *Impatiens sp.* called "touch me not" for its propensity to shower the person bumping it with seeds). The launch involves both vertical and horizontal components of motion.

In exploring free fall, students experiment with balls of the same diameter, but different densities, that they drop from different heights. Entering their data into scatterplots allows the students to search for patterns to learn the rules that govern free fall.

Students then use a straw rocket powered by a bicycle pump (shown at left) to explore the effects of angle of projection and pressure level on the distance a straw travels and its' time to landing, recording their data in scatterplots. Students that have had calculus will be able to compare the theoretical predictions of distance traveled with the actual distances determined experimentally.

In a final exercise on projectile motion, students tackle the classic monkey and a zookeeper problem. The monkey has climbed a tree next to a boundary fence and is hanging from a limb about to drop to freedom. Assuming that the monkey jumps at the exact moment a tranquillizer dart leaves his gun, the

The straw rocket launcher included in the *Biology in a Box* Biomechanics Unit allows students to investigate free fall and projectile motion, as well as to test their solutions to the famous monkey and the zookeeper problem.

Image courtesy of Susan E. Riechert.

zookeeper needs to determine where to aim in order to hit the monkey in the midst of its free fall and thereby capture it before it escapes from the zoo. A magnet holding a stuffed monkey to a metal hanger releases the monkey to free fall simultaneously with depression of the launch button of the straw rocket. Students completing the correct calculations and adjusting the angle of the rocket and pressure with which the straw is launched will hit the monkey with the straw before it reaches the floor.

Examples of open-ended exploration suggestions for projectile motion include (1) web-based research on horny toad size versus that of potential predators and the distances and angles of launch that would be required to hit a particular predator in the face with the toxic blood; (2) construction and tests of a plant model that utilizes a launch mechanism in dispersing its seeds; and (3) a solution to a scenario in which researchers conducting a biodiversity assessment of an underwater community need to shoot animals with paintballs so that they are counted only once. This last problem leads students into Wings, Flying Machines, and Seeds, which addresses the problem of drag.

Wings, Flying Machines, and Seeds. Under Projectile motion, gravity is considered to be the only significant force underlying the time for an object to fall a given distance. However, many animals and seeds have adaptations that introduce air resistance or drag force. Drag is extremely important to organisms for its use in slowing down free fall in animal gliders and in seeds that utilize air currents as a dispersal mechanism. Drag also has disadvantages since there is an energy cost in animal locomotion. In this set of exercises, students learn about the influences of gravity and air resistance on seeds that are dispersed by wind.

All the seeds shown in the figure below disperse by air currents but utilize different morphologies. Plants are for the most part stationary, presenting a problem. That is, seedlings falling below the parent are in competition for water and for light. So there are survival advantages for seeds that can be dispersed to land out of this range. However, if seeds are dispersed *too* far, they could land in an unfavorable habitat, where germination might not occur or in which growth of the new plant would be poor, also reducing fitness. The various mechanisms of seed dispersal, then, reflect adaptations that are responses to each of these (and other) pressures, which vary in intensity among species.

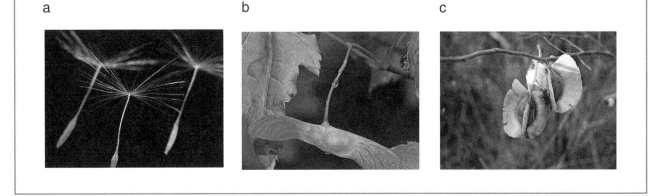

Fruits (with seeds) dispersed by wind. Left: The tuft-like pappus of dandelion fruits allows them to float on even very light breezes. Right: Samaras (winged fruits) from various trees (ash, elm, and maples).

All images from Wikipedia Commons, left to right by Piccolo Namek, Wsiegmund, and Marco Schmidt.

Students in this exercise complete a series of experiments in which they drop paper and cardboard cutouts of different seed shapes (holding mass constant). Their results lead to the discussion of factors that affect the drag force on an object. Using the equation for the drag force, they might modify parameters to examine, for instance, how much drag a cheetah encounters if it is running twice as fast as another cheetah it is trying to outrace for a prey item. Here, students are introduced to the idea of energetic costs to organisms. The technological equivalent is the increased cost of fuel as a car travels faster and faster. The students also can consider the effect of drag on terminal velocity of a seed, and what it might mean for the potential of a seed to drift on air currents away from its parent. The same set of ideas can be applied to analyze a parachute, in which terminal velocity must be low enough to preserve the parachutist's life, but if it is too low the parachutist might be blown too far from the landing target.

Bioacoustics. *Acoustics* is an interdisciplinary science that involves the study of mechanical waves, including vibration and sound. The ability to detect and interpret sounds is important to animal detection of prey, avoidance of predators and other dangers. Most species also use vibrational channels to communicate with each other and even to eavesdrop on others. Animal communication provides the impetus for innumerable engineering applications in acoustics, which may be directed toward sound dampening, amplification, or detection. In our series of exercises, students explore the four methods of animal sound production through analyses of recordings and by experimenting with musical instruments that represent the different mechanisms. Using frog calls, they learn how sound communication patterns can track taxonomic relationships. They also learn about the waveforms of sounds and how they relate to the auditory properties of sounds and learn to interpret graphical representations of sound, matching these sonograms to actual songs produced by frogs and birds. Finally, they consider volume, attenuation as it is influenced by distance and habitat and the technological proofing systems developed to Stop that Noise!

Biology in a Box and the NGSS

The NGSS is built around three dimensions of science learning: crosscutting concepts, science and engineering practices, and core ideas. *Biology in a Box* provides learning experiences in all three dimensions.

Crosscutting Concepts. There is perhaps no better example of the crosscutting concept *structure and function* as exercises in which students observe a natural structure and compare it with a human-made structure or in which they are inspired by a natural object or organism to design a solution to a human need. Biomimetics is the quintessential science for illustrating connections between structure and function—both in the natural world and in the designed world.

Another crosscutting concept that is illustrated by biomimetics is *systems and system models*. Each of the phenomena that students study is an essential element of a biological system. Fur keeps animals warm and feathers enable flight. In *Biology in a Box*, students build and investigate models of these biological mechanisms to study how they function in the natural world, thereby gaining insights into how similar structures may function in the designed world.

Engineering Design Practices. In *Biology in a Box*, students analyze various designs and also create their own, providing opportunities for the students to engage in the following engineering practices:

- Define problems raised by human needs that have already been "solved" by the evolutionary process.
- Develop and use models of natural structures.
- Plan and carry out investigations to determine the properties of natural and human-made structures.
- Analyze data from their investigations.
- Use mathematics to quantify the properties of structures, and use computational thinking to simulate how structures behave under different loads.
- Design and test solutions to problems.
- Argue from evidence about the expected performance of one structure over another to best serve a particular function.
- Obtain, evaluate, and communicate information about structures in the natural world that may serve as models for structures needed to meet human needs.

Core Ideas. Although the units were developed before publication of the NGSS (NGSS Lead States, 2013), many of the units provide opportunities for teachers to help their students meet performance expectations. For example, virtually every organism that students investigate provides opportunities for them to reflect on performance expectations related to core idea LS4 Biological Evolution, Unity, and Diversity. In the biomechanics unit, the cluster of exercises related to projectile motion provides excellent opportunities for students to reflect on the performance expectations related to PS2 Motion and Stability: Forces and Interactions.

We have borrowed from classic exercises in physics and elsewhere in developing our offerings on biomimetics but utilize them in our themes to demonstrate that we can learn much from nature.

References

Bartlett, M. D., Croll, A. B., King, D. R., Paret, B. M., Irschick, D. J., & Crosby, A. J. (2012). Looking beyond fibrillar features to scale gecko-like adhesion. *Advanced Materials, 24*(8), 1078–1083.

Bishop, B. A., & Anderson, C. W. (1990). Student conceptions of natural selection and its role in evolution. *Journal of research in science teaching, 27*(5), 415–427. Retrieved from: http://onlinelibrary.wiley.com/doi/10.1002/tea.3660270503/abstract

Chary, S., Tamelier, J., & Turner, K. (2013). A microfabricated gecko-inspired controllable and reusable dry adhesive. *Smart Materials and Structures, 22*(2), 025013.

NGSS Lead States. (2013). *Next generation science standards: For states, by states, volume 1: The standards.* Washington, DC: National Academies Press.

NRC. (1996). *National Science Education Standards.* Washington, DC: National Academies Press.

Vandebergh, W., & Bossuyt, F. (2012). Radiation and functional diversification of alpha keratins during early vertebrate evolution. *Molecular biology and evolution, 29*(3), 995–1004.

Yurdumakan, B., Raravikar, N. R., Ajayan, P. M., & Dhinojwala, A. Synthetic gecko foot-hairs from multiwalled carbon nanotubes. *Chemical Communications, 2005*, 3799–3780.

Endnote

1. See Unit 10 Animal Behavior Exercise 3 Slap Snack Mimic of the *Biology in a Box* Project (http://biologyinabox.utk.edu).

11

Voyages Through Time and the Evolution of Technology

Pamela Harman and Edna DeVore

SETI Institute, Mountain View, CA

Evolutionary change is a powerful framework for studying our world and our place therein. As the illustration shows, the universe, the planet Earth, life, human technologies, and science all change, although on vastly different scales. Evolution offers scientific answers to the age-old question, "Where did we come from?" This story of epic size, capable of expanding our sense of time and place, is the basis of *Voyages Through Time*.

Image courtesy of NASA.

*V*oyages Through Time™ (Tarter et al., 2003) is a year-long, integrated science curriculum for ninth or tenth grade, based on the theme of evolution. In *Voyages Through Time,* evolution is defined as cumulative change over time that occurs in all realms of the natural and designed world. The evolutionary scope of *Voyages Through Time* (VTT) is billions of years long and ranges from the Big Bang to modern technologies. The evolution of everything provides a compelling "storyline" for the entire curriculum.

The SETI Institute led the development of VTT as a core project in the Center for Education and Outreach. The breadth of the scientific research at the SETI Institute is enormous:

The mission of the SETI Institute is to explore, understand and explain the origin, nature and prevalence of life in the universe.

The scientific research, education and outreach programs are interrelated and focused on this overarching scientific question, "Are we alone?" SETI researchers have pursued a multimodal approach since Frank Drake first formulated the Drake Equation in 1961 (http://www.seti.org/drakeequation). This equation organizes our knowledge and our ignorance about subjects ranging from the birth and death of stars to the evolution of intelligence and technology. More and more, scientists and other researchers are embracing the interdisciplinary approach. In the late 1990s, NASA launched astrobiology research, astrobiology technology development, and created a virtual institute of scientists and educators pursuing interdisciplinary research and education across the United States and internationally.

VTT is an astrobiology curriculum with thousands of users, and the SETI Institute has trained hundreds of high school educators to teach astrobiology in classrooms using VTT and other resources in their summer program. Scientific disciplines are merging and morphing, integrating, and adapting in amazing ways. Biology has become the basis for microchips, and the infant field of computational biology is using the formal systems analysis of electrical engineering to understand in detail the functioning of the cell. Students need to be exposed to the concept that a problem, or a question, defines the scope of today's scientific exploration, and that the tools used to answer that question will be identified, learned, borrowed, and modified from any discipline that promises to move our understanding forward.

This chapter provides a brief overview of *Voyages Through Time* and features the culminating module, Evolution of Technology. This module combines class investigations of the essential role of technology in the development of human civilization with student projects that explore a specific technology as it has evolved over time. Although the module will be most effectively used in the context of the entire VTT series, it can be used as the opening or closing module in an integrated science course or engineering course sequence.

In the experiences of the teachers who helped develop and teach VTT, their students often compartmentalize their classes. For example, students do not often draw connections between scientific domains such as astronomy, biology, and chemistry, yet all those subjects help us understand the habitability of planets, including Earth. VTT aimed to bridge these domains by repeatedly asking the same thematic questions in each module:

- What is changing?
- What is the rate/scale of change?
- What are the mechanisms for change?

Helping students understand the scientific explanation of where they came from and what their future might hold seemed to us to be the most compelling theme possible. Using all time and all space, the VTT curriculum allows students to calibrate their own personal place in the universe and to stretch their concept of past and future. The spatial scales of this curriculum cover the largest thing there is (the universe) down to the cellular and atomic. Time spans measure change over billions of years in *Cosmic Evolution* to just over the 18-month doubling time of digital technology (Moore's Law) in Evolution of Technology. If some students become inspired to wonder about whether intelligent beings on distant planets circling other stars are also trying to figure out how they fit into the scheme of the universe, then VTT has succeeded.

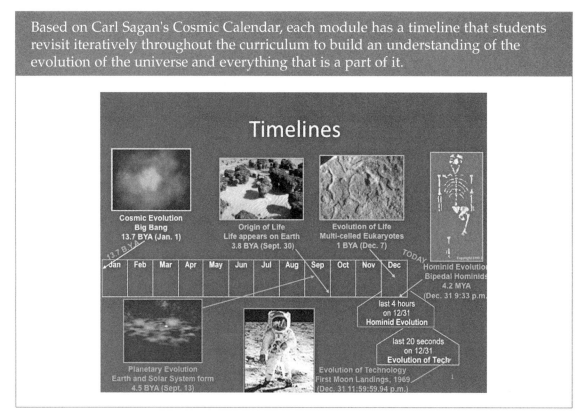

Based on Carl Sagan's Cosmic Calendar, each module has a timeline that students revisit iteratively throughout the curriculum to build an understanding of the evolution of the universe and everything that is a part of it.

Image courtesy of the SETI Institute.

Overview

The year-long VTT curriculum is divided into six modules: Cosmic Evolution, Planetary Evolution, Origin of Life, Evolution of Life, Hominid Evolution, and Evolution of Technology. The modules are unified by key questions about evolutionary change, a consistent pedagogical approach, and timelines. Taken together, the six VTT modules comprise a year-long integrated science course. Each module requires about six weeks of classroom time. Individual modules can stand alone and are used in discipline-based science courses such as biology, earth science, geology, engineering, or astronomy where integrated science is not offered. The overarching goals are for students to understand

- Evolution as cumulative changes over time;
- The various processes underlying these changes;
- The differing time scales and rates of change;
- The connections and relationships across these realms of change;
- Science as a process for advancing our understanding of the natural world.

The first five modules of VTT focus on science that begins with the origin of the universe and culminates in studying the evolution of hominids. The sixth module, Evolution of Technology, focuses on the interactions among invention, engineering and science. Each module is described in greater detail on the VTT website: http://www .voyagesthroughtime.org. (Images in this section are courtesy of Learning in Motion.)

Cosmic Evolution. The universe, the totality of all things that exist, is thought to have begun with an explosion of space and time and the expansion of a hot, dense mass of elementary particles and photons, that has evolved over billions of years into the stars and galaxies we observe today. This grand epic is the story told in the Cosmic Evolution module. The module introduces astronomy, the electromagnetic spectrum as a tool to study the universe at multiple wavelengths, cosmic distances, the origin of the universe in the Big Bang, gravity, and the formation of galaxies and stars, the evolution of stars, and the origin of elements; we are made of star dust.

Planetary Evolution. We live and walk on the surface of a planet rich with life and the resources to sustain it. Two thirds of the Earth is covered with water, and much of the land is lush with plants and animals. But when we look up to the night sky, the Moon, our nearest neighbor, is clearly quite different. It is cold, riddled with craters, and to all appearances, lifeless. A look at the surfaces of Venus and Mars reveals them to be hellishly hot and bone-chillingly cold, respectively, with little chance of life on them today. Planetary Evolution compares our home planet with Venus and Mars and explores what makes it possible for the Earth to support life.

Origin of Life. Current evidence from the rock and fossil record indicates that life on Earth began about 3.8 billion years ago. Yet how life first formed, or even how the biochemical precursors of life developed, and under what conditions these events happened, are not yet understood. The origin of life is an area of active research, with considerable debate among scientists from various disciplines. The Origin of Life module combines what is known about life with the research and debate about life's beginnings and early history.

Evolution of Life. The great diversity of multicelled life on Earth today, how this diversity came to be, the processes that shape diversity, and the relationships among living things are the major topics of this module. The Evolution of Life explores the range of different environments in which living things are found. Students gain an appreciation for the diversity and abundance of life by making estimates of worldwide species richness. Students focus on the changing distributions of living things, the relationship between these changes and geologic changes, and changes in the types of living things over the history of life on Earth.

Hominid Evolution. The hominid family, characterized by bipedal locomotion, appeared between four and five million years ago. This defining event in human evolution was followed by other key events: increased brain size, the initial migration of hominids out of the tropics, and a transition from hunting and gathering to agriculture. While anthropologists agree on this broad sweep of our history, limited data and differing perspectives result in various interpretations and lively debate in the field. In the Hominid Evolution module, the investigation of key events is combined with an examination of this dynamic field.

Evolution of Technology. The Evolution of Technology module provides an introduction and context for students studying the interaction between invention, science, engineering and technology. It can be used in the science classroom to develop understandings of the relationships among science, engineering, invention and technology. It can also be used to introduce an engineering unit or project so that students develop a better understanding of what technology is. Students' understanding of the nature of engineering can be expanded as they explore technologies or processes in a historical context. Changes in technology become apparent, which is evidence of the iterative process of engineering.

The module is divided into six lessons over six weeks. The first lesson, What is Technology? begins with an assessment of students' current understanding about technology. Students then examine and sort a variety of common gadgets to identify the major categories of technology according to the human needs they meet and then pose initial definitions of technology. A student reader article on chopsticks and forks leads to a discussion of the effects of location and culture on the development of technologies.

Lesson two, Technologies Over Time, starts with the construction of a scaled timeline of major events throughout the history of technology in the context of the evolution of everything, beginning with the Big Bang about 13.8 billion years ago. Students are then introduced to the technology poster project, which requires them to research a particular technology and produce a poster on it. This introduction is done via an example project on the radio. Students learn to use the assessment rubric, which outlines the poster requirements, as they explore radio as a sample project. The lesson continues with students beginning their own projects, researching and identifying key events in the histories of their selected technologies and preparing this information for their posters.

Lesson three, How Technologies Work, begins with students building a simple radio and examining its structures and functions. The radio serves as a model to introduce the next part of the students' projects: identifying the scientific principles involved in their own project topics. Class time is provided for students to conduct research and produce a model or other visual display. Some students will disassemble a piece of technology as a part of their research.

In Effects of Technology, lesson four, students first examine a light bulb, learning about the materials from which it is made and the countries from which the United States imports these materials. This prepares students to use a geographical database of natural resources to investigate the materials used to produce the technology they are investigating. They produce a resource map for their posters. Each of these activities engages students in discussions of global effects of technology. Students go on to examine effects of technology on individuals, using the results of surveys they have been conducting (introduced in lesson three) and the interrelationships among technologies in general. Class time is provided for students to work on the effects of technology sections of their posters.

Lesson five, Into the Future, starts with students graphing sample data from each major technology category to determine how these technologies developed over time and to project the potential development into the future. They then discuss how the human needs met by the technologies they researched may be met differently in the future.

The final project is a poster that includes five sections. As students tackle each part of the project, the activity is modeled in the classroom through the study of the radio as a model. These are the poster elements:

- *History*: An extended timeline of important events in the development of the technology drawn from science, engineering, invention, and other technologies, including a timescale.
- *Science*: How does the technology work, or how was it made? A disassembled example, scale or working model, or well-labeled photograph, drawing, or other image.
- *Effects of Technology*: Where do the resources come from to build the technology being studied? Illustrate with a resources map, survey quotes, and relationships diagram.

- *Into the Future*: What is the future of the technology? What might it evolve into?
- *Abstract*: A summary of the general category, the human needs met, how and when the technology evolved, the materials and resources provided and their sources, effects on individuals and society, relationship to other technology categories, and how the technology might evolve in the future.

The final lesson, Closing, begins with a poster session, like those held at scientific conferences, in which students share their completed posters and analyze them for common trends. In their analyses, they are asked to recapitulate the major concepts of the module, including cultural changes and scientific advancements fueled by technology. In some schools, these poster sessions are held so that students from across the school can learn about the projects and discuss the information with the student authors.

There are also three summative assessments of student learning: a take-home essay based on the poster analyses, a concept map, and a reflection on initial and final definitions of technology.

Supporting materials are provided for the teacher, including a comprehensive assessment rubric and strategies for managing projects and student teams. The module identifies resources that support project-specific and general areas of technology studies. Materials are also provided for students, including the scoring rubric, research help, general resources, Student Reader articles, and design suggestions.

Connections to the NGSS

Although Evolution of Technology was developed and published in 2003, the design of the module clearly addresses the core ideas of engineering from the *Framework*. The use of the terms *science, engineering,* and *technology* in the module are consistent with the definitions in the National Research Council's *Framework for K–12 Science Education: Practices, Crosscutting Concepts, and Core Ideas* (NRC, 2012):

In the K–12 context, science is generally taken to mean the traditional natural sciences: physics, chemistry, biology, and (more recently) earth, space, and environmental sciences. . . . Engineering and technology are included as they relate to the applications of science, and in so doing they offer students a path to strengthen their understanding of the role of sciences. We use the term engineering in a very broad sense to mean any engagement in a systematic practice of design to achieve solutions to particular human problems. Likewise, we broadly use the term technology to include all types of human-made systems and processes—not in the limited sense often used in schools that equates technology with modern computational and communications devices. Technologies result when engineers apply their understanding of the natural world and of human behavior to design ways to satisfy human needs and wants. (NRC, 2012, pp. 11–12)

The *Framework* defines practices and knowledge for both science and engineering. The driving engineering questions from the *Framework* are as follows:

- What can be done to address a particular human need or want?
- How can the need be better specified?

- What tools and technologies are available, or could be developed, for addressing this need?
- How does one communicate about phenomena, evidence, explanations, and design solutions?

With the publication of the NGSS (NGSS Lead States, 2013), Engineering, Technology, and the Applications of Science (ETS) is changing the nature of high school science courses. The Evolution of Technology module provides instructional materials and strategies that teachers can employ to help meet the new standards the integrate engineering and technology into the science classroom. Table 11.1 illustrates the correlation between these new standards and the Evolution of Technology curriculum.

Table 11.1 Evolution of Technology Module Alignment With Three Dimensions in the NGSS

Evolution of Technology Lesson Groups	L1	L2	L3	L4	L5	L6
Lesson 1 What Is Technology?						
Lesson 2 Technologies Over Time						
Lesson 3 How Technologies Work						
Lesson 4 Effects of Technology						
Lesson 5 Into the Future						
Lesson 6 Closing						
Performance Expectations						
HS-ETS1-1 Analyze a major global challenge to specify qualitative and quantitative criteria and constraints for solutions that account for societal needs and wants.			✓	✓	✓	✓
HS-ETS1-2 Design a solution to a complex real-world problem by breaking it down into smaller, more manageable problems that can be solved through engineering.		✓				
HS-ETS1-3 Evaluate a solution to a complex real-world problem based on prioritized criteria and trade-offs that account for a range of constraints, including cost, safety, reliability, and aesthetics, as well as possible social, cultural, and environmental impacts.			✓		✓	
Science and Engineering Practices						
Asking questions and defining problems	✓	✓				
Developing and using models	✓	✓	✓	✓	✓	✓
Obtaining, evaluating, and communicating information.			✓	✓	✓	✓
Crosscutting Concepts						
Systems and system models	✓	✓	✓	✓	✓	✓
Stability and change	✓	✓	✓	✓	✓	✓

Instructional Materials

The teacher's manual is digital and includes the media required for lessons, short and extended lesson guides, background articles on lesson content and common student misconceptions, evaluation tools, and all print files for student materials. Because the manual is digital, it has been updated when scientific discoveries changed our understanding of the natural world. For example, when the age of the universe was determined to be 13.8 billion years, rather than 15 billion years, the timelines and age-of-the-universe related materials were all updated throughout the curriculum.

Print files of student materials are provided both as PDFs and text documents that can be edited. Digital materials for student use include a database activity in each module where students explore data with a computer as a scientist might do while conducting research. The materials are available on CD-ROMs and, in some schools, are hosted on servers. In the modules, rich background information is provided for teachers who may be unfamiliar with particular science topics. The expertise of practicing scientists is provided in the articles and video interviews that help students see them as "real people." Finally, there is a Student Reader for each module that includes articles written for the curriculum or drawn from popular science journals. The Student Reader articles are a key part of the lessons and secondarily introduce students to popular science publications that they may continue to read as adults.

Lesson groups and activities are teacher-directed and student-centered. Teachers use the digital files to prepare and to present activities, and students participate in a variety of inquiry-based learning experiences, ranging from microscope explorations of live cultures, to density and differentiation experiments, to computer-based database activities and student readers.

The curriculum uses the guided inquiry approach known as the 5Es—Engage, Explore, Explain, Elaborate, Evaluate—from the Biological Sciences Curriculum Study (Bybee, 1997; Bybee & Landes, 1990). In the 5 Es pedagogy, students are actively involved in developing their own understanding of phenomena through experimentation and observation (Engage, Explore) prior to direct instruction (Explain). Subsequently, students apply new understandings (Elaborate) and finally demonstrate their new knowledge (Evaluate). The modules are designed so that students work individually as well as in teams. All modules include student projects in addition to group activities.

Conclusion

Through the sequence of activities and discussions in Evolution of Technology, students learn that technology involves manipulation of the environment to meet human needs such as food, shelter, communication, and health. Broadly defined, technology is much more than the most recent cell phones and video games.

Students learn that technology has been present throughout human history. The rapid development of technology has had profound effects on human society and the environment, especially within the last 10,000 years, which has seen the development of agriculture, the consolidation of vast numbers of people living in cities, and advances in transportation, construction, medicine and health, energy production and distribution, and communication. They will also recognize how society influences the development and spread of technology. By the time students complete the module, they will recognize that the development and use of technology helps define what it means to be human.

We believe that these ideas are an essential complement to any course in which students develop engineering skills so that they can appreciate the power of engineering and the wider landscape and deep history of the designed world.

Acknowledgments

Just as the big questions in science require an integrated and collaborative effort, so does *Voyages Through Time*. The VTT curriculum development was led by the SETI Institute, in collaboration with scientific researchers and educators at several leading institutions. The VTT science content was developed in conjunction with over forty scientists, who provided current scientific content and extensively reviewed VTT for accuracy.

Teachers and science educators oversaw the pedagogy of VTT for its appropriateness for early high school students and classroom instruction. Scientists from the NASA Ames Research Center worked on the Cosmic Evolution, Planetary Evolution, and Origin of Life modules. Scientists and educators from the California Academy of Sciences collaborated on the Evolution of Life, Hominid Evolution, and Evolution of Technology modules. Scientists and science educators from San Francisco State University and WestEd worked across all modules.

Thanks to our location in the San Francisco Bay Area, additional assistance came from the University of California campuses at Berkeley and Santa Cruz, Stanford University, Santa Clara University, and the United States Geological Survey. Finally, teachers from California and 27 other states were instrumental in the development and classroom testing of VTT. Learning In Motion, the publisher, provided media development.

VTT was funded by a major grant from the National Science Foundation (#9730693) with additional support from Hewlett-Packard Company, the Foundation for Microbiology, NASA Astrobiology Institute, NASA Fundamental Biology Program, the SETI Institute, the Combined Charitable Campaign, and many private donations.

References

Bybee, R. W. (1997). *Achieving scientific literacy: From purposes to practices*. Portsmouth, NH: Heinemann.

Bybee, R. W., & Landes, N. M. (1990, February). Science for life and living: An elementary school science program from Biological Sciences Curriculum Study. *The American Biology Teacher, 52*(2), 92–98.

NGSS Lead States (2013). *Next generation science standards: For states, by states, volume 1: The standards*. Washington, DC: National Academies Press.

NRC. (2012). *A framework for K–12 science education: Practices, crosscutting concepts, and core ideas*. Washington, DC: National Academies Press.

Tarter, J., Burke, M., DeVore, E., Fisher, J., O'Sullivan, K., Pendleton, Y. (2003). *Voyages through time*. Santa Cruz, CA: Learning in Motion. Retrieved from: http://www.voyagesthroughtime.org

12

EPICS High Program

William Oakes, Mindy Hart, Jean Trusedell, Philip Cardella

Purdue University, West Lafayette, IN

Students working in an EPICS lab

Image courtesy of Chantilly Academy

Engineering Projects in Community Service (EPICS) uses service-learning to engage students in real engineering projects to meet needs in their communities. Service-learning and engineering are not traditionally linked but the combination offers a wealth of opportunities for students to experience authentic design as well as connect engineering with people and community needs that matter to them and their families

(Lima & Oakes, 2012). The results of EPICS High projects are delivered to the community and used by real people.

The EPICS High model is based on the internationally recognized University EPICS curriculum that was created at Purdue University and used at more than 20 institutions worldwide (Coyle, Jamieson, & Oakes 2005, 2006). EPICS High is the precollege branch of EPICS that engages students in real design experiences that align with the Next Generation Science Standards (NGSS Lead States, 2013) and leave their community a better place.

Connecting engineering and computing with human and community needs is a critical component cited by the National Academy of Engineering's Report, *Changing the Conversation* (National Academy of Engineering, 2008) to increasing interest among young people and attracting them to pathways into and through engineering. Engineering-based service-learning makes this link explicitly. The approach is consistent with other research on increasing participation and interest in engineering and computing especially among diverse populations. The results confirm the link as EPICS High has grown to more than 50 schools and over 2000 students in 11 states with 44% female participation and more than 50% of the students being students of color. Data also shows that EPICS High increased interest in engineering and STEM and draws students into the STEM pathways who report no interest prior to participating (Oakes et al., 2012; Matusovich, Oakes, & Zoltowski, 2013).

EPICS High is an affordable and flexible curriculum. It starts with teacher training either facilitated by EPICS leaders in person or by an online course that can be taken any time. EPICS also offers a vast network of partners with connections to communities and professionals that can help mentor students as they address authentic community needs. A unique goal of the program is to engage students otherwise underrepresented in STEM courses, with a focus on engaging female and ethnically diverse populations. Highlights of the program and approach are included in this chapter.

EPICS is headquartered at Purdue University and provides some materials for free distribution through the websites and other more in-depth materials for fees that cover costs of developing and maintaining the program. Information is available at the EPICS High website: https://engineering.purdue.edu/EPICSHS.

EPICS High in Action

EPICS High partnerships involve schools of all types. EPICS High programs are underway in rural, suburban, and urban schools. Public, charter, and private schools have found ways to integrate EPICS into their curriculum. The EPICS High curriculum is designed to be flexible. It has been used to create dedicated engineering design classes, to support projects within an existing science, math, agriculture, technology, or computing class, as well as after-school programs. Four examples are highlighted below and other examples can be found at the EPICS High website.

Xavier College Prep in Phoenix, Arizona

An exceptional example of EPICS High at work is Xavier College Prep in Phoenix, Arizona. In the fall of 2013, Xavier began their fourth year using the EPICS model. What sets Xavier apart, aside from outstanding academics, is that it is an all-girls high school. The EPICS model immediately caught on at the school, merging student interest in service-learning and outstanding academics with themes the Catholic school found integrated well with Catholic themes of social service teaching. By its second year, EPICS at Xavier was enrolling approximately 150 young women and involved four teachers.

Some of the EPICS High projects at Xavier have focused on helping their own school community, resulting in a number of innovative and useful designs, including a small footprint technology cart for classroom use, a telescope stand for the astronomy classes, and a redesign of the existing technology classroom and support spaces to make better use of space while improving traffic flow and reducing noise between classroom spaces.

Xavier has also developed partnerships with a number of community organizations, including Weldon House, operated by the National Council on Alcohol and Drug Dependence, with a number of warehouse projects to help store and organize incoming donations, and the Rio Salado Habitat Restoration Project, an inner city area, now a city park, that has been restored to a native riparian habitat. Other projects have included ways to protect the native cottonwood from the resident beaver population, the design of a butterfly garden as a migration stop for Monarch butterflies, education projects, and the development of landscape and seating areas for park-goers.

In addition, Xavier is working with one for-profit company, PetSmart, to aid in their *Zero Waste by 2020* initiative. In this collaboration, student teams will look at possible ways to reuse or recycle the large volume of pet hair clippings, which currently find their way into landfills.

More recent projects include Arizona Forward's Grand Canalscape project, designed to revitalize the area around the centuries-old canal system in central Phoenix, and the City of Phoenix and the PHX Renews Project, a pilot program with a vision to turn vacant urban lots into public art and education spaces. At the PHX Renews pilot site in downtown Phoenix, student teams have designed and will be installing an outdoor classroom with an interactive sundial built into the classroom stage. The PHX Renews site also includes collaboration between Xavier EPICS and the Arizona Science Center to develop and install an interactive pervious concrete demonstration exhibit.

In 2012, EPICS High students at Xavier partnered with a mission in Ghana to help find cost-effective and healthier alternatives to charcoal and wood-burning fireplaces for native families to cook meals and bake food. A variety of alternatives have been explored and students are hoping to develop an appropriate technology using either biofuel or solar options. Additionally, the team will produce an instructional video and documentation that the mission can share with local residents to teach them how to make and maintain their own ovens using available resources.

Another way that the EPICS teams at Xavier engage local schools is through a program they call Girls Have IT (Information Technology) Camp. The camps were modeled after their own annual Girls Have IT Day. This mini summer camp engages middle school girls in a wide variety of STEAM (science, technology, engineering, art, and math) activities. This camp shows middle school girls that they can really "do math and science." Data collected by the EPICS team at Xavier from their annual event has shown that many of the attendees do not even know what engineering is when they arrive, yet leave knowing they "can do this" and are excited, and encouraged, that they can be successful in STEM classes in high school and college.

George Westinghouse College Prep, Chicago, Illinois

George Westinghouse College Prep (GWCP) is a public, selective enrollment school in Chicago, Illinois, that opened its doors in 2009. The mission of the school is to empower students with the academic, social, career, and technological skills necessary for postsecondary success. EPICS has been used by students at the school to meet the requirement that all students donate 40 hours to service-learning projects.

Students in the EPICS program at GWCP began with projects that addressed local needs identified by the students, ranging from a cell phone app for self-guided tours for the Chicago Center for Green Technology, to creating manipulative tools for 4th graders that teach the younger students fractions, to a project with a program called the Alliance for the Great Lakes benefiting the Chicago Park District.

A recent project was designed to improve the plant collection database for the Garfield Park Conservatory, to benefit visitors and those who work at the conservatory. As is typical with all EPICS Projects, the student teams used the EPICS model to identify community needs and stakeholders, partner with community members to assess those needs, design a proposed solution, and deliver a product to the stake holders. When they completed the project, the students provided a user manual for the database so the staff could make updates after it was delivered. GWCP is an exemplar of integrating other disciplines (such as computer science) into an engineering design course aimed at meeting local needs.

Columbus Area Career Connection (C4), Columbus, Indiana

The Columbus Area Career Connection provides career and technical education to high school students in Columbus, Indiana, population 45,000. EPICS High has been a part of the program for several years, with 25–35 students working on projects. Their initial project was a community holiday light display that students continue to work on and improve each year. The display integrated lights with music and was a very visible success for the student teams.

Utopia Eagle Pen Constructed by C4 EPICS Students

Image courtesy of Becki Combs

EPICS High in Columbus has been very successful in building long-term partnerships with established local organizations so that the students can meet local needs while earning academic credit. For example, a recent project, shown at left, was to design and build an Eagle Pen and Flight Pen at the Utopia Wildlife Rehabilitation Center. The project was completed as part of an Architecture class and a Construction Technology class.

Another project involved students in a 3-D Visualization and Animation class, who developed 3-D models of Columbus's architecturally significant buildings for the Columbus Visitor's Center, giving the Visitor's Center more visibility on the Internet.

Agawam High School, Agawam, Massachusetts

Agawam High School began its program in 2007 as part of the national expansion of EPICS with the support from a Learn and Serve America dissemination grant. Led by teachers John T. Burns and Deborah Hunter, the team partnered with the local Lions Club chapter to provide handicap accessibility to the Lions Club Eye Mobile, a large motor home used for the purpose of health screens.

Today, EPICS has been integrated into many of the classes at the high school and one of the latest projects involves engineering and aquaculture. With the assistance of a disabled veteran who donates time and expertise to teach tenth-grade biology, EPICS students are redesigning a marine tank in the school library and are planning to build a reef tank with an originally designed and built sump-type system. Agawam has expanded the EPICS Program by starting a similar program at their junior high, where students have built and maintained a fresh water system.

EPICS High: Equipping Educators

EPICS High seeks to equip educators to guide students through the process of identifying needs within their communities and developing designs to meet those needs. The process starts with teacher training on the EPICS design process: how to manage teams and projects, and how to assess students' accomplishments. The curriculum is designed to engage students and provide frameworks for teachers to guide and assess student progress. Partnerships are key to the EPICS program, and the EPICS program helps link teachers and schools with partners in their communities as well as professionals to provide expertise and additional mentoring for student teams.

Teacher Training: In Person and Online

The EPICS High Program equips teachers with the information and curriculum they need to create learning environments that engage students in hands-on design experiences to address the needs of their local communities. Training sessions introduce teachers to service-learning, human-centered design, project management, and other topics that enable them to manage and coach design teams. The training is designed to involve teachers from any discipline and provide experiences that would equip them to support the development of best practices related to design-based service-learning. The training capitalizes on best practices that integrate standards with the experiential learning of the EPICS projects. Additional best practices include project management, design, teamwork, reading, writing, and discourse with teachers and

Students from Agawam High School EPICS Class

Image courtesy of Agawam High School

EPICS Human Centered Design Model

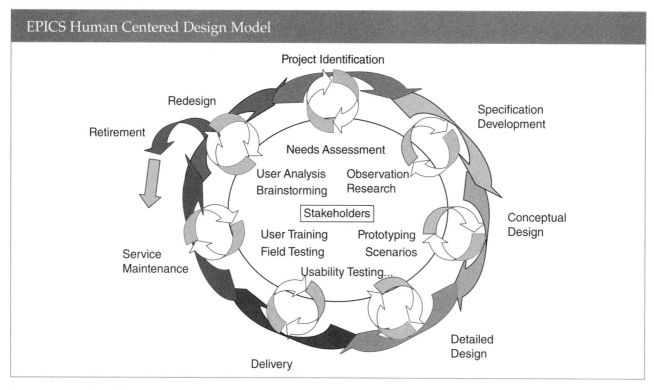

Image courtesy of EPICS

students. The training guides teachers through the EPICS design process, shown above.

EPICS High training promotes the "teacher as facilitator" model that encourages youth voice and student ownership. Students are empowered to drive the projects by conducting a community needs assessment and identifying initial projects. This empowers students and results in greater interest in and ownership of the projects. The approach has been proven to make the EPICS classes attractive to students who are not necessarily interested in engineering but are motivated by the projects. Training provides the scaffolding that teachers need to become comfortable with the facilitator model.

A key principle of service-learning is reciprocal partnerships with the community. Models are discussed to identify, cultivate, and manage partnerships with community members. Reciprocal partnerships seek mutual benefits and empowerment. A hallmark of the EPICS model is the establishment of long-term partnerships with community members. After projects are delivered, the partnerships continue, through new projects or service of fielded projects.

Teacher training is held annually at Purdue University in West Lafayette, Indiana, as well as several sites across the country. An online version of the training is also available through Purdue and allows teachers to participate in training per their availability. Information on the training sites and the online version are available on the EPICS website: http://engineering.purdue.edu/EPICSHS.

The EPICS High Curriculum

The EPICS High curriculum is comprised of flexible modules created to meet the diverse needs of teachers, students, and communities. The core of the learning in EPICS is the experience of the design projects. The role of curriculum modules is to provide learning and assessment frameworks around the projects. The overarching goal of the modules is to give every student a sense of empowerment and involvement in their own communities, as well as an introduction to engineering, computing, and design.

Teachers Engaged in Activities During Training

The initial curriculum modules include activities that help EPICS schools build teaming skills, develop community partnerships, and explore the basics of service-learning. Additional curricular modules include human-centered design, cultural context and ethics, and communication skills. EPICS High curriculum modules include the following:

Lesson Plans—Lesson plans are aligned with the NGSS, Common Core ELA, and Mathematics integrated with the Scientific Method and the EPICS Engineering Process.

Background Information—Lessons have background information to set context and lay foundations to build on.

Student Sheets—Student sheets are formatted to be inserted in Engineering Composition Notebooks and provide scaffolding for data collection and reflection.

Teacher Reflection—As a way for teachers to continue to monitor the progress of their students through the Engineering Design Process, each lesson has a Teacher Reflection sheet to allow teachers to record student performance.

Image courtesy of Agawam High School

Exit Slips—Reflection is an integral part of the educational process and each lesson has reflection sheets for the students.

The curriculum was developed for use in varying geographic, socioeconomic, and cultural contexts in schools in rural, suburban, urban, public, or private settings. The curriculum includes many resources and tools to ensure fidelity when EPICS High curricular modules are implemented.

With many states adopting the Common Core State Standards (NGA & CCSSO, 2010) and the NGSS (NGSS Lead States, 2013), the EPICS program is updating, revising, and aligning the curriculum to meet these rigorous educational benchmarks. Since each school and community is unique, each EPICS High project is unique and may meet different standards. Though no project is likely to be able to target all the NGSS standards, every EPICS project can be used to meet a broad range of the standards.

Since each project is unique, it is difficult to predict in advance which standards will be addressed. However, teachers will be able to ensure that more standards will be met as they gain experience with the NGSS and with EPICS. Table 12.1 illustrates how several Next Generation Science Standards can be met through the EPICS process using an example project with a local zoo that sought to improve the simulated environment for the North American River Otter. The team designed a feeding system that stimulated the otters' natural hunting instincts. Multiple standards can be met at different points in the EPICS design process and these are just examples.

Table 12.1 Connections Between NGSS and an EPICS Lesson

NGSS Performance Expectations, Concepts and Practices	Sample EPICS Design Activities
NGSS Life Science Performance Expectations	
HS-LS2-1. Use mathematical and/or computational representations to support explanations of factors that affect carrying capacity of ecosystems at different scales.	The students investigate conditions in the 18,500 gallon pool at the local zoo that is home to three river otters.
HS-LS2-2. Use mathematical representations to support and revise explanations based on evidence about factors affecting biodiversity and populations in ecosystems of different scales.	The students compare the carrying capacity of the otters' natural environment with their environment in the zoo and find that the captive environment mimics overpopulation of the species.
HS-LS2-6. Evaluate the claims, evidence, and reasoning that the complex interactions in ecosystems maintain relatively consistent numbers and types of organisms in stable conditions, but changing conditions may result in a new ecosystem.	The students conduct research to determine what other zoos and aquariums have done to meet the needs of marine animals and to determine the natural behaviors of the otter in the wild.
CCSS English Language Arts—Technical Subjects	
ELA/Literacy-RST.9-10.8 Assess the extent to which the reasoning and evidence in a text support the author's claim or a recommendation for solving a scientific or technical problem.	Students search, evaluate, and summarize materials from different sources as they research the best ways to improve living conditions for the otters.
NGSS Engineering Design Performance Expectations	
HS-ETS1-2. Design a solution to a complex real-world problem by breaking it down into smaller, more manageable problems that can be solved through engineering.	Using the EPICS design model, the students create a prototype to simulate the naturalistic feeding of the otters as a feasible approach of improving the living conditions in the exhibit.
HS-ETS1-3. Evaluate a solution to a complex real-world problem based on prioritized criteria and trade-offs that account for a range of constraints, including cost, safety, reliability, and aesthetics, as well as possible social, cultural, and environmental impacts.	Students compare concepts using decision matrices that capture the project specifications and feedback from zoo personnel to narrow their ideas to a final conceptual design.
Crosscutting Concepts	
Cause and Effect—In grades 9–12, students . . . suggest cause and effect relationships to explain and predict behaviors in complex natural and designed systems.	Students develop a prototype to test their concept and determine how the new feeder would mimic the natural feeding habits of the otters.
Systems and System Models—In grades 9–12, students . . . use models and simulations to predict the behavior of a system and recognize that these predictions have limited precision and reliability because of the assumptions and approximations inherent in the models.	Students construct a computer model to evaluate different holding capacities and flow rates for the feeder system.
NGSS Science and Engineering Practices	
Engaging in argument from evidence in Grades 9–12 builds from K–8 experiences and progresses to using appropriate and sufficient evidence and scientific reasoning to defend and critique claims and explanations about the natural and designed world(s).	Throughout the project, the EPICS students explain how the new feeder can help the otters function in a more naturalistic way by showing the simulation of the predator-prey relationship to stakeholders and external reviewers.

EPICS High Curricular and Extracurricular Models

EPICS High was designed to allow flexibility in program structure. Consequently, three models have evolved: embedded within the school-day curriculum, after-school programs, and a hybrid in-school and after-school program.

EPICS High programs embedded within the school day can offer separate classes dedicated to their projects that include engineering design classes (especially in states with engineering standards), technology education classes, and environmental science and career exploration courses. The projects can also be integrated into existing math, science, computer science, career education, or social science classes. Projects that are integrated into existing courses are used primarily as curricular connections between STEM courses and social studies, communication, art, or English.

After-school programs leverage students' interests in community service to engage them in learning new skills, while it reinforces previously learned material from STEM disciplines. Schools that have community service requirements for academic diplomas can utilize EPICS High as a way to fulfill those requirements while teaching students about design and careers in engineering, technology, and computing fields.

The hybrid in-school and after-school programs have sometimes been implemented to allow more students to participate, since some students who want to participate have difficulty accommodating both required courses and EPICS High courses. Other students may be able to participate in class but are too busy after school to attend meetings at that time. This two-pronged approach gives schools and students more flexibility while managing the kinds of diverse projects that are addressed by EPICS High programs occurring outside of school hours. As shown in Table 12.2, EPICS High projects are categorized by four main areas of impact: Access and Abilities, Human Services, Education and Outreach, and Environmental.

Table 12.2 Example EPICS High Partners and Projects

Area of Impact	Community Partners	Projects
Access and Abilities	Muscular Dystrophy Association, Lions Club, Leader Dogs for the Blind, special needs classrooms	Wheel chair swing, accessibility ramp and railing, tactile map, learning experiences for students with special needs
Human Services	Food banks, Habitat for Humanity, homeless shelters, Parks and Recreation	Software for data, volunteer and client management, play structures for children, sustainability analyses, playground designs
Education and Outreach	School districts, environmental agencies, local museums	Hands-on and lab equipment for middle and elementary classrooms, models for community education, mobile science centers
Environmental	Governmental environmental agencies, planning commissions, school districts, local universities	Recycling processes, energy audits, sustainability analyses, rain gardens, green roofs

Partnerships: Community, Corporate, and Professionals

A core value of EPICS High is long-term, reciprocal partnerships. In some schools, community partnerships are new or need to be established. While the partnerships are ultimately between the local schools and their community, the EPICS High Program provides resources and assistance to connect the schools and their community partners. Assistance may involve drawing on connections with national organizations such as United Way and Habitat for Humanity to help connect teachers with organizations within their community.

Another kind of partnership is with the engineering and computing communities. EPICS High not only teaches engineering but engages students in engineering. While teachers are introduced to engineering and design concepts, it is not the intention or belief that the training can equip them to be engineers. The concept of EPICS is to build partnerships using practicing engineers as part of the process. Experienced engineers mentor the student teams, provide reviews for the designs, and assist teachers in the design process. The experienced engineers can come from industry, retired community members, university faculty, or students. The EPICS High staff assists teachers in making connections with engineers in their own community.

Sometimes the professional contacts come through the network of EPICS Universities. In the examples highlighted earlier in the chapter, Xavier has been supported by Arizona State University and Westinghouse has been supported by the Illinois Institute of Technology. The C4 program in Columbus, Indiana, is supported by Cummins Engines, which has their world headquarters in the same town. Other companies support programs locally or regionally. IEEE (the world's largest professional association for the advancement of technology) has an EPICS initiative, and IEEE members are encouraged to serve as mentors.

Each EPICS project and community partnership is unique. The EPICS staff works with each school to help initiate their program and identify the needed partners. When EPICS works well, it engages partners on multiple levels to work with the students to make their community a better place. Motorola, Habitat for Humanity, the Lions Club, and many other organizations' employees provide EPICS High students with a precious resource: their time. Students work and partner with real-world professionals from companies and universities such as these to provide real world outstanding products that serve a real community need. Each EPICS High site relies on partnerships such as these and the types of partnerships that exist between the professional world, the school, and the community is unique.

Acknowledgments

EPICS High would not have been possible without the generous support from Learn and Serve America, the Martinson Family Foundation, and the Motorola Solutions Foundation. Intel provided initial support for EPICS and has supported the growth of the program in Arizona. Google has supported expansion in California. State Farm and Rolls Royce have supported teacher training at Purdue. IEEE has supported expansion globally.

Conclusion

The EPICS High program has the capacity to fundamentally change how the world views engineering and is already changing the equation in schools with high percentages of girls and minorities engaged in EPICS High projects. By providing opportunities to bring students together with local not-for-profit agencies, both groups benefit. Students gain real-world educational and design-based experiences that meet NGSS and Common Core State Standards and prepare them for college. Partnering agencies gain technology to improve the services they provide. The approach offers an affordable method to teach authentic design as projects are scoped to meet the available resources. Even if students choose not to pursue a degree in engineering, they learn about how they can change their community with the help of technology and a logical, thoughtful process. The result of every successful EPICS project leaves our students' communities in a better place.

References

Coyle, E. J., Jamieson, L. H., & Oakes, W. C. (2005, February). "EPICS: Engineering projects in community service," *International Journal of Engineering Education*, 21(1), 139–150.

Coyle, E. J., Jamieson, L. H., & Oakes, W. C. (2006, January). "Integrating engineering education and community service: Themes for the future of engineering education," *Journal of Engineering Education*, 95(1), 7–11.

Lima, M., & Oakes, W. (2013). *Service learning: Engineering in your community* (2nd Ed.). New York: Oxford University Press.

Matusovich, H. M., Oakes, W., & Zoltowski, C. B. (2013). Why women choose service-learning: Seeking and finding engineering-related experiences. *International Journal of Engineering Education*, 29(2), 388–402.

National Academy of Engineering. (2008). *Changing the conversation: Messages for improving public understanding of engineering*. Washington, DC: National Academies Press.

NGA, & CCSSO. (2010). *Common core state standards: English language arts*. Washington, DC: Author.

NGSS Lead States. (2013). *Next generation science standards: For states, by states, volume 1: The standards*. Washington, DC: National Academies Press.

Oakes, W., Dexter, P., Thompson, M., Hunter, J., Baygents, J., and Filley, R. (2012, June). Early engineering through service-learning: Adapting a university model to high school. *Proceedings of the 2012 ASEE Annual Conference*, San Antonio, Texas.

Index

A SAGE Company

Corwin is committed to improving education for all learners by publishing books and other professional development resources for those serving the field of PreK–12 education. By providing practical, hands-on materials, Corwin continues to carry out the promise of its motto: **"Helping Educators Do Their Work Better."**